Figure 6-1　RGB Image and Greyscale Image

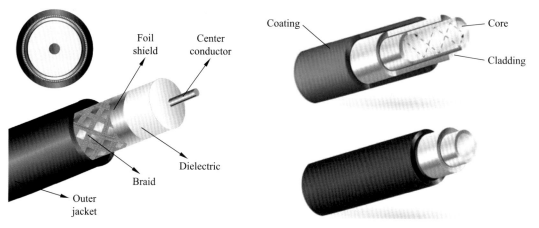

Figure 7-6　Coaxial Cable

Figure 7-7　Optical Fiber

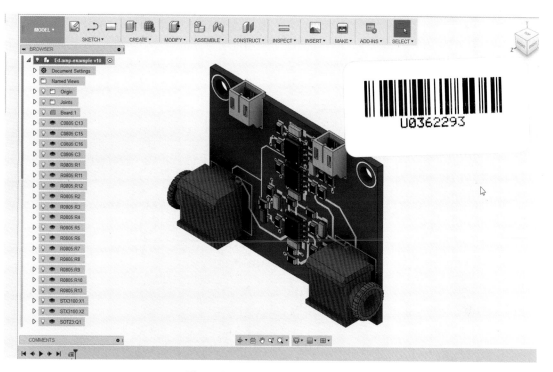

Figure 9-1　EAGLE Work Window

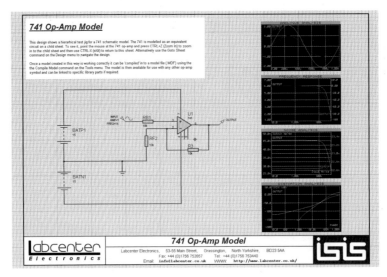

Figure 9-2　Proteus Work Window

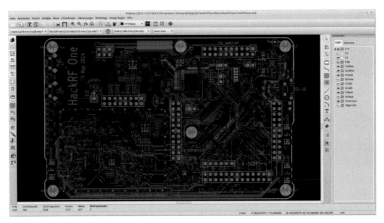

Figure 9-3　KiCad Work Window

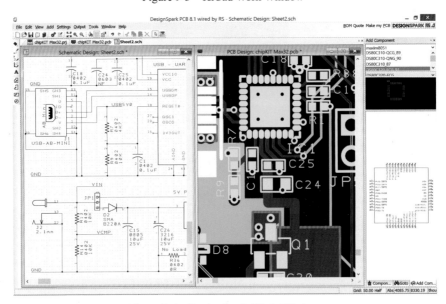

Figure 9-4　DesignSpark Work Window

教育部高等学校电子信息类专业教学指导委员会规划教材

高等学校电子信息类专业系列教材

电子信息英语教程

张强华 司爱侠 编著

清华大学出版社

北京

内 容 简 介

本书是电子信息专业英语教材，内容包括电子工程、电子器件的类型、电测仪器、模拟信号与数字信号、集成电路、VHDL、纳米电子技术简介、计算机硬件与软件的不同类型、传感器的类型及无线传感器网络、数字信号处理、数字图像处理、文本处理、计算机网络、计算机网络拓扑和传输介质、控制系统、PLC、工业机器人、EDA、电路仿真、印刷电路设计软件、物联网、云计算、人工智能及大数据等。

每个单元均包含以下部分：课文——选材广泛、风格多样、切合实际的两篇专业文章；单词——给出课文中出现的新词，读者由此可以积累电子信息专业的基本词汇；词组——给出课文中的常用词组；缩略语——给出课文中出现的缩略语；参考译文——让读者对照理解以提高翻译能力；习题——针对课文的练习；阅读材料——增加了本书的深度和广度。本书提供听力材料、教学大纲、PPT、参考试卷、习题答案及总词汇表等资源。

本书可作为高等院校电子信息类专业的专业英语教材，也可供从业人员自学。

图书在版编目（CIP）数据

电子信息英语教程/张强华，司爱侠编著. —北京：清华大学出版社，2023.3
高等学校电子信息类专业系列教材
ISBN 978-7-302-62632-9

Ⅰ. ①电…　Ⅱ. ①张…　②司…　Ⅲ. ①电子信息－英语－高等学校－教材　Ⅳ. ①G203

中国国家版本馆 CIP 数据核字（2023）第 019693 号

责任编辑：安　妮
封面设计：李召霞
责任校对：申晓焕
责任印制：沈　露

出版发行：清华大学出版社
　　　　　网　　　址：http://www.tup.com.cn, http://www.wqbook.com
　　　　　地　　　址：北京清华大学学研大厦 A 座　　　　　邮　　编：100084
　　　　　社 总 机：010-83470000　　　　　　　　　　　邮　　购：010-62786544
　　　　　投稿与读者服务：010-62776969，c-service@tup.tsinghua.edu.cn
　　　　　质量反馈：010-62772015，zhiliang@tup.tsinghua.edu.cn
　　　　　课件下载：http://www.tup.com.cn，010-83470236
印 装 者：三河市龙大印装有限公司
经　　销：全国新华书店
开　　本：185mm×260mm　　印　张：16.75　　插　页：1　　字　数：408 千字
版　　次：2023 年 4 月第 1 版　　　　　　　　　　　　印　次：2023 年 4 月第 1 次印刷
印　　数：1～1500
定　　价：59.00 元

产品编号：096959-01

前 言
PREFACE

在《普通高等学校本科专业目录》中，电子信息类是属于工学的一级学科，它培养具备电子信息领域内宽厚的理论基础、实验能力和专业知识的人才。他们工作于电子技术、信息通信、信息工程、光电信息以及计算机等相关领域内，从事各种电子材料、元器件、集成电路、集成电子系统和光电子系统的设计、制造、新产品研发、网络运营以及技术管理等方面的工作。

如今，该行业的新技术、新设备、新工具不断出现，要掌握这些新知识和新技能，从业人员必须不断地学习，这需要具备专业英语能力。专业英语水平已经成为决定工作能力的因素之一。要提高专业英语水平，就必须专门进行针对性的学习。本书旨在切实提高读者实际使用专业英语的能力。

本书特色

（1）适应"宽口径"人才培养模式。本书内容不仅包含电子信息类专业的基础知识和基本理论，还包含物联网、云计算、人工智能及大数据等新内容。一方面，这些新技术正在改变传统的电子信息专业；另一方面，越来越多的电子信息专业的毕业生进入这些新领域。

（2）针对就业环境，面向未来发展。在本书的编写过程中，我们针对学生毕业后的就业环境，根据未来工作实际的要求，做了切合实际的精心加工。

体例结构

本书由 11 个单元组成，每个单元均包含以下部分：课文——选材广泛、风格多样、切合实际的两篇专业文章，**配有听力音频文件，扫码即可播放**；单词——给出课文中出现的新词，读者由此可以积累电子信息专业的基本词汇；词组——给出课文中的常用词组；缩略语——给出课文中出现的、业内人士必须掌握的缩略语；参考译文——让读者对照理解以提高翻译能力；习题——既有针对课文的练习，也有一些开放性的练习；阅读材料——提供内容丰富的阅读材料，增加了本书的深度和广度，不仅可以进一步扩大读者的视野，还可供教师选作"翻转课堂"等教学改革的资料；总词汇表——便于读者复习、记忆单词，也可作为小词典长期查阅，**请扫描下方二维码下载**。

教学支持

我们为教师提供听力材料、教学大纲、教学课件、模拟试卷、习题答案及总词汇表等资源，请访问清华大学出版社官网或公众号"书圈"获取。

本书可作为高等院校电子信息类专业的专业英语教材，也可供从业人员自学。

扫码下载
总词汇表

作　者

2022 年 10 月

目 录
CONTENTS

Electronic Engineering

扫码听课文

Electronic engineering is a form of engineering associated with electronic circuits, devices and the equipment and systems that use them.

1 Electronic Engineering Fields

When asking the question "What is electronic engineering?", it is necessary to understand that there are many different fields and disciplines involved in the overall topic.

Some of the fields within electronic engineering include:

(1) Analog electronic engineering: analog electronics is still a major sector within the overall electronic engineering scene. With many analog elements still being needed, analog circuits are still widely used. While analog electronic engineering is not as large as it used to be many years ago before digital electronics took off in a big way, the growth in the overall electronics market has compensated for this. Analog electronic engineering can provide a stimulating environment in which to work and a good career.

(2) Radio frequency electronic engineering: radio frequency electronic engineering has grown in its size in recent years. With many more systems using wireless links, everything from mobile phones to WiFi, IoT, short range links and much more, wireless technology is needed.

(3) Digital development engineering: many functions are now undertaken using digital techniques. Accordingly many digital circuits are needed and this means that some digital / logic electronic engineering is needed.

(4) Programmable logic engineering: with the complexity of many logic / digitally based circuits, an approach that is being used increasingly is one where programmable logic chips are used. FPGAs and other programmable logic chips are widely used, enabling large amounts of logic circuits to be incorporated into programmable chips. Using high level design languages like VHDL, the design is brought to within manageable limits. Also if the design needs optimizing or changing, this can be achieved by changing the logic programme. This sector of the electronic engineering arena is growing, and the tools becoming more sophisticated and very interesting to use.

(5) Software engineering: there is an increasing amount of software contained within electronic products these days. As a result, software engineering is becoming increasingly

important. In many projects, at least two thirds of the development budgets are allocated to developing the software.

(6) Systems engineering: systems engineering is a particularly important element of the design of any item. In terms of this sector of electronic engineering, a system is any complete object. It may be a radio receiver, it may be a mobile phone, or it could be an item consisting of several individual items.

The term "systems engineering" refers to the fact that this form of engineering looks at the complete object or system, including smaller items, everything from boards to complete units. It focuses on the operation of the overall system and ensures that the initial requirements are correct. It finally tests the item to ensure that it operates to its specification, and also to the initial requirements that were placed upon it.

There are also many other niche areas of electronic engineering: component engineering, reliability engineering, risk management, quality assurance and many more. All are very important and need basic electronic engineering skills.

While most electronic engineers will tend to specialize in one area for their career, it is important to have a knowledge of other areas. This helps the engineer to interact effectively with others from slightly different disciplines as always happens on large projects.

Take one every day example: a mobile phone base station has many elements, each requiring electronic engineers with different specialities. There are the radio frequency parts used for the transmitter and receiver as well as the antennas. However large amounts of software are required as the system is complicated and it requires a lot of elements to be controlled. Signals have complex functions along with acknowledgements of messages sent and received. Software engineering is required for this. Also programmable logic is used for many of the logic requirements and this links into both software and also the logic hardware design as well as many analog functions.

Other engineering skills including system design, installation planning, cellular coverage planners and many others will be needed as well.

It can be seen that something as common as a mobile phone base station requires many engineers with a variety of skills.

2　Opportunities in Electronic Engineering

Electronic engineering is normally focused on creating electronic items, from small electronic gadgets right up to huge systems like aircraft, monitoring systems, and many more items.

In many areas electronic engineers can be creating items that benefit others: medical equipment has a huge amount of electronic elements; safety systems also have electronics; there are many ecological projects that have electronics at their core.

There are in fact many industry sectors in which electronic engineering is used and where electronic engineers are needed, including general electronics design and development;

telecommunications; automation and IoT; medical electronics; defence electronic engineering; manufacturing engineering; broadcast; aeronautical electronics; consumer products electronic engineering; and research and development.

3 Activities within Electronic Engineering Projects

There are many stages in an electronic engineering project, from the initial design concept right through its design, testing, production and then in services. There are many activities which can be interesting, captivating and can provide an interesting career.

Some of the activities may include development of initial design concept; field trials of initial concept; initial design; development; design testing; introduction into production; post design services; customer liaison; and sales and marketing support.

These are some of the many activities that are undertaken by electronic engineers during projects. While much of the electronic engineering is undertaken at the base laboratory, it is sometimes necessary to travel to support customers, undertake liaison with suppliers or even with other contractor companies supplying an overall system. This can be challenging and rewarding and it can provide an additional insight into how the overall engineering environment operates.

New Words

electronic	[ɪˌlekˈtrɒnɪk]	adj.电子的；电子设备的
engineering	[ˌendʒɪˈnɪərɪŋ]	n.工程（学）
circuit	[ˈsɜːkɪt]	n.电路
device	[dɪˈvaɪs]	n.设备，装置，器具
field	[fiːld]	n.领域
discipline	[ˈdɪsəplɪn]	n.学科；训练
analog	[ˈænəlɒg]	adj.模拟的
compensate	[ˈkɒmpenseɪt]	v.补偿，弥补
provide	[prəˈvaɪd]	v.提供；规定
stimulate	[ˈstɪmjuleɪt]	vt.刺激，激励
radio	[ˈreɪdiəʊ]	n.无线电；收音机
		v.用无线电发送讯息
frequency	[ˈfriːkwənsi]	n.频率
wireless	[ˈwaɪələs]	adj.无线的
link	[lɪŋk]	n.链接
		v.使联系在一起；连接
logic	[ˈlɒdʒɪk]	n.逻辑（学）
programmable	[ˈprəʊgræməbl]	adj.可编程的

manageable	['mænɪdʒəbl]	adj.易控制的，易处理的，可管理的
optimize	['ɒptɪmaɪz]	vt.使最优化
programme	['prəʊɡræm]	n.程序
		v.为（机器或系统）设定程序
budget	['bʌdʒɪt]	n.预算
		v.把……编入预算
operate	['ɒpəreɪt]	v.运转；操作
specification	[ˌspesɪfɪ'keɪʃn]	n.规格；详述；说明书
engineer	[ˌendʒɪ'nɪə]	n.工程师
project	['prɒdʒekt]	n.项目，工程；方案，计划
		v.规划，计划
transmitter	[træns'mɪtə]	n.发射机
antenna	[æn'tenə]	n.天线
complicate	['kɒmplɪkeɪt]	v.使复杂化
control	[kən'trəʊl]	n.&v.控制
signal	['sɪɡnəl]	n.信号
		v.发信号
acknowledgement	[ək'nɒlɪdʒmənt]	n.确认
opportunity	[ˌɒpə'tjuːnətɪ]	n.机会，时机
huge	[hjuːdʒ]	adj.巨大的
ecological	[ˌiːkə'lɒdʒɪkl]	adj.生态（学）的
telecommunication	[ˌtelɪkəˌmjuːnɪ'keɪʃn]	n.电信
fix	[fɪks]	v.固定；确定
manufacturing	[ˌmænju'fæktʃərɪŋ]	n.制造业，工业
aeronautical	[ˌeərə'nɔːtɪkl]	adj.航空（学）的
liaison	[li'eɪzn]	n.联络，联络人
laboratory	[lə'bɒrətrɪ]	n.实验室；研究室
insight	['ɪnsaɪt]	n.洞察力；领悟

Phrases

electronic engineering	电子工程
a form of ...	一种
be associated with	和……联系在一起；与……有关
electronic circuit	电子电路
analog electronic	模拟电子
analog circuit	模拟电路
radio frequency	无线电频率

high level design language	高级设计语言
software engineering	软件工程
electronic product	电子产品
systems engineering	系统工程
focus on	聚焦，集中，关注
risk management	风险管理
quality assurance	质量保证
interact with ...	与……相互作用，与……相互影响；与……相互配合
base station	基地；基站
a variety of	各种各样的
monitoring system	监视系统
consumer product	消费品
field trial	现场试验
liaison with	联络

Abbreviations

WiFi (wireless fidelity)	无线保真
FPGA (field programmable gate array)	现场可编程门阵列
VHDL (VHSIC hardware description language)	高速集成电路硬件描述语言

参考译文

电 子 工 程

电子工程是一种与电子电路、器件以及使用它们的设备和系统相关的工程。

1 电子工程领域

当问到"什么是电子工程？"时，知道这个主题涉及许多不同的领域和学科是很有必要的。电子工程包括以下领域：

（1）模拟电子工程：在整个电子工程领域，模拟电子仍然是一个主要领域。由于仍需要许多模拟元件，因此，模拟电路仍被广泛使用。虽然模拟电子工程的范围不如多年前数字电子产品还未蓬勃发展时那么庞大，但整个电子市场的增长弥补了这一点。模拟电子工程可以提供一个令人振奋的工作环境和良好的职业生涯。

（2）射频电子工程：近年来，射频电子工程的规模不断扩大。越来越多的系统使用无线链路（从手机到 WiFi、物联网、短程链路等），这些都需要无线技术。

（3）数字开发工程：现在许多功能都是使用数字技术实现的。因此，许多地方都需要数字电路，这意味着需要一些数字/逻辑电子工程。

（4）可编程逻辑工程：由于许多基于逻辑/数字的电路的复杂性，人们越来越多地使用可编程逻辑芯片。FPGA 和其他可编程逻辑芯片被广泛使用，使得大量的逻辑电路能够被集成到可编程芯片中。通过使用 VHDL 等高级设计语言，将设计控制在可管理的范围内。如果设计需要优化或更改，则可以通过更改逻辑程序来实现。电子工程的该领域正在增长，工具变得更加先进而且使用起来也非常有趣。

（5）软件工程：如今，电子产品中包含的软件越来越多。因此，软件工程变得越来越重要。在许多项目中，至少三分之二的开发预算用于开发软件。

（6）系统工程：系统工程在任何项目设计中都特别重要。就电子工程这一领域而言，系统是任何完整的对象。它可能是一个无线电接收器，可能是一部手机，也可能是由几个单独的项目组成的整体。

"系统工程"指这种工程着眼于完整的对象或系统，包括更小的项目，如从电路板到完整的单元。它关注整个系统的运行，并确保初始要求是正确的。最后，它会测试该项目，以确保它按照规范和初始要求运行。

电子工程还有许多其他领域，如组件工程、可靠性工程、风险管理、质量保证等。所有这些领域都非常重要，而且需要基本的电子工程技能。

虽然大多数电子工程师在职业生涯中倾向专注于一个领域，但了解其他领域的知识也很重要。这有助于工程师与来自不同学科的其他人进行高效地互动，就像大型项目中经常发生的那样。

例如，手机基站有许多元件，每个元件都需要具有不同专业知识的电子工程师。发射器、接收器和天线都使用射频部件。由于系统很复杂，并且需要控制很多元件，因此需要大量的软件。信号的功能复杂，还可用于对发送和接收的消息的确认。这就需要软件工程。此外，可编程逻辑用于许多逻辑需求，并与软件、逻辑硬件设计以及许多模拟功能相关联。

还需要其他工程技能，包括系统设计、安装规划、蜂窝覆盖规划等。

可以看出，像手机基站这样常见的东西需要许多具有各种技能的工程师。

2 电子工程的机会

电子工程通常专注于创建电子产品，从小型电子产品到大型系统，如飞机、监控系统等。

在许多领域，电子工程师都可以创造出有益于他人的产品：医疗设备有大量的电子元件；安全系统也有电子设备；许多生态项目的核心都是电子产品。

事实上，许多行业都使用电子工程，也需要电子工程师，包括通用电子设计与开发、电信、自动化和物联网、医用电子学、国防电子工程、制造工程、广播、航空电子、消费品电子工程以及研究与开发。

3 电子工程项目内的活动

电子工程项目有很多阶段：从最初的设计概念到设计、测试、生产，再到投入使用。许多活动是有趣的、吸引人的，可以提供一个有趣的职业生涯。

其中一些活动可能包括初步设计概念的开发、初始概念的现场试验、初步设计、开发、设计测试、投入生产、后期设计服务、客户联络以及销售和市场支持。

这些是电子工程师在项目期间进行的许多活动中的一部分。虽然大部分电子工程是在基地实验室进行的，但有时需要出差去支持客户，与供应商进行联络，甚至与提供整个系统的其他承包商公司进行联络。这可能具有挑战性和回报性，并且可以对整个工程环境如何运行提供额外的见解。

Text B

扫码听课文

Types of Electronic Devices

1   Resistors

The resistor is a passive electrical component, whose function is to introduce resistance to the flow of electric current in an electrical circuit to limit the current. The magnitude of the opposition to the flow of current is called the resistance of the resistor. A larger resistance value indicates a greater opposition to current flow. The resistance is measured in ohms (Ω), and its equation is as follows.

$$R = \frac{V}{I}$$

The voltage (V), current (I), and resistance (R) are related by Ohm's law. i.e. $V = IR$. The higher the resistance R, the lower is the current I for a given voltage V across it. It is a linear device.

Resistors dissipate electrical energy given by $P = I^2R$ Watts or Joules/sec.

Resistors are made using different materials such as carbon film, metal film, etc.

Different types of resistors by application: common resistor (which is used in current limiter, setting biases, voltage dividers, filtering, termination resistors, load resistors, etc.), precision resistor (for voltage feedback circuits, voltage references), current sense resistors, and power resistors.

Resistor selection parameters: while selecting any resistor in the circuit, the designer needs to consider the following parameters: resistance value (R), power (Wattages) dissipated across it, and tolerance (+/− %).

2   Capacitor

The capacitor is a passive electrical component, whose function is to store electrical energy and deliver it to the circuit when needed. The capacity of a capacitor to store electrical charge is known as the capacitance of that capacitor. It is denoted by C. The unit of capacitance is Farad (F).

Various uses of capacitors: Blocking the flow of DC voltage and permitting the flow of AC, hence used for coupling of the circuits; phase shifting and creating time delays; filtration, especially in removing ripples from the rectified waveform; getting the tuned frequency; and as a motor starter.

Capacitor selection parameters: While selecting a capacitor in any circuit users need to take care of the following parameters: capacitance value, maximum operating voltage of the capacitor, tolerance, breakdown voltage, frequency range, equivalent series resistance (ESR) and size.

3 Inductors

The inductors (also called as a coil or choke) is a passive two-terminal electrical component. It stores magnetic energy when an electric current is passed through it. It's an insulated wire wound into a coil around a core of some material (air, iron, powdered iron, or ferrite material) in a spiral form.

The inductor is denoted by inductance L and the measuring unit is Henry (H).

An ideal inductor has zero resistance and zero capacitance. However, real inductors have a small value resistance associated with the winding of the coil and whenever current flows through it, energy is lost in the form of heat.

Applications of inductors: in buck/boost power regulators, in filter circuits in DC power supplies, isolating signals, in transformer to step up/down the AC voltage level, in oscillator and tuning circuits, and generating voltage surges in fluorescent lamp sets.

Types of inductors: inductors are mainly classified depending on the core material used and operating frequency. The different types of inductors are iron cored inductors, air cored inductors, powdered iron cored inductors, ferrite cored inductors, variable inductors, audio frequency inductors and radio frequency inductors.

Inductor selection parameters: while selecting an inductor in any circuit user needs to take care of the following parameter apart from the application: inductance value, tolerance , maximum current rating, shielded and non-shielded, size, Q ratings, frequency range, the resistance of the inductor and type of core used.

4 Diodes

The diode is a two-terminal semiconductor device that allows an electric current to pass in one direction while blocking it in the reverse direction. The diode is made up of a semiconductor device with P-type material and N-type material. Typical material used in a diode is silicon and germanium. They conduct when a minimum forward voltage (around 0.7V for Silicon) is applied across it and remain off during reverse bias condition.

Applications of diodes: power conversion (AC to DC) / rectification , clamping the voltage, zener diode as a voltage regulator, over voltage protection, ESD protection, and demodulation of signals.

Type of diodes: rectifier diode, switching diode, light emitting diode, zener diode, Schottky diode, ESD diode, tunnel diode, varicap diode, photodiode, and laser diode in optical communication.

Diode selection parameters: while selecting a diode in any circuit users needs to take care of the following parameters: forward bias voltage, maximum forward current, average forward current , power dissipation , reverse breakdown voltage/peak inverse voltage, maximum reverse current, operating junction temperature, reverse recovery time, and size.

5   Quartz Crystals

The quartz crystal is made from a thin piece of quartz wafer. This wafer is made from silicon-material. The wafer is tightly fitted and controlled between two parallel metalized surfaces which make an electrical connection. When an external voltage is applied to the plates, the crystal vibrates with a certain fundamental frequency which creates alternating waveform which swings between high and low levels. This phenomenon is known as the piezoelectric effect. Due to this property, they are used in electronic circuits along with active components to create stable clock input to the processor.

Quartz crystal applications: used in oscillator circuit to provide a clock input to the processor device, and source of reference signals for RF.

Quartz crystal selection parameters: load capacitance, fundamental frequency, frequency tolerance, frequency stability, ESR, and operating voltage.

6   Relays

A relay is an electromagnetic switch that opens and closes potential-free contacts. An electro-mechanical relay consists of an armature, coil, spring and contacts. When the voltage is applied to a coil, it generates a magnetic field. This attracts the armature and causes a change in the open/closed state of the circuit. It is mainly used to control a high powered circuit using a low power signal.

There are mainly two types of relays based on constructions: electromechanical relays (EMR) and solid state relays (SSR).

A solid state relay has a photodiode at its input side and a switching device such as transistor/FET at its output side. When a specific voltage is applied at its input, photodiode conducts and triggers the base of the transistor to cause the switching. Due to its fast switching, miniaturized form factor, low voltage requirement, and eliminating the mechanical arching, electrical noise and contact bounce, it's more widely used in applications compared with electromechanical relay.

Applications of relays: controlling the high powered circuit with isolated low power, such as controlling 230V AC circuits with a +5V signal; switching voltage ON/OFF; and connecting or disconnecting electrical MCB (Micro Circuit Breaker).

Selection parameters for relays: output load type (AC/DC), input coil voltage for a electromechanical relay, photodiode voltage for SSR, output switching voltage, output current, on-state resistance, number of switching, number of poles and contacts, and type of output contacts.

7　Transistor

The transistor is a non-linear three-terminal semiconductor device. The transistor is considered to be one of the most important devices in the field of electronics. The transistor has transformed many aspects of man's life. There are two main functions of transistors, to act as solid state switches and to amplify input signals. The transistor acts as a switch when operated either in saturation or cut-off region. It amplifies signals when used in the active region. It offers very high input resistance and very low output resistance.

Transistors are categorized into BJT (bipolar junction transistor) and FET (field effect transistor) based on their construction.

Types of transistors: BJT: NPN and PNP ; FET: JFET and MOSFET.

Applications of transistors (BJT/FET): amplification of analog signals; as switching devices in SMPS, microcontrollers, etc.; oscillators; over/under voltage protection; modulation circuits and demodulation of signals; and power control in invertors and chargers (high current power transistors).

New Words

resistor	[rɪˈzɪstə]	n.电阻器
passive	[ˈpæsɪv]	adj.被动的
resistance	[rɪˈzɪstəns]	n.电阻
magnitude	[ˈmægnɪtjuːd]	n.量级
indicate	[ˈɪndɪkeɪt]	v.表明，指示
voltage	[ˈvəʊltɪdʒ]	n.电压，伏特数
current	[ˈkʌrənt]	n.电流
linear	[ˈlɪnɪə]	adj.线性的
dissipate	[ˈdɪsɪpeɪt]	vt.消耗
bias	[ˈbaɪəs]	n.偏差

filtering	[ˈfɪltərɪŋ]	n.过滤器
termination	[ˌtɜːmɪˈneɪʃn]	n.终端
precision	[prɪˈsɪʒn]	n.精确度，准确性
Wattage	[ˈwɒtɪdʒ]	n.瓦特数，瓦数
tolerance	[ˈtɒlərəns]	n.宽差
capacitor	[kəˈpæsɪtə]	n.电容器
Farad	[ˈfæræd]	n.法拉（电容单位）
filtration	[fɪlˈtreɪʃn]	n.过滤；筛选
waveform	[ˈweɪvfɔːm]	n.波形
tune	[tjuːn]	v.调谐
motor	[ˈməʊtə]	n.马达，发动机
starter	[ˈstɑːtə]	n.（发动机的）启动装置，启动器
inductor	[ɪnˈdʌktə]	n.电感器
coil	[kɔɪl]	n.线圈
choke	[tʃəʊk]	n.扼流圈
magnetic	[mæɡˈnetɪk]	adj.磁性的
insulate	[ˈɪnsjuleɪt]	vt.使绝缘
regulator	[ˈreɡjuleɪtə]	n.调节器，调整器，校准器
isolate	[ˈaɪsəleɪt]	vt.使隔离，使绝缘
oscillator	[ˈɒsɪleɪtə]	n.振荡器；振子
surge	[sɜːdʒ]	v.激增
shield	[ʃiːld]	vt.屏蔽；保护
diode	[ˈdaɪəʊd]	n.二极管
germanium	[dʒɜːˈmeɪnɪəm]	n.锗
rectification	[ˌrektɪfɪˈkeɪʃn]	n.整流
demodulation	[diːˈmɒdjʊleɪʃn]	n.解调，检波
rectifier	[ˈrektɪfaɪə]	n.整流器
laser	[ˈleɪzə]	n.激光，激光器
optical	[ˈɒptɪkl]	adj.光学的
junction	[ˈdʒʌŋkʃn]	n.结；接合点
recovery	[rɪˈkʌvərɪ]	n.恢复
quartz	[kwɔːts]	n.石英
wafer	[ˈweɪfə]	n.圆片，晶片
vibrate	[vaɪˈbreɪt]	v.振动；摆动
phenomenon	[fəˈnɒmɪnən]	n.现象
property	[ˈprɒpətɪ]	n.特性；属性
processor	[ˈprəʊsesə]	n.处理机，处理器
relay	[ˈriːleɪ]	n.继电器
		v.转播；转送

electromagnetic	[ɪˌlektrəʊmægˈnetɪk]	*adj.*电磁的
electromechanical	[ɪˈlektrəʊmɪˈkænɪkəl]	*adj.*电动机械的，机电的
armature	[ˈɑːmətʃə]	*n.*电枢；转子；衔铁
spring	[sprɪŋ]	*n.*弹簧
		*v.*跳跃
construction	[kənˈstrʌkʃn]	*n.*结构
trigger	[ˈtrɪɡə]	*n.*触点，触发器
non-linear	[nɒn ˈlɪnɪə]	*adj.*非线性的
amplify	[ˈæmplɪfaɪ]	*v.*放大，增强
saturation	[ˌsætʃəˈreɪʃn]	*n.*（达到）饱和状态；饱和度
amplification	[ˌæmplɪfɪˈkeɪʃn]	*n.*扩大，放大
invertor	[ɪnˈvɜːtə]	*n.*变频器，逆变器
charger	[ˈtʃɑːdʒə]	*n.*充电器

Phrases

electrical circuit	电路
be measured in ...	以……方式测量，以……方式度量
carbon film	碳膜
metal film	金属薄膜，金属膜
current limiter	电流限制器
electrical charge	电荷
be denoted by	表示为
phase shifting	相位偏移，移相
apart from ...	除了……外；此外
breakdown voltage	击穿电压
insulated wire	绝缘导线
powdered iron	铁粉
ferrite material	铁氧体材料
tuning circuit	调谐电路
fluorescent lamp	荧光灯（管），日光灯（管）
variable inductor	可变电感器
forward voltage	正向电压
reverse bias voltage	反向偏压，逆偏压
light emitting diode	发光二极管
tunnel diode	隧道二极管
forward bias voltage	正向偏压
power dissipation	功率消耗，功耗

peak inverse voltage	反向峰值电压，最大反向电压
operating junction temperature	工作结温度
quartz wafer	石英晶片
fundamental frequency	基频
piezoelectric effect	压电效应
active component	有源元件
load capacitance	负载电容
electrical noise	电气噪声
contact bounce	触点抖动
cut-off region	截止区
over voltage protection	过压保护
under voltage protection	低压保护

Abbreviations

AC (alternating current)	交流电
DC (direct current)	直流电
ESR (equivalent series resistance)	等效串联电阻
ESD (electro static discharge)	静电放电
RF (radio frequency)	射频
EMR (electro mechanical relay)	机电继电器
SSR (solid state relay)	固体继电器
FET (field effect transistor)	场效应晶体管
MCB (micro circuit breaker)	微型断路器
BJT (bipolar junction transistor)	双极结晶体管
JFET (junction field effect transistor)	结型场效应晶体管
MOSFET (metal-oxide-semiconductor field effect transistor)	金属-氧化物-半导体场效应晶体管
SMPS (switched mode power supply）	开关（型）电源

参考译文

电子器件的类型

1　电阻器

电阻器是一种无源电气元件，其功能是向电路中的电流引入电阻，以限制电流。对电流的阻力称为电阻器的电阻。电阻值越大，表明电流的阻力越大。电阻的测量单位为欧姆（Ω），其公式如下所示。

$$R = \frac{V}{I}$$

电压（V）、电流（I）和电阻（R）与欧姆定律有关。即 $V = IR$。电阻 R 越高，给定电压 V 下的电流 I 越低。这是一个线性器件。

电阻器的电能消耗为 $P = I^2R$，P 的单位为瓦特或焦耳/秒。

电阻器是用不同的材料制成的，如碳膜、金属膜等。

按应用类型可以把电阻器分为以下不同类型：普通电阻器（用于电流限制器、设置偏置、分压器、滤波器、终端电阻器、负载电阻器等）、精密电阻器（用于电压反馈电路、电压基准）、电流感测电阻器和功率电阻器。

电阻器的选择参数：在选择电路中的任何电阻器时，设计者需要考虑电阻值（R）、其上消耗的功率（瓦特数）以及容差（+/-%）。

2 电容器

电容器是一种无源电气元件，其功能是存储电能，并在需要时将其输送至电路。电容器存储电荷的能力称为电容器的电容。它用 C 表示。电容的单位是法拉（F）。

电容器的各种用途包括：阻止直流电压的流动，并允许交流电流的流动，因此用于电路的耦合；移相和产生时间延迟；过滤，尤其是去除整流波形中的波纹；获得调谐频率以及用作电动机起动器。

电容器选择参数：在任何电路中选择电容器时，需要注意电容值、电容器的最大工作电压、容差、击穿电压、频率范围、等效串联电阻（ESR）及大小。

3 电感器

电感器（也称为线圈或扼流圈）是一种无源双端电气元件。当电流通过时，它会存储磁能。它用绝缘导线螺旋形地绕在某种材料（空气、铁、铁粉或铁氧体材料）的磁芯上构成。

电感用 L 表示，度量单位为亨利（H）。

理想的电感器具有零电阻和零电容。然而，真正的电感器有一个与线圈绕组相关的值很小的电阻，只要电流流过它，能量就会以热的形式损失。

电感器的应用：用于降压/升压功率调节器、用于直流电源的滤波电路、隔离信号、在变压器中提高/降低交流电压水平、用于振荡和调谐电路以及用于在荧光灯组中产生电压浪涌。

电感器的类型：电感器主要根据使用的芯材料和工作频率进行分类。以下是不同类型的电感器：铁心电感器、空心电感器、铁粉芯电感器、铁氧体芯电感器、可变电感器、音频感应器和射频感应器。

电感器的选择参数：在任何电路中选择电感器时，需要注意电感值、容差、最大额定电流、屏蔽和非屏蔽、大小、Q 值、频率范围、电感器的电阻以及使用的芯材类型。

4　二极管

二极管是双端半导体器件，允许电流从一个方向通过，同时阻止电流从相反方向通过。该二极管由具有 P 型材料和 N 型材料的半导体器件组成。二极管中使用的典型材料是硅和锗。当施加最小正向电压（硅的最小正向电压约 0.7V）时，它们将导通，并在反向偏置条件下保持关闭。

二极管的应用：电源转换（交流到直流）/整流、钳位电压、稳压二极管用作稳压器、过压保护、静电放电防护以及信号解调。

二极管的类型：整流二极管、开关二极管、发光二极管、稳压二极管、肖特基二极管、静电放电二极管、隧道二极管、变容二极管、光电二极管和光通信中的激光二极管。

二极管的选择参数：在任何电路中选择二极管时，需要注意正向偏置电压、最大正向电流、平均正向电流、功耗、反向击穿电压/反向峰值电压、最大反向电流、工作结温度、反向恢复时间及大小。

5　石英晶体

石英晶体是由一片薄薄的石英晶片制成的。晶片由硅材料制成，它被紧密地安装在两个平行的金属化表面之间，形成电气连接。当外部电压被施加到极板上时，晶体以一定的基频振动，从而产生在高电平和低电平之间摆动的交替波形。这种现象被称为压电效应。由于这一特性，它们与有源元件一起用于电子电路中，为处理器创建稳定的时钟输入。

石英晶体的应用：在振荡器电路中，为处理器设备提供时钟输入；射频参考信号源。

晶体的选择参数：负载电容、基频、频率容差、频率稳定性、等效串联电阻以及工作电压。

6　继电器

继电器是一种电磁开关，用于打开和关闭无电势触点。机电继电器由电枢、线圈、弹簧和触点组成。当电压施加到线圈上时，它会产生磁场。这会吸引电枢，并导致电路的打开/关闭状态发生变化。它主要用于使用低功率信号控制高功率电路。

按照结构分类，继电器主要有两种类型：机电继电器（EMR）和固态继电器（SSR）。

固态继电器的输入端有一个光电二极管，输出端有一个开关器件，如晶体管/FET。当在其输入端施加特定电压时，光电二极管导通并触发晶体管的基极以启动开关。由于其开关速度快、外形尺寸小、电压要求低，且消除了机械起拱、电气噪声和触点抖动，与机电继电器相比，它得到了更广泛的应用。

继电器的应用：用隔离的低功率控制高功率电路（如用+5V 信号控制 230V 交流电路）、切换电压开关，以及连通或断开电子微型断路器。

继电器的选择参数：输出负载类型（AC/DC）、机电继电器的输入线圈电压、用于固态继电器的光电二极管电压、输出开关电压、输出电流、导通状态电阻、开关次数、极数和触点数以及输出触点类型。

7 晶体管

晶体管是一种非线性的三端半导体器件。晶体管被认为是电子领域最重要的器件之一。晶体管改变了人类生活的许多方面。它有两个主要功能：充当固态开关和放大输入信号。晶体管在饱和或截止区工作时起开关的作用。当在活动区域中使用时，它会放大信号。它提供了非常高的输入电阻和非常低的输出电阻。

根据结构，晶体管分为 BJT（双极结晶体管）和 FET（场效应晶体管）。

晶体管的类型：BJT 包括 NPN 和 PNP；FET 包括 JFET 和 MOSFET。

晶体管（BJT/FET）的应用：模拟信号的放大；用作开关电源、微控制器等的开关设备；振荡器；过压/低压保护；调制电路和信号解调；以及逆变器和充电器中的功率控制（高电流功率晶体管）。

Exercises

[Ex. 1] Answer the following questions according to Text A.

1. What is electronic engineering?

2. What is still a major sector within the overall electronic engineering scene?

3. What can analog electronic engineering provide?

4. How much of the development budget is allocated to developing the software in many projects?

5. What does the term systems engineering refer to?

6. What are many other niche areas of electronic engineering mentioned in the passage?

7. What is electronic engineering normally focused on?

8. What are the industry sectors in which electronic engineering is used and where electronic engineers are needed?

9. What may some of the activities may within electronic engineering projects include?

10. While much of the electronic engineering is undertaken at the base laboratory, what is it sometimes necessary?

[Ex. 2] Answer the following questions according to Text B.

1. What is the resistor?

2. What are the different types of resistors by application?

3. What is the capacity of a capacitor to store electrical charge known as? How is it denoted?

4. What are the applications of inductors?

5. What is the diode? What is it made up of?

6. Where are quartz crystals used?

7. What is a relay?

8. What are the applications of relays?

9. What is the transistor considered to be?

10. What are transistors categorized into based on their construction? What are their applications?

[Ex. 3] Translate the following terms or phrases from English into Chinese and vice versa.

1. analog circuit	1.
2. electronic circuit	2.
3. radio frequency	3.
4. active component	4.
5. electrical noise	5.
6. *adj.*模拟的	6.
7. *n.&v.*控制	7.
8. *n.*设备，装置，器具	8.
9. *n.*频率	9.
10. *n.*解调，检波	10.

[Ex. 4] Translate the following passage into Chinese.

Electronics and Electronics Engineering Technology

Electronics is a branch of physics and electrical engineering. It deals with the emission, behavior, and effects of electrons and with electronic devices.

Electronics encompasses an exceptionally broad range of technology. The term originally was applied to the study of electron behavior and movement, particularly as observed in the first electron tubes. It came to be used in its broader sense with advances in knowledge about the fundamental nature of electrons and about the way in which the motion of these particles could be utilized. Today many scientific and technical disciplines deal with different aspects of electronics. Research in these fields has led to the development of such key devices as transistors, integrated circuits, lasers, and optical fibres. These in turn have made it possible to manufacture a wide array of electronic consumer, industrial, and military products. Indeed, it can be said that the world is in the midst of an electronic revolution.

Electronic engineering technology (EET) is an engineering technology field that implements and applies the principles of electrical engineering. EET deals with the design, application, installation, manufacturing, operation and maintenance of electronic systems. However, EET is a specialized discipline that has more focused on application, theory, and applied design, and implementation, while electronics may focus more of a generalized emphasis on theory and conceptual design. Electronic engineering technology is the largest branch of engineering technology and includes a diverse range of sub-disciplines, such as applied design, electronics, embedded systems, control systems, instrumentation, telecommunications, and power systems.

Reading

9 Types of Electrical Measuring Instruments① and Their Functions

Electricity is a flow that contains an electric charge and is related to physical phenomena②. It has various purposes in supporting daily activities. When using electricity in your daily life, you need a device to measure electric voltage.

There are many types of measuring instrument whose function is to measure electrical quantities which include current magnitude, endurance③, electrical power, light power, voltage and frequency.

1   Ohm Meter

Ohm meter is a device that functions to measure the amount of electricity from a switch. According to ohm's law, the circuit of electric current is directly proportional④ to the voltage. This device focuses more on resistance only.

Ohm meters are divided into two types. One is analog ohm meters, the other is digital ohm meter⑤. Analog ohm meter is a simpler device because it measures with a needle. You have to be more precise in seeing where the number is located. Digital ohm meter is an ohm meter that provides more accurate and detailed results. The disadvantage of digital ohm meter is that it is difficult to monitor when the voltage fluctuates⑥. This ohm meter also has the function of knowing the damage to an electrical circuit, so it can help your work faster.

---

① instrument ['ɪnstrəmənt] *n.*仪器；工具

② phenomena [fɪ'nɒmɪnə] *n.*现象

③ endurance [ɪn'djʊərəns] *n.*耐久性

④ proportional [prə'pɔːʃənl] *adj.*比例的，成比例的

⑤ ohm meter：欧姆表，欧姆计

⑥ fluctuate ['flʌktʃueɪt] *vi.*波动，涨落 *vt.*使波动

2 Frequency Meter

Another type of electric measuring instrument is the frequency meter. This device has a function to measure the repetition of periodic[①] movements per second. The frequency meter also consists of two types, analog and digital. The analog frequency meter works by manual needle, and the digital frequency meters use more detailed numbers.

3 Volt Meter

The next type of measuring instrument is a volt meter. This device has a function to measure the amount of voltage of an electric current flowing per second. This volt meter can measure the electric voltage within a predetermined maximum limit. If the voltage exceeds the limit it will cause damage to the device.

Volt meters also consist of two types. They are analog volt meters and digital volt meters[②]. Analog volt meter works by using a needle, while digital volt meter can show you the number in detail.

4 Ampere Meter

The fourth type of electric measuring instrument is the ampere meter[③]. This tool serves to measure the electric voltage current in a closed circuit. You only need to attach this ampere meter to the circuit of electric current you want to measure.

5 Watt Meter

The watt meter[④] has a function to measure direct current power. This electric measuring device is a combination of an ampere meter and a volt meter. Besides being able to measure direct current power, the watt meter can also measure the power of a single phase alternating current[⑤] and the power of a three phase alternating current[⑥].

6 Megger

Megger stands for mega ohm meter. Megger is a measuring device to give you information

---

① periodic [ˌpɪərɪˈɒdɪk] adj.周期的；定期的
② digital volt meter：数字电压表
③ ampere meter：安培表，电流表
④ watt meter：瓦特计，电表，功率表
⑤ single phase alternating current：单相交流电
⑥ three phase alternating current：三相交流电

whether the conductor of the instances has a direct connection. Its general function is to measure the insulation resistance of power tools. The minimum is 1000 x working voltage.

7 Kwh Meter

Kwh meter is used to calculate electrical energy consumption. Meanwhile, the induction of kwh meter is one of the type that is useful for calculating household electrical power.

In general, this kwh meter is easy to find in every house, because this kwh meter is required to know each electricity consumption in households and other buildings that use this device.

8 Oscilloscope[①]

This device has a function to map the signal from electricity. This type of electric measuring device consists of a physical frequency component. Oscilloscope has measurement results based on digital as well as graphs that are easy to read. There are so many benefits of this oscilloscope, such as differentiating AC and DC voltages in electrical components, knowing noise and checking electronic circuit signals.

9 Avo Meter

Avo meter[②] stands for ampere, voltage and ohm meter. Avo meter is a multifunctional electric measuring instrument for measuring electric current, voltage and resistance of electronic components. Avo meter consists of analog and digital.

These are some types of electric measuring instruments that can be used as needed. It's critical to note that many instruments are designed to be used on DC or AC only, while others can be used interchangeably[③]. So it is very important to use each meter only with the type of current for which the meter is designed. Using a meter with an incorrect type of current can result in damage to the meter and may cause injury[④] to the user.

---

① oscilloscope [əˈsɪləskəup] *n.*示波仪

② avo meter：万用电表

③ interchangeably [ɪntəˈtʃeɪndʒəblɪ] *adv.*可交换地，可交替地

④ injury [ˈɪndʒərɪ] *n.*伤害，损伤

Unit 2

扫码听课文

Analog Signals and Digital Signals (I)

A signal is an electromagnetic or electrical current that carries data from one system or network to another. In electronics, a signal is often a time-varying voltage that is also an electromagnetic wave carrying information, though it can take on other forms, such as current. There are two main types of signals used in electronics: analog signals and digital signals. This article discusses the corresponding characteristics, uses, advantages and disadvantages, and typical applications of analog vs. digital signals.

1 Analog Signal

An analog signal is time-varying and is generally bound to a range (e.g. +12V to –12V), but there is an infinite number of values within that continuous range. An analog signal uses a given property of the medium to convey the signal's information, such as electricity moving through a wire. In an electrical signal, the voltage, current, or frequency of the signal may be varied to represent the information. Analog signals are often calculated responses to changes in light, sound, temperature, position, pressure, or other physical phenomena.

When plotted on a amplitude vs. time graph, an analog signal should produce a smooth and continuous curve. There should not be any discrete value changes (see Figure 2-1).

Figure 2-1   Analog Signal

2 Digital Signal

A digital signal is a signal that represents data as a sequence of discrete values. A digital signal can only take on one value from a finite set of possible values at a given time. With digital signals, the physical quantity representing the information can be many things:

(1) Variable electric current or voltage.

(2) Phase or polarization of an electromagnetic field.

(3) Acoustic pressure.

(4) The magnetization of a magnetic storage media.

Digital signals are used in all digital electronics, including computing equipment and data transmission devices. When plotted on a voltage vs. time graph, digital signals are one of two values, and are usually between 0V and VCC (usually 1.8V, 3.3V, or 5V) (see Figure 2-2).

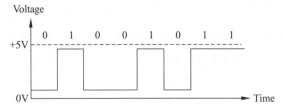

Figure 2-2　Digital Signal

3　Analog Electronics

Most of the fundamental electronic components — resistors, capacitors, inductors, diodes, transistors, and operational amplifiers (op amps) — are all inherently analog components. Circuits built with a combination of these components are analog circuits (see Figure 2-3).

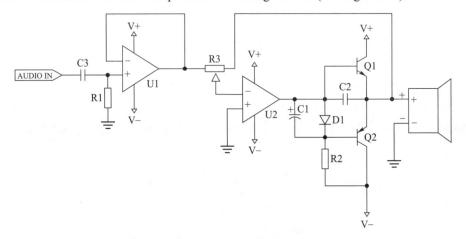

Figure 2-3　Analog Circuit

Analog circuits can be complex designs with multiple components, or they can be simple, such as two resistors that form a voltage divider. In general, analog circuits are more difficult to design than digital circuits that accomplish the same task. A designer who is familiar with analog circuits is needed to design an analog radio receiver, or an analog battery charger, since digital components have been adopted to simplify those designs.

Analog circuits are usually more susceptible to noise, with "noise" being any small, undesired variations in voltage. Small changes in the voltage level of an analog signal can produce significant errors when being processed.

Analog signals are commonly used in communication systems that convey voice, data, image, signal, or video information using a continuous signal. There are two basic kinds of analog transmission, which are both based on how they adapt data to combine an input signal with a carrier signal. The two techniques are amplitude modulation (AM) and frequency modulation (FM). AM adjusts the amplitude of the carrier signal. FM adjusts the frequency of the carrier signal. Analog transmission may be achieved via many methods:

(1) Through a twisted pair or coaxial cable.

(2) Through an optical fiber cable.

(3) Through radio.

(4) Through water.

4   Digital Electronics

Digital circuits implement components such as logic gates or more complex digital ICs. Such ICs are represented by rectangles with pins extending from them (see Figure 2-4).

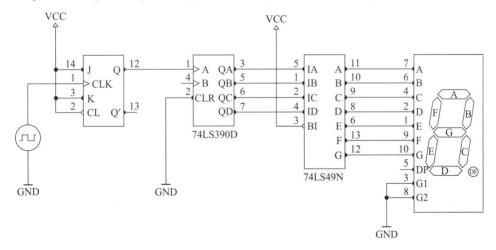

Figure 2-4   Digital Circuit

Digital circuits commonly use a binary scheme. Although data values are represented by just two states (0s and 1s), larger values can be represented by groups of binary bits. For example, in a 1-bit system, a 0 represents a data value of 0, and a 1 represents a data value of 1. However, in a 2-bit system, a 00 represents a 0, a 01 represents a 1, a 10 represents a 2, and a 11 represents a 3. In a 16-bit system, the largest number that can be represented is 2^{16}, or 65536. These groups of bits can be captured either as a sequence of successive bits or a parallel bus. This allows large streams of data to be processed easily.

Unlike analog circuits, most useful digital circuits are synchronous, meaning there is a reference clock to coordinate the operation of the circuit blocks, so they operate in a predictable manner. Analog electronics operate asynchronously, meaning they process the signal as it arrives at the input.

Most digital circuits use a digital processor to manipulate the data. This can be in the form of a simple microcontroller unit (MCU) or a more complex digital signal processor (DSP), which can filter and manipulate large streams of data such as video.

Digital signals are commonly used in communication systems where digital transmission can transfer data over point-to-point or point-to-multipoint transmission channels, such as copper wires, optical fibers, wireless communication media, storage media, or computer buses. The transferrable data is represented as an electromagnetic signal, such as a microwave, radio wave, electrical voltage, or infrared signal.

In general, digital circuits are easier to design, but they often cost more than analog circuits that are intended for the same tasks.

5　Analog-to-Digital and Digital-to-Analog Signal Conversion

Many systems must process both analog and digital signals. It is common in many communication systems to use an analog signal. These analog signals are converted to digital signals, which filter, process, and store the information.

Figure 2-5 shows a common architecture in which the RF analog front-end (AFE) consists of all analog blocks to amplify, filter, and gain the analog signal. Meanwhile, the digital signal processor (DSP) filters and processes the information. To convert signals from the analog subsystem to the digital subsystem, an analog-to-digital converter (ADC) is used. To convert signals from the digital subsystem to the analog subsystem, a digital-to-analog converter (DAC) is used.

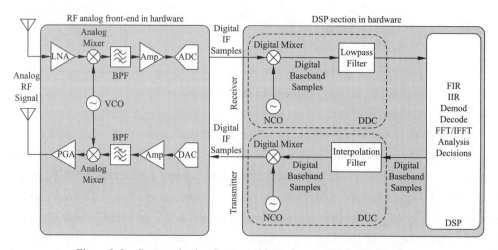

Figure 2-5　Communication System with Analog and Digital Subsystems

A digital signal processor (DSP) is a specialized microprocessor chip that performs digital signal processing operations. DSPs are fabricated on MOSFET integrated circuit chips, and are widely used in audio signal processing, telecommunications, digital image processing, high-definition television products, common consumer electronic devices such as mobile phones, and in many other significant applications.

A DSP is used to measure, filter, or compress continuous real-world analog signals. Dedicated DSPs often have higher power efficiency, making them suitable in portable devices due to their power consumption constraints. A majority of general-purpose microprocessors are also able to execute digital signal processing algorithms.

New Words

carry	[ˈkærɪ]	v.携带；传输；传播
form	[fɔːm]	n.类型；形态；状态
analog	[ˈænəlɔg]	n.模拟
		adj.模拟的
characteristic	[ˌkærəktəˈrɪstɪk]	n.特色；特点
range	[reɪndʒ]	n.区间，范围
infinite	[ˈɪnfɪnət]	adj.无限的，无穷的；极大的
continuous	[kənˈtɪnjuəs]	adj.连续的，没有间隔的
calculate	[ˈkælkjuleɪt]	v.计算；估算
pressure	[ˈpreʃə]	n.压力；气压
smooth	[smuːð]	v.使光滑
		adj.光滑的
variable	[ˈveərɪəbl]	adj.变化的，可变的；变量的
		n.变量
phase	[feɪz]	n.相位
polarization	[ˌpəʊləraɪˈzeɪʃn]	n.产生极性；极化；（光）偏振
acoustic	[əˈkuːstɪk]	adj.听觉的；声学的；原声的
magnetization	[ˌmægnətɪˈzeɪʃn]	n.磁化；磁化强度；磁化作用
transmission	[trænzˈmɪʃn]	n.播送；传送
amplifier	[ˈæmplɪfaɪə]	n.放大器
accomplish	[əˈkʌmplɪʃ]	v.完成，达成
simplify	[ˈsɪmplɪfaɪ]	v.使简化
susceptible	[səˈseptəbl]	adj.易受影响的
significant	[sɪgˈnɪfɪkənt]	adj.重要的；显著的
communication	[kəˌmjuːnɪˈkeɪʃn]	n.通信（系统）
convey	[kənˈveɪ]	v.表达；传送

adapt	[əˈdæpt]	v.（使）适应/适合
adjust	[əˈdʒʌst]	v.调整，调节；适应；校准
rectangle	[ˈrektæŋgl]	n.长方形，矩形
binary	[ˈbaɪnərɪ]	adj.二进制的；二态的；二元的
scheme	[skiːm]	n.方案，模式，计划
state	[steɪt]	n.状态
bit	[bɪt]	n.位；比特
parallel	[ˈpærəlel]	adj.并行的；并联的
bus	[bʌs]	n.总线
synchronous	[ˈsɪŋkrənəs]	adj.同步的
coordinate	[kəʊˈɔːdɪneɪt]	v.(使)协调
		adj.坐标的
filter	[ˈfɪltə]	v.过滤；筛选
		n.过滤器；滤波器
video	[ˈvɪdiəʊ]	n.视频
transfer	[trænsˈfɜː]	v.传输；使转移
channel	[ˈtʃænl]	n.通道
transferrable	[trænsˈfɜːrəbl]	adj.可传输的，转移的，可转换的
microwave	[ˈmaɪkrəweɪv]	n.微波
conversion	[kənˈvɜːʃn]	n.转换，转变
store	[stɔː]	v.存储，保存
architecture	[ˈɑːkɪtektʃə]	n.体系结构；结构；架构
subsystem	[ˈsʌbsɪstəm]	n.子系统，分系统
path	[pɑːθ]	n.路径，路线
fabricate	[ˈfæbrɪkeɪt]	v.制造，组装
portable	[ˈpɔːtəbl]	adj.轻便的，可携带的
microprocessor	[ˌmaɪkrəʊˈprəʊsesə]	n.微处理器
execute	[ˈeksɪkjuːt]	v.执行；实施
algorithm	[ˈælgərɪðəm]	n.算法

Phrases

time-varying voltage	时变电压
electromagnetic wave	电磁波
analog signal	模拟信号
digital signal	数字信号
continuous curve	连续曲线
discrete value	离散值，不连续值

a sequence of	一系列的
finite set	有限集
electromagnetic field	电磁场
storage media	存储介质
a combination of ...	……的组合
analog circuit	模拟电路
voltage divider	分压器
carrier signal	载波信号
coaxial cable	同轴电缆
optical fiber cable	光纤电缆
digital circuit	数字电路，数字线路
logic gate	逻辑门，逻辑闸
digital transmission	数字传输
copper wire	铜线；铜丝
radio wave	无线电波
audio signal	音频信号
digital image processing	数字图像处理

Abbreviations

VCC (volt current condenser)	电路的供电电压
AM (amplitude modulation)	调幅
FM (frequency modulation)	调频
IC (integrated circuit)	集成电路
MCU (microcontroller unit)	微控制器单元
AFE (analog front-end)	模拟前端
ADC (analog-to-digital converter)	模数转换器
DAC (digital-to-analog converter)	数模转换器

参考译文

模拟信号与数字信号(一)

　　信号是将数据从一个系统或网络传输到另一个系统或网络的电磁波或电流。在电子学中，信号通常是一种时变电压，它也是一种携带信息的电磁波，它还可以采取其他形式，如电流。电子学中使用的信号主要有两种：模拟信号和数字信号。下面将讨论模拟信号与数字信号的相应特性、用途、优缺点以及典型应用。

1 模拟信号

模拟信号是时变的，通常被限定在一个范围内（如+12V 至−12V），但在该连续范围内有无限多个值。模拟信号使用介质的给定特性来传递信号的信息，如通过导线的电流。在电信号中，可以通过改变信号的电压、电流或频率来表示信息。模拟信号通常是根据光、声、温度、位置、压力或其他物理现象的变化计算出来的。

当绘制振幅-时间曲线图时，模拟信号应产生平滑且连续的曲线，不应有任何离散值变化，如图 2-1 所示。

（图略）

2 数字信号

数字信号是将数据表示为一系列离散值的信号。数字信号在给定时间只能从有限的可能值集中获取一个值。对于数字信号，代表信息的物理量可以为：

（1）可变电流或电压。

（2）电磁场的相位或极化。

（3）声压。

（4）磁性存储介质的磁化。

数字信号用于所有数字电子设备，包括计算设备和数据传输设备。当绘制电压-时间曲线图时，数字信号是两个值之一，通常在 0V 和 VCC 之间（通常为 1.8V、3.3V 或 5V），如图 2-2 所示。

（图略）

3 模拟电子

大多数基本电子元件（电阻器、电容器、电感器、二极管、晶体管和运算放大器）本质上都是模拟元件。由这些元件组合而成的电路是模拟电路，如图 2-3 所示。

（图略）

模拟电路可以是由多个元件组成的复杂设计，也可以是很简单的设计，如两个电阻器构成一个分压器。一般来说，模拟电路比完成相同任务的数字电路更难设计。因为已经采用数字元件来简化设计，所以需要熟悉模拟电路的设计师来设计模拟无线电接收器或模拟电池充电器。

模拟电路通常更容易受到噪声的影响，噪声是指电压中任何微小的、不希望出现的变化。在处理模拟信号时，电压水平的微小变化可能会产生显著的误差。

模拟信号通常用于使用连续信号传输语音、数据、图像、信号或视频信息的通信系统。模拟传输有两种基本类型，它们都基于如何调整数据以将输入信号与载波信号结合。这两种技术是调幅和调频。调幅（AM）调整载波信号的振幅。调频（FM）调整载波信号的频率。模拟信号可通过多种介质传输，如：

（1）通过双绞线或同轴电缆。

（2）通过光纤电缆。

（3）通过无线电。

（4）通过水。

4　数字电子

数字电路实现逻辑门或更复杂的数字 IC 等组件。此类 IC 由矩形表示，其引脚从矩形延伸，如图 2-4 所示。

（图略）

数字电路通常使用二进制方案。尽管数据值仅由两种状态（0 和 1）表示，但较大的值可以由二进制位组表示。例如，在 1 位系统中，0 表示数据值 0，1 表示数据值 1。在 2 位系统中，00 代表 0，01 代表 1，10 代表 2，11 代表 3。在 16 位系统中，可以表示的最大数字是 2^{16} 或 65536。这些位组可以用一系列连续位或并行总线捕获，这样就可以轻松地处理大数据流。

与模拟电路不同，数字电路是同步的，这意味着有一个参考时钟来协调电路块的操作，因此它们以可预测的方式运行。模拟电子设备异步工作，这意味着它们在信号到达输入端时对其进行处理。

大多数数字电路使用数字处理器来处理数据。它是一个简单的微控制器单元（MCU）或更复杂的数字信号处理器（DSP）。它可以过滤和处理大量数据流，如视频。

数字信号通常用于通信系统中，其中数字传输可以通过点对点或点对多点传输信道（如铜线、光纤、无线通信介质、存储介质或计算机总线）传输数据。可传输的数据表示为电磁信号，如微波、无线电波、电压或红外信号。

一般来说，数字电路更容易设计，但它们通常比用于相同任务的模拟电路的成本更高。

5　模数信号和数模信号转换

很多系统都必须处理模拟信号和数字信号。在很多通信系统中，使用模拟信号是很常见的。这些模拟信号被转换为数字信号，用来过滤、处理和存储信息。

图 2-5 显示了一种常见的架构，其中 RF 模拟前端（AFE）由所有模拟模块组成，用于放大、过滤和增益模拟信号。同时，数字信号处理器（DSP）部分对信息进行过滤和处理。为了将信号从模拟子系统转换到数字子系统，需要使用模数转换器（ADC）。为了将信号从数字子系统转换到模拟子系统，需要使用数模转换器（DAC）。

（图略）

数字信号处理器（DSP）是执行数字信号处理操作的专用微处理器芯片。DSP 是在 MOSFET 集成电路芯片上制造的，广泛应用于音频信号处理、电信、数字图像处理、高清电视产品、手机等常见消费电子设备，以及许多其他重要应用。

DSP 用于测量、过滤或压缩连续的真实模拟信号。专用 DSP 通常具有更高的功率效率，由于其功耗限制，因此适用于便携式设备。大多数通用微处理器也能够执行数字信号处理算法。

Text B
Analog Signals and Digital Signals (II)

1   ADC Operation

Figure 2-6 shows ADC operation. The input is the analog signal, which is processed through a sample-hold (S/H) circuit to create an approximated digital representation of the signal. The amplitude no longer has infinite values, and has been "quantized" to discrete values, depending on the resolution of the ADC. An ADC with a higher resolution will have finer step sizes, and will more accurately represent the input analog signal. The last stage of the ADC encodes the digitized signal into a binary stream of bits that represents the amplitude of the analog signal. The digital output can now be processed in the digital domain.

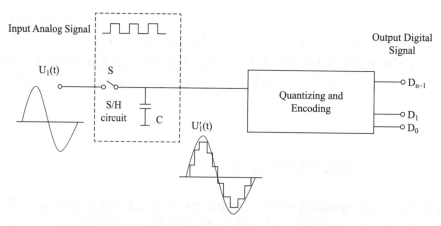

Figure 2-6   Typical ADC Architecture for Analog to Digital Signal

2   DAC Operation

A DAC provides the reverse operation. The DAC input is a binary stream of data from the digital subsystem, and it outputs a discrete value, which is approximated as an analog signal. As the resolution of the DAC increases, the output signal more closely approximates a true smooth and continuous analog signal (see Figure 2-7). There is usually a post filter in the analog signal chain to further smooth out the waveform.

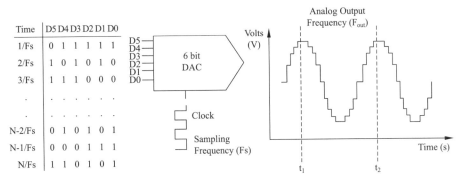

Figure 2-7   6-Bit DAC for Digital-to-Analog Signal Conversion

As mentioned before, many systems used today are "mixed signal", meaning they rely on both analog and digital subsystems. These solutions require ADCs and DACs to convert information between the two domains.

3   Advantages and Disadvantages of Digital Signals and Analog Signals

As with most engineering topics, there are pros and cons for both analog and digital signals. The specific application, performance requirements, transmission medium, and operating environment can determine whether analog or digital signals (or a combination) should be used.

3.1   Advantages and Disadvantages of Digital Signals

Advantages of using digital signals, including digital signal processor (DSP) and communication systems, include the following:

(1) Digital signals can convey information with less noise, distortion, and interference.

(2) Digital circuits can be reproduced easily in mass quantities at comparatively low costs.

(3) Digital signal processing is more flexible because DSP operations can be altered using digitally programmable systems.

(4) Digital signal processing is more secure because digital information can be easily encrypted and compressed.

(5) Digital systems are more accurate, and the probability of error occurrence can be reduced by employing error detection and correction codes.

(6) Digital signals can be easily stored on any magnetic media or optical media using semiconductor chips.

(7) Digital signals can be transmitted over long distances.

Disadvantages of using digital signals include the following:

(1) A higher bandwidth is required for digital communication when compared to analog transmission of the same information.

(2) DSP processes the signal at high speeds, and comprises more top internal hardware resources. This results in higher power dissipation compared to analog signal processor, which includes passive components that consume less energy.

(3) Digital systems and processing are typically more complex.

3.2　Advantages and Disadvantages of Analog Signals

Advantages of using analog signals, including analog signal processor (ASP) and communication systems, include the following:

(1) Analog signals are easier to process.

(2) Analog signals are best suited for audio and video transmission.

(3) Analog signals are of much higher density, and can present more refined information.

(4) Analog signals use less bandwidth than digital signals.

(5) Analog signals provide a more accurate representation of changes in physical phenomena, such as sound, light, temperature, position, or pressure.

(6) Analog communication systems are less sensitive in terms of electrical tolerance.

Disadvantages of using analog signals, including analog signal processor (ASP) and communication systems, include the following:

(1) Data transmission at long distances may result in undesirable signal disturbances.

(2) Analog signals are prone to generation loss.

(3) Analog signals are subject to noise and distortion, as opposed to digital signals which have much higher immunity.

(4) Analog signals are generally lower quality signals than digital signals.

4　Systems and Applications of Analog Signals and Digital Signals

Traditional audio and communication systems use analog signals. However, with advances in silicon process technologies, digital signal processing capabilities, encoding algorithms, and encryption requirements — in addition to increases in bandwidth efficiencies — many of these systems have become digital. There are still some applications where analog signals have legacy use or benefits. Most systems that interface to real-world signals (such as sound, light, temperature, and pressure) use an analog interface to capture or transmit the information. A few analog signal applications are listed below:

(1) Audio recording and reproduction.

(2) Temperature sensors.

(3) Image sensors.

(4) Radio signals.

(5) Telephones.

(6) Control systems.

Although many original communication systems used analog signals (telephones), recent technologies use digital signals because of their advantages with noise immunity, encryption, bandwidth efficiency, and the ability to use repeaters for long-distance transmission. A few digital signal applications are listed below:

(1) communication systems (broadband, cellular).

(2) Networking and data communications.

(3) Digital interfaces for programmability.

5　Conclusion

This article introduces some of the basic concepts of analog and digital signals, and their uses in electronics. They each have their own advantages and disadvantages. Knowing your application's needs and performance requirements will help you determine which signals to choose.

New Words

sample	[ˈsɑːmpl]	vt.采样，取样
		n.样品；样本
quantize	[ˈkwɒntaɪz]	vt.数值化；使量子化
resolution	[ˌrezəˈluːʃn]	n.分辨率
reverse	[rɪˈvɜːs]	adj.相反的，反面的
		v.（使）反转；（使）颠倒
domain	[dəˈmeɪn]	n.领域，范围
distortion	[dɪˈstɔːʃn]	n.失真，变形
interference	[ˌɪntəˈfɪərəns]	n.干扰，干涉
reproduce	[ˌriːprəˈdjuːs]	v.重复生产，复制
flexible	[ˈfleksəbl]	adj.柔韧的；灵活的
alter	[ˈɔːltə]	v.改变；变更
encrypt	[ɪnˈkrɪpt]	v.加密，将……译成密码
accurate	[ˈækjərət]	adj.精确的，精准的
probability	[ˌprɒbəˈbɪlətɪ]	n.可能性；概率
dissipation	[ˌdɪsɪˈpeɪʃn]	n.消耗；浪费
energy	[ˈenədʒɪ]	n.能量
immunity	[ɪˈmjuːnətɪ]	n.免除，豁免；免疫力

capability	[ˌkeɪpəˈbɪlətɪ]	n.能力
cellular	[ˈseljələ]	n.蜂窝网络
		adj.蜂窝的
programmability	[prəʊgræməˈbɪlətɪ]	n.可编程性

Phrases

sample-hold (S/H) circuit	采样保持电路
step size	步长
mixed signal	混合信号，复合信号
performance requirement	性能需求
error detection	误差检测，错误检测
correction code	校正码
magnetic media	磁性媒体，磁介质
optical media	光学媒体，光介质
semiconductor chip	半导体芯片，半导体晶片
result in	导致；造成

参考译文

模拟信号与数字信号(二)

1　模数转换操作

图 2-6 显示了模数转换操作。输入是模拟信号，通过采样保持（S/H）电路对其进行处理，以创建信号的近似数字表示。振幅不再具有无限值，并已"量化"为离散值，具体取决于模数转换的分辨率。具有更高分辨率的模数转换将具有更精细的步长，并将更准确地表示输入模拟信号。模数转换的最后一级将数字化信号编码为代表模拟信号振幅的二进制比特流。现在可以在数字域中处理数字输出。

（图略）

2　数模转换操作

数模转换提供反向操作。数模转换输入是来自数字子系统的二进制数据流，它输出一个与模拟信号近似的离散值。随着数模转换分辨率的增加，输出信号更接近于真实的平滑连续模拟信号，如图 2-7 所示。在模拟信号链中通常有一个后滤波器来进一步平滑波形。

（图略）

如前所述，如今使用的许多系统都是"混合信号"，这意味着它们依赖模拟子系统和数字子系统。这些解决方案需要模数转换和数模转换在两个域之间转换信息。

3 数字信号和模拟信号的优缺点

与大多数工程主题一样，模拟信号和数字信号各有利弊。具体的应用、性能要求、传输介质和操作环境可以决定应使用模拟信号或数字信号（或组合）。

3.1 数字信号的优缺点

使用数字信号（包括数字信号处理器和通信系统）的优点包括：

（1）数字信号可以以较少的噪声、失真和干扰传递信息。

（2）数字电路可以用相对较低的成本轻松地大量复制。

（3）数字信号处理更加灵活，因为可以使用数字可编程系统替换 DSP 操作。

（4）数字信号处理更安全，因为数字信息容易加密和压缩。

（5）数字系统更精确，通过使用错误检测和校正码，可以降低错误发生的概率。

（6）使用半导体芯片可以将数字信号很容易地存储在任何磁性介质或光学介质上。

（7）数字信号可以远距离传输。

使用数字信号的缺点包括：

（1）与具有相同信息的模拟传输相比，数字通信需要更高的带宽。

（2）DSP 高速处理信号，并包含更多的顶级内部硬件资源。与模拟信号处理器（包含能耗较低的无源组件）相比，它会导致更高的功耗。

（3）数字系统和处理通常更复杂。

3.2 模拟信号的优缺点

使用模拟信号（包括模拟信号处理器和通信系统）的优点包括：

（1）模拟信号更容易处理。

（2）模拟信号非常适合音频和视频传输。

（3）模拟信号的密度更高，可以提供更精确的信息。

（4）模拟信号比数字信号使用的带宽更少。

（5）模拟信号能更准确地表示物理现象的变化，如声音、光线、温度、位置或压力。

（6）模拟通信系统在电气容差方面不太敏感。

使用模拟信号（包括模拟信号处理器和通信系统）的缺点包括：

（1）长距离的数据传输可能导致不良的信号干扰。

（2）模拟信号容易产生损耗。

（3）模拟信号易受噪声和失真的影响，而数字信号的抗扰度要高得多。

（4）模拟信号通常比数字信号质量低。

4　模拟信号和数字信号的系统和应用

传统的音频和通信系统使用模拟信号。然而，随着硅工艺技术、数字信号处理能力、编码算法和加密要求的进步及带宽效率的提高，很多系统已经成为数字系统。在一些应用中，模拟信号仍有传统用途或优点。大多数与真实信号（如声音、光、温度和压力）连接的系统都使用模拟接口来捕获或传输信息。下面列出了一些模拟信号的应用：

（1）录音和复制。

（2）温度传感器。

（3）图像传感器。

（4）无线电信号。

（5）电话。

（6）控制系统。

尽管许多原始通信系统使用模拟信号（电话），但最近的技术使用数字信号，因为它们具有抗噪性、加密、带宽效率的优点以及使用中继器进行远程传输的能力。以下列出了一些数字信号的应用：

（1）通信系统（宽带、蜂窝）。

（2）网络和数据通信。

（3）可编程的数字接口。

5　结论

本文介绍了模拟信号和数字信号的一些基本概念，以及它们在电子学中的应用。它们各有优缺点。了解应用的需求和性能要求将有助于确定要选择哪种信号。

Exercises

[Ex. 1]　Answer the following questions according to Text A.

1. What is a signal in electronics?

2. What are analog signals?

3. What is a digital signal?

4. What can the physical quantity representing the information be with digital signals?

5. What can analog circuits be?

6. How may analog transmission be achieved?

7. What does "most useful digital circuits are synchronous" mean?

8. Where are digital signals commonly used?

9. What is a digital signal processor (DSP)?

10. What is a DSP used to do?

[Ex. 2] Answer the following questions according to Text B.

1. What is the input in ADC operation?

2. What does the last stage of the ADC do?

3. What is the DAC input?

4. What can determine whether analog or digital signals (or a combination) should be used?

5. Why is digital signal processing more secure?

6. What is the first disadvantage of using digital signals mentioned in the passage?

7. What do analog signals provide?

8. What are a few analog signal applications listed in the passage?

9. Why do recent technologies use digital signals?

10. What are a few digital signal applications listed in the passage?

[Ex. 3] Translate the following terms or phrases from English into Chinese and vice versa.

1. carrier signal	1.
2. digital transmission	2.
3. electromagnetic wave	3.
4. logic gate	4.
5. semiconductor chip	5.
6. *n.*算法	6.
7. *n.*放大器	7.
8. *n.*通道	8.
9. *n.*微处理器	9.
10. *vt.*采样，取样 *n.*样品；样本	10.

[Ex. 4] Translate the following passage into Chinese.

Analog vs. Digital FAQ

1 What is the difference between analog and digital technology?

Both analog and digital signals carry information. The difference lies in how signals are encoded. In analog technology, waves or signals are stored in the original form, as in the case of an analog recorder where signals are recorded in the tape directly from the microphone. However, in digital technology, waves or signals are sampled at intervals and then converted into numbers before being stored in a digital device.

2   Is WiFi digital or analog?

Signals are neither analog nor digital because they are simply waves of information. It's the way they are encrypted that makes them analog or digital. So, in this way, WiFi technology sends information in digital form. Thus, WiFi is digital technology.

3   What are the advantages of digital technology?

Signals that are digitally transmitted require less bandwidth than analog transmitted signals. Moreover, as data is stored in the form of numbers in digital technology, it makes it compact, compressible and easy to process via digital signal processors (DSPs).

4   What are the advantages and disadvantages of analog technology?

In analog technology, signals are easy to synchronize with smaller bandwidth. Another advantage is that they are easy to process and allow an infinite range of values to be stored. However, a major con of analog signals is that they produce unwanted noise and disturbance in the transmitted data.

5   Are digital watches more accurate than analog watches?

When it comes to accuracy, digital watches are more accurate than analog because they have less variation in electronic signals.

Reading

Microprocessor

Microprocessor is a controlling unit of a micro-computer, which is fabricated on a small chip capable of performing ALU (arithmetic logical unit[①]) operations and communicating with the other devices connected to it.

Microprocessor consists of an ALU, register[②] array, and a control unit. ALU performs arithmetical and logical operations on the data received from the memory or an input device. Register array consists of registers identified by letters like B, C, D, E, H, L and accumulator[③]. The control unit controls the flow of data and instructions within the computer.

1   How Does a Microprocessor Work?

The microprocessor follows a sequence: fetch[④], decode[⑤], and then execute.

---

① arithmetic logical unit: 算术逻辑单元
② register ['redʒɪstə] n.寄存器
③ accumulator [ə'kjuːmjəleɪtə] n.累加器
④ fetch [fetʃ] v.获取
⑤ decode [ˌdiː'kəʊd] vt.译码，解码

Initially, the instructions are stored in the memory in a sequential order. The microprocessor fetches those instructions from the memory, then decodes and executes those instructions till STOP instruction is reached. Later, it sends the result in binary to the output port[①]. Between these processes, the register stores the temporary[②] data and ALU performs the computing functions.

Here is a list of some of the frequently used terms in a microprocessor:

(1) Instruction set[③]: it is the set of instructions that the microprocessor can understand.

(2) Bandwidth: it is the number of bits processed in a single instruction.

(3) Clock speed: it determines the number of operations per second the processor can perform. It is expressed in megahertz[④] (MHz) or gigahertz[⑤] (GHz).It is also known as clock rate.

(4) Word length[⑥]: it depends upon the width of internal data bus, registers, ALU, etc. A 16-bit microprocessor can process 16-bit data at a time. The word length ranges from 4 bits to 64 bits depending upon the type of the microcomputer.

(5) Data types: the microprocessor has multiple data type formats like binary, BCD[⑦], ASCII[⑧], signed and unsigned numbers[⑨].

2　Features of a Microprocessor

Here is a list of some of the most prominent features of any microprocessor:

(1) Cost-effective: the microprocessor chips are available at low prices and low cost.

(2) Size: the microprocessor is of small size chip, hence it is portable.

(3) Low power consumption: microprocessors are manufactured by using metaloxide[⑩] semiconductor technology, which has low power consumption.

(4) Versatility[⑪]: the microprocessors are versatile as we can use the same chip in a number of applications by configuring the software program.

(5) Reliability: the failure rate[⑫] of an IC in microprocessors is very low, hence it is reliable.

---

① port [pɔ:t] *n.*端口

② temporary ['temprərɪ] *adj.*短暂的，临时的

③ instruction set：指令集

④ megahertz ['megəhɜ:ts] *n.*兆赫

⑤ gigahertz ['gɪgəhɜ:ts] *n.*千兆赫

⑥ word length：字长

⑦ BCD：二进制编码数据

⑧ ASCII：美国信息交换标准代码

⑨ unsigned number：无符号数

⑩ metaloxide [metə'lɒksaɪd] *n.*金属氧化物

⑪ versatility [ˌvɜ:sə'tɪlətɪ] *n.*通用性

⑫ failure rate：失效率，故障率

3. Classification

3.1　RISC Processor

RISC stands for reduced instruction set computer[①]. It is designed to reduce the execution time by simplifying the instruction set of the computer. Using RISC processors, each instruction requires only one clock cycle to execute results in uniform execution time. This reduces the efficiency as there are more lines of code, hence more RAM is needed to store the instructions. The compiler also has to work more to convert high-level language instructions into machine code[②].

Architecture of RISC: RISC microprocessor architecture uses highly-optimized set of instructions. It is used in portable devices like Apple iPod due to its power efficiency.

The major characteristics of a RISC processor are as follows:

(1) It consists of simple instructions.

(2) It supports various data-type formats.

(3) It utilizes simple addressing modes[③] and fixed length instructions for pipelining.

(4) It supports register to use in any context.

(5) One cycle execution time.

(6) "LOAD" and "STORE" instructions are used to access the memory location.

(7) It consists of larger number of registers.

(8) It consists of less number of transistors.

3.2　CISC Processor

CISC stands for complex instruction set computer[④]. It is designed to minimize the number of instructions per program and ignore[⑤] the number of cycles per instruction. The emphasis is on building complex instructions directly into the hardware.

The compiler[⑥] has to do very little work to translate a high-level language into assembly level language/machine code because the length of the code is relatively short, so very little RAM is required to store the instructions.

Architecture of CISC: its architecture is designed to decrease[⑦] the memory cost because more storage is needed in larger programs. To solve this problem, the number of instructions per program can be reduced by embedding the number of operations in a single instruction.

---

① reduced instruction set computer：精简指令集计算机

② machine code：机器代码

③ addressing mode：寻址模式

④ complex instruction set computer：复杂指令集计算机

⑤ ignore [ɪɡˈnɔː] v.忽略，不顾

⑥ compiler [kəmˈpaɪlə] n.编译器；编译程序

⑦ decrease [dɪˈkriːs] v.减少

Characteristics of CISC:

(1) Variety of addressing modes.

(2) Larger number of instructions.

(3) Variable length of instruction formats.

(4) Several cycles may be required to execute one instruction.

(5) Instruction-decoding logic is complex.

(6) One instruction is required to support multiple addressing modes.

3.3　Special Processors

These are the processors which are designed for some special purposes.

3.3.1　Coprocessor[①]

A coprocessor is a specially designed microprocessor, which can handle its particular function many times faster than the ordinary microprocessor.

For example: Math Coprocessor.

3.3.2　Input/Output Processor

It is a specially designed microprocessor having a local memory of its own, which is used to control I/O devices with minimum CPU involvement[②].

For example:

(1) DMA (direct memory access[③]) controller.

(2) Keyboard/mouse controller.

(3) Graphic display controller.

(4) SCSI[④] port controller.

3.3.3　DSP (digital signal processor)

This processor is specially designed to process the analog signals into a digital form. This is done by sampling the voltage level at regular time intervals and converting the voltage at that instant into a digital form. This process is performed by a circuit called an analog-to-digital converter or ADC.

A DSP contains the following components:

(1) Program memory: it stores the programs that DSP will use to process data.

(2) Data memory: it stores the information to be processed.

---

① coprocessor [ˈkəʊˌprəʊsesə] n.协处理器

② involvement [ɪnˈvɒlvmənt] n.参与；牵连

③ direct memory access：直接存储器存取，直接存储器访问

④ SCSI：小型计算机系统接口

(3) Compute engine[①]: it performs the mathematical processing, accessing the program from the program memory and the data from the data memory.

(4) Input/Output: it connects to the outside world.

Its applications are:

(1) Sound and music synthesis[②].

(2) Audio and video compression[③].

(3) Video signal processing.

(4) 2D and 3D graphics acceleration[④].

---

① engine [ˈendʒɪn] n.引擎
② synthesis [ˈsɪnθəsɪs] n.合成
③ compression [kəmˈprɛʃn] n.压缩
④ acceleration [əkˌseləˈreɪʃn] n.加速

Unit 3

Integrated Circuit (IC)

扫码听课文

Over the years, we have observed how technology has managed to squeeze itself into a more compact and concise structure. For instance, the first computers that were made were the size of 1000 laptops which we use today. How has this been made possible? The integrated circuit is the answer to it.

1 Why Was Integrated Circuit Developed?

The circuits that were made previously were large and bulky, consisting of circuit components like resistor, capacitor, inductor, transistor, diodes, etc., which were connected with copper wires. This factor limited the use of the circuits to big machines. It was not possible to create small and compact appliances with these big circuits. Moreover, they were not entirely shockproof and reliable.

As it is said, necessity is the mother of all inventions. So there was a need to develop smaller size circuits with more power and safety to incorporate them into devices. Three American scientists invented transistors that simplified things to a large extent, but the development of integrated circuits changed electronics technology's face.

2 Definition of Integrated Circuit

Integrated circuit is a small chip of a semiconductor material that mounts an entire circuit on itself. It is very small when compared to the standard circuits, which are made of independent circuit components. The most commonly used IC is the monolithic integrated circuit.

IC is defined as a microchip on which thousands and hundreds of electrical components, such as resistors, capacitors and transistors, are fabricated. An IC functions as an oscillator, amplifier, microprocessor, timer or even as a computer memory.

3 Integrated Circuit Design

Certain logic techniques and circuit designs are used to design an integrated circuit. There are three categories of IC design. They are digital design, analog design and mixed design.

3.1　Digital Design

When used as computer memories (such as RAM and ROM), ICs are designed by the digital design method. This design method ensures that the circuit density is maximum and the overall efficiency is maximum. The ICs designed using this method work with binary input data such as 0 and 1. Figure 3-1 shows the steps involved in designing digital integrated circuits.

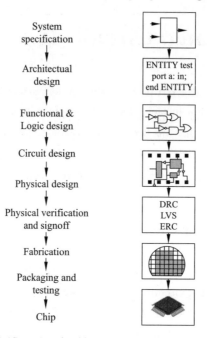

System
specification

Architectual
design

Functional &
Logic design

Circuit design

Physical design

Physical verification
and signoff

Fabrication

Packaging and
testing

Chip

ENTITY test
port a: in;
end ENTITY

DRC
LVS
ERC

Figure 3-1　The Steps Involved in Designing Digital Integrated Circuits

3.2　Analog Design

When ICs are used as oscillators, filters and regulators, analog design method is employed to design the integrated chip. This design method is used when the power dissipation, gain and resistance are required to be perfect.

3.3　Mixed Design

The mixed design integrates the analog and digital design principles. The mixed ICs function as digital-to-analog converters, analog-to-digital converters (D/A and A/D converters) and clock/timing ICs.

4　Integrated Circuit Construction

An integrated circuit is a complex layering of semiconductors, coppers, and other interconnected materials to form resistors, transistors and other components.

The semiconductor wafers that make up the ICs are fragile, and the connections between the layers very intricate. As an IC die is too small to solder and connect to, the ICs are packaged. The IC package turns the delicate and tiny die into a black chip we are familiar with. There are many different types of packages, each having unique dimensions and mounting types.

All ICs are polarized, and every pin in an IC is unique both in location and function. Integrated chips use a notch or a dot to indicate the first pin.

Once the first pin is identified, the remaining pins increase sequentially counterclockwise direction around the chip.

5 Integrated Circuit Features

5.1 Construction & Packaging

An integrated circuit is made of semiconducting materials such as silicon. The integrated chips are tiny and delicate to be handled; hence they are bonded into a set of tiny gold and aluminium wires and cast into a flat block of plastic or ceramic. The block has metal pins on the outside that leads to the wires inside. The solid block prevents overheating of the chip and keeps it cool.

5.2 Size of an IC

The size of the integrated chip varies between 1 square mm to more than 200 square mm.

5.3 Integration of an IC

Integrated chips get their name because they combine different devices on the same chip. A microcontroller is an IC that incorporates a microprocessor, memory and interface all in the same device.

6 Commonly Used ICs

6.1 Logic Gate ICs

Logic gate ICs are combinational circuits that provide a logical output based on different input signals. It can have two to three inputs but only one output.

6.2 Timer ICs

A timer IC is produced with accurate timing cycles with a 100 percent or 50 percent duty cycle.

6.3　Operational Amplifiers

An operational amplifier or an OpAmp is a high gain voltage amplifier with a differential input and a single-ended output.

6.4　Voltage Regulators

A voltage regulator IC provides a constant DC output irrespective of the changes in DC input.

7　Moore's Law

In 1965, Gordon Moore posited that roughly every two years, the number of transistors on microchips will double. Commonly referred to as Moore's Law, this phenomenon suggests that computational progress will become significantly faster and more efficient over time. Widely regarded as one of the hallmark theories of the 21st century, Moore's Law carries significant implications for the future of technological progress.

Moore's Law has had a direct impact on the progress of computing power. What this means specifically is that transistors in integrated circuits have become faster. Transistors conduct electricity, which contain carbon and silicon molecules that can make the electricity run faster across the circuit. The faster the integrated circuit conducts electricity, the faster the computer operates.

Integrated circuits revolutionized electronics and computing during the 1960s and 1970s. First, engineers were putting dozens of components on a chip in what was called small scale integration (SSI). Medium scale integration (MSI) soon followed, with hundreds of components in an area the same size. Around 1970, large scale integration (LSI) brought thousands of components, very large scale integration (VLSI) gave us tens of thousands, and ultra large scale integration (ULSI) millions—and the physical size of all chips is no larger than that before.

8　Why Are Integrated Circuits Important?

Integrated circuits revolutionized the electronic industry and made way for devices such as computers, CD players, televisions and many appliances around the home. In addition, the spread of the chips helped to bring advanced electronic devices to all parts of the world.

9　What Is the Difference Between a Semiconductor and an IC?

IC is a thin device made of silicon that contains at least two interconnected semiconductor devices. On the other hand, a semiconductor is a substance with electrical properties intermediate between a good conductor and a good insulator.

New Words

squeeze	[skwi:z]	v.挤压，压缩
concise	[kənˈsaɪs]	adj.简明的，简洁的
laptop	[ˈlæptɒp]	n.便携式计算机
bulky	[ˈbʌlkɪ]	adj.庞大的；笨重的
factor	[ˈfæktə]	n.因素；系数
shockproof	[ˈʃɒkpru:f]	adj.防震的
reliable	[rɪˈlaɪəbl]	adj.可靠的
necessity	[nəˈsesətɪ]	n.必要，需要
invention	[ɪnˈvenʃn]	n.发明
independent	[ˌɪndɪˈpendənt]	adj.独立的；无关联的
monolithic	[ˌmɒnəˈlɪθɪk]	adj.单片的；整体的
microchip	[ˈmaɪkrəʊtʃɪp]	n.微晶片；微型集成电路片
		v.植微芯片于……
gain	[geɪn]	n.增益
		v.获得；受益；增加
integrate	[ˈɪntɪgreɪt]	v.集成，合并
combination	[ˌkɒmbɪˈneɪʃn]	n.结合（体）；联合（体）
fragile	[ˈfrædʒaɪl]	adj.脆弱的；易碎的
intricate	[ˈɪntrɪkət]	adj.错综复杂的
solder	[ˈsəʊldə]	v.焊接，焊合
dimension	[daɪˈmenʃn]	n.尺寸；规模；维度
polarize	[ˈpəʊləraɪz]	v.使极化；使偏振
notch	[nɒtʃ]	n.(V 字状的)槽口
identify	[aɪˈdentɪfaɪ]	vt.识别；确定
counterclockwise	[ˌkaʊntəˈklɒkwaɪz]	adj.逆时针方向的，自右向左的
		adv.逆时针方向地，自右向左地
delicate	[ˈdelɪkət]	adj.精致的；纤细的
overheat	[ˌəʊvəˈhi:t]	v.变得过热
square	[skweə]	adj.平方的
microcontroller	[ˌmaɪkrəʊkɒnˈtrəʊlə]	n.微控制器
interface	[ˈɪntəfeɪs]	n.界面；接口
combinational	[ˌkɒmbəˈneɪʃənəl]	adj.组合的，结合的，联合的
input	[ˈɪnpʊt]	n.输入；输入电路；输入端

output	[ˈaʊtpʊt]	n.输出；输出端；输出量
		v.输出
timer	[ˈtaɪmə]	n.定时器；计时器
constant	[ˈkɒnstənt]	adj.恒定的
		n.常量
irrespective	[ˌɪrɪˈspektɪv]	adj.不考虑的，不顾的；无关的
phenomenon	[fəˈnɒmɪnən]	n.现象，事件
hallmark	[ˈhɔːlmɑːk]	n.特点，标志
		vt.使具有……标志
implication	[ˌɪmplɪˈkeɪʃn]	n.影响
carbon	[ˈkɑːbən]	n.碳
substance	[ˈsʌbstəns]	n.物质，材料
conductor	[kənˈdʌktə]	n.导体
insulator	[ˈɪnsjuleɪtə]	n.绝缘体

Phrases

computer memory	计算机存储器
digital design	数字设计
analog design	模拟设计
mixed design	混合设计
make up	构成；形成
semiconducting material	半导体材料
be bonded into	结合在一起
input signal	输入信号
Moore's law	摩尔定律
electrical property	电气特性

Abbreviations

RAM (random access memory)	随机存储器
ROM (read only memory)	只读存储器
SSI (small scale integration)	小规模集成电路
MSI (medium scale integration)	中规模集成电路
LSI (large scale integration)	大规模集成电路
VLSI (very large scale integration)	甚大规模集成电路
ULSI (ultra large scale integration)	超规模集成电路

参考译文

集成电路(IC)

多年来，我们观察技术如何设法将自己压缩成一个更紧凑、更简洁的结构。例如，最早制造的计算机的大小是今天使用的笔记本电脑的 1000 倍。这是如何实现的？集成电路就是答案。

1   为什么要开发集成电路?

以前制造的电路体积很大且笨重，由电阻器、电容器、电感器、晶体管、二极管等电路元件组成，这些元件用铜线连接。这一因素限制了电路在大型机器上的使用。用这些大电路制造小型、紧凑的电器是不可能的。此外，它们并非完全防震和可靠。

正如人们所说，需求是一切发明之母。因此，有必要开发更小尺寸、更大功率和更安全的电路，以便将其整合到设备中。三位美国科学家发明的晶体管在很大程度上简化了这一需求，但集成电路的发展改变了电子技术的面貌。

2   集成电路的定义

集成电路是一种由半导体材料制成的小型芯片，它将整个电路安装在自身上。与由独立电路元件构成的标准电路相比，它非常小。最常用的集成电路是单片集成电路。

集成电路被定义为一种微芯片，在其上可以制造成百上千的电子元件，如电阻、电容和晶体管。集成电路可以作为振荡器、放大器、微处理器、定时器，甚至是计算机存储器。

3   集成电路设计

某些逻辑技术和电路设计用于设计集成电路。IC 设计分为数字设计、模拟设计和混合设计三类。

3.1   数字设计

当用作计算机存储器（如 RAM 和 ROM）时，集成电路采用数字设计方法。这种设计方法保证电路密度最大且整体效率最高。使用这种方法设计的集成电路可以处理二进制输入数据，如 0 和 1。图 3-1 显示了设计数字集成电路涉及的步骤。

（图略）

3.2   模拟设计

当集成电路用作振荡器、滤波器和调节器时，采用模拟设计方法来设计集成芯片。当要求最佳功耗、增益和电阻时，可采用该设计方法。

3.3 混合设计

混合设计融合了数字和模拟设计原理。混合集成电路用作数模转换器、模数转换器（D/A 和 A/D 转换器）和时钟/定时集成电路。

4 集成电路的构造

集成电路是由半导体、铜和其他互连材料组成的复杂分层，以形成电阻、晶体管和其他组件。

构成集成电路的半导体晶片很脆弱，层与层之间的连接非常复杂。由于 IC 晶粒太小，无法焊接和连接，因此需要对其进行封装。IC 封装将精密微小的晶粒变成我们熟悉的黑色芯片。封装有许多不同类型，每种类型都有独特的尺寸和安装类型。

所有集成电路都是极化的，集成电路中的每个引脚在位置和功能上都是唯一的。集成芯片使用槽口或点指示第一个引脚。

一旦识别出第一个引脚，其余引脚围绕芯片逆时针方向依次增加。

5 集成电路的特性

5.1 构造和包装

集成电路是由硅等半导体材料制成的。集成芯片小巧、易碎，不易于操作，因此它们被粘合成一组细小的金丝和铝丝，并被铸造成一块扁平的塑料或陶瓷块。该模块的外部有金属引脚，连接到内部的电线。实心块可防止芯片过热并保持冷却。

5.2 集成电路的尺寸

集成芯片的尺寸为 $1\sim200\text{mm}^2$。

5.3 集成电路的集成

集成芯片之所以得名，是因为它们将不同的设备组合在同一个芯片上。微控制器是一种集成电路，它在同一个元件中集成了微处理器、存储器和接口。

6 常用的集成电路

6.1 逻辑门集成电路

逻辑门集成电路是基于不同输入信号提供逻辑输出的组合电路。它可以有 2~3 个输入，但只有一个输出。

6.2　定时器集成电路

定时器集成电路具有精确的定时周期，占空比为 100% 或 50%。

6.3　运算放大器

运算放大器（OpAmp）是一种具有差分输入和单端输出的高增益电压放大器。

6.4　电压调节器

电压调节器集成电路提供恒定的直流输出，与直流输入的变化无关。

7　摩尔定律

1965 年，戈登·摩尔提出，大约每两年，微芯片上的晶体管数量就会翻一番。它通常被称为摩尔定律。这种现象表明，随着时间的推移，计算过程将显著加快，效率更高。摩尔定律被广泛认为是 21 世纪的标志性理论之一，它对未来的技术进步具有重要意义。

摩尔定律直接影响了计算能力的发展。具体来说，集成电路中的晶体管变得更快。晶体管导电，其中包含碳和硅分子，可以使电流在电路中运行得更快。集成电路的导电速度越快，计算机的运行速度就越快。

在 20 世纪 60 年代和 70 年代，集成电路彻底改变了电子学和计算技术。首先，工程师们在一个芯片上放置了几十个组件，这就是所谓的小规模集成电路（SSI）。接着，中规模集成电路（MSI）在一个相同大小的区域中放置了数百个组件。大约在 1970 年，大规模集成电路（LSI）提供了数千个组件，甚大规模集成电路（VLSI）提供了数万个组件，超大规模集成电路（ULSI）提供了数百万个组件——所有芯片的物理尺寸都不比以前大。

8　为什么集成电路很重要?

集成电路彻底改变了电子行业，为计算机、CD 播放器、电视和许多家用电器等设备开辟了道路。此外，芯片的普及有助于将先进的电子设备带到世界各地。

9　半导体和集成电路有什么区别?

集成电路是一种由硅制成的薄器件，至少包含两个相互连接的半导体器件。半导体是一种电性能介于良导体和良绝缘体之间的物质。

Text B

VHDL

1　What Is VHDL?

VHDL (VHSIC hardware description language) is becoming increasingly popular as a way to capture complex digital electronic circuits for both simulation and synthesis. VHSIC stands for very high speed integrated circuit.

VHDL is a programming language that has been designed and optimized for describing the behavior of digital circuits and systems. It combines features of the following:

1.1　A Simulation Modeling Language

VHDL has many features appropriate for describing in great detail the behavior of electronic components ranging from simple logic gates to complete microprocessors and custom chips. Features of VHDL allow electrical aspects of circuit behavior (such as rise and fall times of signals, delays through gates, and functional operation) to be precisely described. The resulting VHDL simulation models can then be used as building blocks in larger circuits for the purpose of simulation.

1.2　A Design Entry Language

Just as high-level programming languages allow complex design concepts to be expressed as computer programs, VHDL allows the behavior of complex electronic circuits to be captured into a design system for automatic circuit synthesis or for system simulation. Like Pascal, C and C++, VHDL includes features useful for structured design techniques, and offers a rich set of control and data representation features. Unlike these other programming languages, VHDL provides features allowing concurrent events to be described. This is important because the hardware being described using VHDL is inherently concurrent in its operation. Users of PLD programming languages such as PALASM, ABEL, CUPL and others will find the concurrent features of VHDL quite familiar. Those who have only programmed using software programming languages will, however, have some new concepts to grasp.

1.3　A Test Language

One of the most important aspects of VHDL is its ability to capture the performance specification for a circuit in a form commonly referred to as a test bench. Test benches are VHDL descriptions of circuit stimulus and corresponding expected outputs that verify the behavior of a circuit over time. Test benches should be an integral part of any VHDL project, and should be created in parallel with other descriptions of the circuit.

1.4　A Netlist Language

VHDL is a powerful language with which to enter new designs at a high level, but it is also useful as a low-level form of communication between different tools in a computer-based design environment. VHDL's structural language features allow it to be effectively used as a netlist language, replacing (or augmenting) other netlist languages such as EDIF.

1.5　A Standard Language

One of the most compelling reasons for you to become experienced with and knowledgable in VHDL is its adoptance as a standard in the electronic design community. Using a standard language such as VHDL will virtually guarantee that you will not have to throw away and re-capture design concepts simply because the design entry method you have chosen is not supported in a newer generation of design tools. Using a standard language also means that you are more likely to be able to take advantage of the most up-to-date design tools, and will have access to a knowledge-base of thousands of other engineers, many of who are solving problems similar to your own.

2　How Is VHDL Used?

VHDL is a general-purpose programming language optimized for electronic circuit design. As such, there are many points in the overall design process at which VHDL can help.

2.1　For Design Specification

VHDL can be used right up front, while you are still designing at a high level, to capture the performance and interface requirements of each component in a large system. This is particularly useful for large projects involving many team members. Using a top-down approach, a system designer may define the interface to each component in the system, and describe the acceptance requirements of those components in the form of a high-level test bench. The interface definition (typically expressed as a VHDL entity declaration) and high-level performance specification (the test bench) can then be passed on to other team members for completion or refinement.

2.2　For Design Capture

Design capture is the phase in which the details of the system are entered (captured) in a computer-based design system. In this phase, you may express your design (or portions of your design) as schematics (either board-level or purely functional) or using VHDL descriptions. If you are going to be using synthesis technology, then you will want to write the VHDL portions of the design using a style of VHDL that is appropriate for synthesis.

The design capture phase may include tools and design entry methods other than VHDL. In many cases, design descriptions written in VHDL are combined with other representations, such as schematics, to form the complete system.

2.3 For Design Simulation

Once entered into a computer-based design system, you will probably want to simulate the operation of your circuit to find out if it will meet the functional and timing requirements developed during the specification process. If you have created one or more test benches as a part of your design specification, then you will use a simulator to apply the test bench to your design as it is written for synthesis (a functional simulation) and possibly using the post-synthesis version of the design as well.

2.4 For Design Documentation

The structured programming features of VHDL, coupled with its configuration management features, make VHDL a natural form in which to document a large and complex circuit.

2.5 As an Alternative to Schematics

Schematics have long been a part of electronic system design, and it is unlikely that they will become extinct anytime soon. Schematics have their advantages, particularly when used to depict circuitry in block diagram form. For this reason, many VHDL design tools now offer the ability to combine schematic and VHDL representations in a design.

2.6 As an Alternative to Proprietary Languages

If you have used programmable logic devices in the past, then you have probably already used some form of hardware description language (HDL). Proprietary languages such as PALASM, ABEL, CUPL and Altera's AHDL have been developed over the years by PLD device vendors and design tool suppliers, and remain in widespread use today. In fact, there are probably more users of PLD-oriented proprietary languages in the world today than all other HDLs (including Verilog and VHDL) combined.

3 Why Should You Use VHDL?

Why choose to use VHDL for your design efforts? There are many likely reasons; if you ask most VHDL tool vendors this question, the first answer you will get is, "It will dramatically improve your productivity."

How will VHDL increase your productivity? By making it easy to build and use libraries of commonly-used VHDL modules, VHDL makes design reuse feel natural. As you discover the benefits of reusable code, you will soon find yourself thinking of ways to write your VHDL statements in ways that will make them general-purpose; writing portable code will become an automatic reflex.

Another important reason to use VHDL, and another way that your productivity can be improved (or destroyed, if you are not careful), is the rapid pace of development in electronic design automation (EDA) tools and in target technologies. Using a standard language such as VHDL can greatly improve your chances of moving into more advanced tools without having to re-enter your circuit descriptions. Your ability to retarget circuits to new types of device targets will also be improved by using a standard design entry method.

New Words

capture	[ˈkæptʃə]	vt.&n.描述，表达，表示
appropriate	[əˈprəʊprɪət]	adj.适当的，合适的
custom	[ˈkʌstəm]	adj.定制的，定做的
concurrent	[kənˈkʌrənt]	adj.同时发生的
inherently	[ɪnˈhɪərəntlɪ]	adv.天性地，固有地
grasp	[grɑːsp]	v.&n.掌握；理解
integral	[ˈɪntɪgrəl]	adj.完整的；基本的；必需的
netlist	[ˈnɪtlɪst]	n.网络列表
replace	[rɪˈpleɪs]	v.替换；更新
augment	[ɔːgˈment]	v.增加，提高；扩大
knowledgable	[ˈnɒlɪdʒəbl]	adj.知识渊博的
community	[kəˈmjuːnətɪ]	n.社团，社区
guarantee	[ˌgærənˈtiː]	v.担保；确保
		n.保证；保修单
up-to-date	[ˌʌptəˈdeɪt]	adj.新式的
knowledge-base	[ˈnɒlɪdʒbeɪs]	n.知识库
top-down	[ˌtɒpˈdaʊn]	adj.自上而下的
approach	[əˈprəʊtʃ]	n.方法，方式
		v.对付，处理
entity	[ˈentətɪ]	n.实体
declaration	[ˌdekləˈreɪʃn]	n.声明
refinement	[rɪˈfaɪnmənt]	n.改进，改良
computer-based	[kəmˈpjuːtəbeɪst]	adj.基于计算机的

express	[ɪkˈspres]	vt.表达
schematics	[skiːˈmætɪks]	n.原理图，示意图
board-level	[ˈbɔːd ˈlevl]	adj.板级的
style	[staɪl]	n.方式；样式；风格
documentation	[ˌdɒkjumenˈteɪʃn]	n.文档；记录
depict	[dɪˈpɪkt]	v.描述，描绘
supplier	[səˈplaɪə]	n.供应商；供应者
widespread	[ˈwaɪdspred]	adj.广泛的，普遍的
dramatically	[drəˈmætɪklɪ]	adv.显著地
productivity	[ˌprɒdʌkˈtɪvətɪ]	n.生产率，生产力
library	[ˈlaɪbrərɪ]	n.库
module	[ˈmɒdjuːl]	n.模块；组件
reuse	[ˌriːˈjuːz]	vt.再用，复用，重新使用
statement	[ˈsteɪtmənt]	n.语句
reflex	[ˈriːfleks]	n.反应
rapid	[ˈræpɪd]	adj.瞬间的；快速的
pace	[peɪs]	n.速度；节奏
re-enter	[riːˈentə]	v.重新进入
retarget	[rɪˈtɑːgɪt]	vt.把……作为新目标（或对象），把……指向新目标

Phrases

stand for	代表
programming language	程序设计语言，编程语言
simulation modeling language	仿真建模语言，模拟建模语言
for the purpose of	为了……，因……起见
high-level programming language	高级程序设计语言
be expressed as	表示为
test bench	测试台
structural language	结构化语言
be passed on to	传给
synthesis technology	集成技术
block diagram	方框图，分块图
proprietary language	专有语言
reusable code	可重用代码，可复用代码
portable code	可移植的代码

Abbreviations

VHSIC (very-high speed integrated circuit)	超高速集成电路
PLD (programmable logic device)	可编程逻辑器件
EDIF (electronic design interchange format)	电子设计交换格式
HDL (hardware description language)	硬件描述语言
AHDL (Altera HDL)	Altera 硬件描述语言

参考译文

超高速集成电路硬件描述语言

1 什么是 VHDL？

VHDL（VHSIC 硬件描述语言）作为一种描述复杂数字电子电路以进行仿真和综合的方法，正在变得越来越流行。VHSIC 代表超高速集成电路。

VHDL 是一种为描述数字电路和系统的行为而设计和优化的编程语言。它结合了以下特点。

1.1 仿真建模语言

VHDL 有许多适合详细描述电子元件的行为的特性，从简单的逻辑门到完整的微处理器和定制芯片。VHDL 具有可以精确描述电路电气行为的特性（如信号的上升和下降时间、通过门的延迟及功能操作）。由此产生的 VHDL 仿真模型可以用作更大电路中的构建块，以用于仿真。

1.2 设计入门语言

正如高级编程语言允许将复杂的设计概念表示为计算机程序一样，VHDL 允许将复杂电子电路的行为描述到设计系统中，用于自动电路集成或系统仿真。与 Pascal、C 和 C++一样，VHDL 包括对结构化设计技术有用的特性，并提供了丰富的控制和数据表示特征集。与其他编程语言不同，VHDL 提供了允许描述并发事件的功能。这一点很重要，因为本质上，使用 VHDL 描述的硬件在其操作中是并发的。PLD 编程语言（如 PALASM、ABEL、CUPL 等）的用户会发现对 VHDL 的并发特性非常熟悉。然而，那些只使用软件编程语言编程的用户将需要掌握一些新概念。

1.3 测试语言

VHDL 最重要的一个方面是它能够以通常称为测试台的形式描述电路的性能规格。测试台是电路刺激和相应预期输出的 VHDL 描述，用于验证电路随着时间推移的行为。测试台应该是任何 VHDL 项目不可分割的一部分，并且应该与电路的其他描述并行创建。

1.4 网络列表语言

VHDL 是一种功能强大的语言，可以在较高的层次上输入新的设计，但在基于计算机的设计环境中，VHDL 作为不同工具之间的低层次通信形式也很有用。VHDL 的结构化语言特性使其能够有效地用作网络列表语言，取代（或扩充）EDIF 等其他网络列表语言。

1.5 标准语言

VHDL 作为一个电子设计界的标准而被采纳，这是迫切地需要积累 VHDL 经验和知识的原因之一。实际上，使用标准语言（如 VHDL）可以保证不必仅仅因为新一代设计工具不支持选择的设计输入方法而抛弃和重新描述设计概念。使用标准语言还意味着更有可能利用最新的设计工具，访问数千名其他工程师的知识库，这些工程师正在解决类似的问题。

2 如何使用 VHDL？

VHDL 是一种为电子电路设计而优化的通用编程语言。因此，在整个设计过程中，VHDL 在很多方面都可以提供帮助。

2.1 设计规范

VHDL 可以在进行高级别设计时直接用于描述大型系统中每个组件的性能和接口需求，这对于涉及很多团队成员的大型项目非常有用。使用自上而下的方法，系统设计师可以定义系统中每个组件的接口，并以高级测试台的形式描述这些组件的验收要求。然后，可以将接口定义（通常表示为 VHDL 实体声明）和高级性能规范（测试台）传递给其他团队成员以完成或细化。

2.2 设计描述

设计描述是在基于计算机的设计系统中输入系统细节的阶段。在此阶段，可以将设计（或部分设计）表示为示意图（板级或纯功能性）或使用 VHDL 描述。如果打算使用集成技术，那么将需要使用适合集成的 VHDL 方式编写设计的 VHDL 部分。

设计输入阶段可能包括 VHDL 以外的工具和设计输入方法。在许多情况下，用 VHDL 编写的设计描述与其他表示（如原理图）相结合，以形成完整的系统。

2.3 设计仿真

一旦进入基于计算机的设计系统，可能会想要仿真电路的运行，以确定它是否满足规范过程中制定的功能和时序要求。如果已经创建了一个或多个测试台作为设计规范的一部分，那么将使用模拟器将测试台应用到设计中，因为它是为集成（功能模拟）编写的，可能还使用设计的集成后版本。

2.4 设计文件

VHDL 的结构化编程特性和配置管理特性，使它成为记录大型复杂电路的自然形式。

2.5 作为原理图的替代方案

长期以来，原理图一直是电子系统设计的一部分，不太可能会很快消失。原理图有其优点，尤其是用于以方框图的形式描述电路时。出于这个原因，许多 VHDL 设计工具提供了在设计中结合原理图和 VHDL 表示的能力。

2.6 作为专有语言的替代方案

如果过去使用过可编程逻辑设备，那么可能已经使用了某种形式的硬件描述语言（HDL）。专有语言（如 PALASM、ABEL、CUPL 和 Altera 的 AHDL）多年来由 PLD 设备供应商和设计工具供应商开发，至今仍在广泛使用。事实上，当今世界中使用面向 PLD 的专有语言的用户可能比使用所有其他 HDL（包括 Verilog 和 VHDL）的用户加起来还要多。

3 为什么应该使用 VHDL？

为什么选择使用 VHDL 进行设计？有很多可能的原因。如果你问大多数 VHDL 工具供应商这个问题，你会得到的第一个答案是，"它将极大地提高你的生产力。"

VHDL 将如何提高生产力？通过简化常用 VHDL 模块库的构建和使用，VHDL 使设计重用变得自然。当你发现可重用代码的好处时，很快就会发现自己在思考如何编写 VHDL 语句，使其具有通用性。编写可移植代码将成为一种自动反应。

使用 VHDL 的另一个重要原因是电子设计自动化 (EDA) 工具和目标技术的快速发展，这也是提高（或破坏，如果不小心的话）生产力的另一种方式。使用 VHDL 等标准语言可以极大地增加使用更高级工具的机会，而无须重新输入电路描述。通过使用标准设计输入方法，还可以提高将电路重新定位到新型器件目标的能力。

Exercises

[Ex. 1] Answer the following questions according to Text A.

1. What were the circuits that were made previously?

2. What is integrated circuit (IC)? What is the most commonly used IC?

3. How many categories of IC design are there? What are they?

4. What does digital design method ensure?

5. What do the remaining pins do once the first pin is identified?

6. How does the size of the integrated chip vary?

7. What is a microcontroller?

8. What are logic gate ICs?

9. What did Gordon Moore of the Intel Company, a leading chip maker, notice in 1965?

10. Why are integrated circuits important?

[Ex. 2] Answer the following questions according to Text B.

1. What is VHDL?

2. What feature does VHDL combine?

3. What can be used as building blocks in larger circuits for the purpose of simulation?

4. What is one of the most important aspects of VHDL?

5. What is one of the most compelling reasons for you to become experienced with and knowledgable in VHDL?

6. What will using a standard language such as VHDL virtually guarantee? Why?

7. What may a system designer do using a top-down approach?

8. What is design capture?

9. Once entered into a computer-based design system, what will you probably do?

10. What is the first answer you get for the question "Why choose to use VHDL for your design efforts?" if you ask most VHDL tool vendors?

[Ex. 3] Translate the following terms or phrases from English into Chinese and vice versa.

1. electrical property	1.
2. semiconducting material	2.
3. portable code	3.
4. simulation modeling language	4.
5. synthesis technology	5.
6. n.导体	6.
7. n.增益 v.获得；受益；增加	7.
8. adj.独立的；无关联的	8.
9. n.绝缘体	9.
10. n.微控制器	10.

[Ex. 4] **Translate the following passage into Chinese.**

Microelectronics

Microelectronics is a field in electronics that utilizes tiny, or micro, components to manufacture electronics. As demand for small and less expensive devices grows, the field continues to expand. The main areas of focus generally are research, reliability and manufacture.

1　What Do Microelectronics Do?

Microelectronics engineers develop plans and construct prototypes of electronic circuit chips, circuit boards, and semiconductors. They apply knowledge of mechanical systems, new materials, and electronics to construct prototypes of new designs.

2　What Are Microelectronic Devices?

These devices are typically made from semiconductor materials. Many components of normal electronic design are available in a microelectronic equivalent. These include transistors, capacitors, inductors, resistors, diodes and (naturally) insulators and conductors can all be found in microelectronic devices.

3　Why Do We Need Microelectronics?

Microelectronics is one of the most important key technologies for innovations. Important applications include power supply in industrial processes, drive technology, information and communication technologies, and lighting equipment.

4　Are Microelectronics Devices Semiconductors?

Microelectronic devices are made by using semiconductor materials like Silicon and Germanium. The components that make up microelectronic devices comprises the capacitors, transistors, resistors, diode, inductors and conductors and insulators.

5　What Is the Difference Between Microelectronics and Nanoelectronics?

Microelectronics and nanoelectronics are subfields of electronics in which the nominal feature sizes of electronic components are between 100 and 0.1 micrometers in magnitude (microelectronics) or 100 nanometers or smaller (nanoelectronics).

6　What Is the Difference Between Semiconductors and Microelectronics?

While SMT technology generally incorporates semiconductor products, semiconductor products do not typically include SMT components. Microelectronics can incorporate both, and the result is smaller and usually faster final products.

Reading

An Introduction to Nanoelectronics

Electronic devices and the components within them are getting smaller year by year. This has been driven by consumer demand for smaller devices that have the same capabilities and performance as the pre-existing[①] "bulkier" technology. Here, we will explore in more detail how nanoelectronics[②] not only reduces the size of electronic devices, but also provides the same or enhanced performance.

1   The Introduction of Nanoelectronics

Traditional materials can only go so far before they reach a point where they can't get any smaller. This is where nanotechnology[③] comes in and has enabled nanoelectronics to emerge. The electronic components created using nanomaterials[④] are much smaller than the components made from conventional bulk materials[⑤]. One example of a nanoelectronic device is a graphene-based battery[⑥]. This is a bulk device that uses nanomaterials, but compared to lithium ion (Li-ion) batteries[⑦], it can possess up to 5-6 times the energy density and still be smaller than their Li-ion equivalents. Another example — focusing purely on nanosized electronic components — is transistors made out of carbon nanotubes[⑧]. Such small transistors push beyond the limits of conventional technology and because they are so small (yet efficient enough to function well) that more transistors can be fitted onto circuits and computer chips, thus increasing the speed of devices.

The use of nanomaterials — i.e., materials which are between 1 and 100 nanometers[⑨] in size — has many advantages. Not only are nanomaterials inherently small (often very thin), which can help to make the components of a device smaller (which can help to reduce the size of the device itself), they are usually very efficient. Because of their small size, they have a very high relative[⑩] surface area, which in many cases is very active — with the best example of an active surface being graphene. Graphene's surface interacts very strongly with its surroundings, be it through the conduction of electrons between surfaces or the interaction with environmental stimulus/molecules in sensing mechanisms[⑪], among others.

Most nanoelectronic devices are developed using either 2D materials or semiconductors, which are very active materials. Due to these properties, nanomaterials can provide electrical efficiencies as high as the bulk materials used in traditional components, but with the added bonus of being much smaller. This is especially true for conductive or semi-conductive[⑫] nanomaterials that often have

---

① pre-existing [ˌpriːɪɡˈzɪstɪŋ] *adj.*先已存在的，早已存在的

② nanoelectronics [nənəʊɪˈlektrɒnɪks] *n.*纳米电子学

③ nanotechnology [ˌnænəʊtekˈnɒlədʒɪ] *n.*纳米技术

④ nanomaterial [ˌnænəʊməˈtɪərɪəl] *n.*纳米材料

⑤ bulk material：粒状材料

⑥ graphene-based battery：石墨烯基电池

⑦ lithium ion (Li-ion) battery：锂离子电池

⑧ nanotube [ˈneɪməʊtjʊb] *n.*纳米管

⑨ nanometer [ˈneɪnəmiːtə] *n.*纳米

⑩ relative [ˈrelətɪv] *adj.*相对的；比较的

⑪ sensing mechanism：感知机制，感觉机制

⑫ semi-conductive [ˈsemɪkənˈdʌktɪv] *adj.*半导体的

electrical conductivities[①] and charge carrier mobilities. In addition, many nanomaterials are inherently stable to high temperatures, pressure and chemicals, which are often needed depending on the components in question. The thermal stability[②] is very important when devices get hot.

But it is not only the conductive nanomaterials that are efficient. While electrically conducting nanomaterials get the most attention, there are also plenty of electrically insulating nanomaterials that can be just as important for protecting certain areas of a nanoelectronic device. In fact, in some cases, heterostructures[③] composed of a conductive nanomaterial layer sandwiched between two insulating nanomaterial layers works better, because the conductivity and the subsequent electrical current can be better directed (which results in a lower electrical energy loss). Other properties of nanomaterials include their ability to realize and utilize quantum[④] phenomena, which can lead to more effective electronic currents as there is little to no resistance when the electrons travel between quantumly confined regions. These phenomena are also the building blocks for what will hopefully be the next generation of technologies, i.e., quantum technologies. So, there is a wide range of materials, with varying properties that can be used.

Aside from the property benefits, the way nanomaterials are fabricated enables the development of smaller components. Most non-nanomaterial components have to be fabricated using a top-down approach, that is a larger material is broken down into smaller structures. But there are limits to how small you can go if the structural accuracy is to be maintained, especially if it is a complex architecture. Nanomaterials can also be made in this way, but if you want to have nanomaterials that are structurally accurate, pure, and very small, then they can be made using a bottom-up approach, which is the process of creating nanomaterials atom[⑤] by atom. It is a more controlled approach that enables the size of the components to be reduced, while the active nanomaterials are pure and architecturally designed to fit their specific application. In many cases, both methods can be used together to first create the thin nanoelectronics components through a bottom-up approach, followed by patterning it with a top-down etching[⑥] or lithography[⑦] approach.

2　Scope of Nanoelectronics

So, what falls into the scope of nanoelectronics? Aside from being a smaller version of electronics, it encompasses everything from nanoscale[⑧] components to quantum technology,

---

① conductivity [ˌkɒndʌkˈtɪvəti] *n.*传导性，传导率，电导率
② thermal stability：热稳定性
③ heterostructure [hetərəʊˈstrʌktʃə] *n.*异质结构
④ quantum [ˈkwɒntəm] *n.*量子
⑤ atom [ˈætəm] *n.*原子
⑥ etching [ˈetʃɪŋ] *n.*蚀刻
⑦ lithography [lɪˈθɒɡrəfɪ] *n.*光刻
⑧ nanoscale [ˈneɪnəskeɪl] *n.*纳米级

spintronics[1], and molecular[2] electronics (i.e., single molecule electronics). In terms of the actual individual components that are present within the sphere of nanoelectronics, there are many, as nanoelectronics covers everything from energy storage and energy generation systems, to transistors, to flexible and printable circuits, switches, photodetectors[3], sensors, displays, memory storage systems, nanosized radio transmitters, and quantum devices. And there are many more in between, these are just the most notable components.

All these devices are made up of different nanomaterials, and the same components can be made with very different nanomaterials depending on the desired efficiencies, ease of fabrication and cost. It's also safe to say that nanoelectronics makes use of most nanomaterial forms, from 2D materials and other thin-film[4] layers to nanotubes, fullerenes[5], nanowires[6], nanoparticles[7] and quantum dots.

3 Conclusion

Nanomaterial-based components can be made much smaller than those made of traditional bulk materials, which helps to reduce the overall size of the electronic device. Moreover, many nanomaterials are stable in most environments, whether it's in a sensor within a harsh[8] chemical processing environment, or in an electronic device that gives out a lot of residual[9] heat to the internal components. While there are many areas of nanoelectronics, some of the more widely studied systems include nanomaterial-inspired energy storage[10] and energy generation systems, various types of nanosized and molecular transistors, optoelectronic devices, and flexible/printable circuits[11] — where the nanomaterials are often formulated into an ink and printed.

---

[1] spintronics [spɪnˈtrɒnɪks] n.自旋电子学
[2] molecular [məˈlekjələ] adj.分子的
[3] photodetector [fəʊtəʊdɪˈtektə] n.光电探测器；光检测器
[4] thin-film [ˈθɪnfɪlm] n.薄膜
[5] fullerene [ˈfʊləriːn] n.富勒烯
[6] nanowire [ˈnænəʊaɪər] n.纳米线
[7] nanoparticle [ˈnænəʊpɑːtɪkl] n.纳米粒子，纳米微粒
[8] harsh [hɑːʃ] adj.严格的；残酷的；恶劣的
[9] residual [rɪˈzɪdjuəl] adj.残余的；残留的
[10] nanomaterial-inspired energy storage：由纳米材料激发的储能器
[11] printable circuit：可打印电路

Unit 4

Text A

Computer Hardware

扫码听课文

1　Introduction

Hardware is the most visible part of any information system: the equipment such as computers, scanners and printers that is used to capture data, transform it and present it to the user as output. Although we will focus mainly on the personal computer (PC) and the peripheral devices that are commonly used with it, the same principles apply to the complete range of computers:

(1) Supercomputers, a term used to denote the fastest computing engines available at any given time, which are used for running exceptionally demanding scientific applications.

(2) Mainframe computers, which provide high-capacity processing and data storage facilities to hundreds or even thousands of users operating from terminals.

(3) Servers, which have large data storage capacities enabling users to share files and application software, although processing will typically occur on the user's own machine.

(4) Workstations, which provide high-level performance for individual users in computationally intensive fields such as engineering.

(5) Personal computers (including laptop/notebook computers), which have a connected monitor, keyboard and CPU, and have developed into a convenient and flexible business tool capable of operating independently or as part of an organizational network.

(6) Mobile devices such as personal digital assistants or the latest generation of cellular telephones, which offer maximum portability plus wireless connection to the internet, although they do not offer the full functionality of a PC.

2　Input Devices

Data may enter an information system in a variety of different ways, and the input device that is most appropriate will usually depend on the type of data being entered into the system, how frequently this is done, and who is responsible for the activity. For example, it would be more efficient to scan a page of typed text into an information system rather than retyping it, but if this happens very seldom, and if typing staff are readily available, then the cost of the scanner might not be justified. However, all of the input devices described in this chapter have at least one thing in common: the ability to translate non-digital data types such as text, sound or graphics into digital format for processing by a computer.

2.1　The Keyboard

A lot of input still happens by means of a keyboard. Usually, the information that is entered by means of a keyboard is displayed on the monitor. The layout of most keyboards is similar to that of the original typewriter on which it was modeled.

2.2　Pointing Devices

The now ubiquitous electronic mouse is an essential input device for use with any graphical user interface. Buttons on the mouse can be used to select icons or menu items, or the cursor can be used to trace drawings on the screen.

Touchscreens are computer monitors that incorporate sensors on the screen panel itself or its sides. The user can indicate or select an area or location on the screen by pressing a finger onto the monitor. Light and touch pens work on a similar principle, except that a stylus is used, allowing for much finer control. Touch pens are more commonly used with handheld computers such as personal organizers or digital assistants. They have a pen-based interface whereby a stylus is used on the small touch-sensitive screen of the handheld computer, mainly by means of ticking off pre-defined options, although the fancier models support data entry either by means of a stylized alphabet, which resembles a type of shorthand, or some other more sophisticated handwriting recognition interface.

Digitizer tablets, also known as graphics tablets, use a pressure sensitive area with a stylus. This can be used to trace drawings.

Data glove looks like a hand glove but it contains a large number of sensors and has a data cable attached, though data cable is being replaced by means of infrared cordless data transmission. Not only does the data glove allow for full three-dimensional movement but it also senses the position of individual fingers and translates this into a grip. The glove is currently used in virtual reality simulators where the user moves around in an artificially rendered environment projected onto tiny LCD screens fitted into vision goggles. The computer generates various imaginary objects, which the user can "pick up" and manipulate by means of the glove. Advanced models even allow for tactile feedback by means of small pressure pockets built into the glove.

2.3　Optical Scanners and Readers

There are a number of different optical scanner technologies on the market.

(1) Optical scanners use light-emitting devices to illuminate the printing on paper. Depending on how much light is reflected, a light sensor determines the position and darkness (or color) of the markings on the paper. Special-purpose optical scanners are in use by postal services to read and interpret hand-written postal codes. General-purpose scanners are used with personal computers to scan in images or text. A common use of optical scanners is the scanning of black-and-white or color images and pictures. When scanning text, it is necessary to load additional optical character recognition (OCR) software that converts the scanned raster-image of the text into the equivalent character symbols, so that they can be edited using word processing software.

(2) Barcode scanners detect sequences of vertical lines of different widths. These scanners have become very popular with retailers due to the fact that all pre-packaged products are now required to have a product barcode on their packaging. Libraries now also commonly use barcode scanners. They are more generally used for tracking large numbers of physical items, such as luggage handling by airlines.

(3) Optical mark readers are capable of reading dark marks on specially designed forms. The red multiple choice answer sheets in use at many educational and testing institutions are a good example.

2.4   Other Input Devices

A magnetic card reader reads the magnetized stripe on the back of plastic credit-card size cards. These cards need to be pre-recorded following certain standards. Although the cards can hold only a tiny amount of information, they are very popular for access control.

Biometric devices are used to verify personal identity based on fingerprints, iris or retinal scanning, hand geometry, facial characteristics, etc. A scanning device is used to capture key measurements and compare them against a database of previously stored information. This type of authentication is becoming increasingly important in the control of physical access.

Finally, voice input devices are coming of age. Voice-recognition has recently made a strong entry into the market with the availability of low-cost systems that work surprisingly well with today's personal computers. These systems allow for voice control of most standard applications.

3   Central Processing Unit (CPU)

Once data has been entered into a computer, it is acted on by the CPU, which is the real brain of the computer.

3.1   Components of the CPU

The CPU has two major components.

(1) The arithmetic and logic unit (ALU) executes the actual instructions. It knows how to add

or multiply numbers, compare data, or convert data into different internal formats.

(2) The control unit does the "housekeeping". It ensures that the instructions are processed on time, in the proper sequence, and operate on the correct data.

3.2 Speed of Processing

One can measure the speed of the CPU by checking the time it takes to process one single instruction. However, instead of indicating the time it takes to execute a single instruction, the processing speed is usually indicated by how many instructions (or computations) a CPU can execute in a second.

In practice, the speed of a processor is dictated by four different elements: the "clock speed", which indicates how many simple instructions can be executed per second; the word length, which is the number of bits that can be processed by the CPU at any one time; the bus width, which determines the number of bits that can be moved simultaneously in or out of the CPU; and then the physical design of the chip, in terms of the layout of its individual transistors.

4 Main Memory

The function of main memory (also referred to as primary memory, main storage or internal storage) is to provide temporary storage for instructions and data during the execution of a program. Main memory is usually known as RAM, which stands for random access memory.

4.1 Random Access Memory (RAM)

RAM consists of standard circuit-inscribed silicon microchips that contain many millions of tiny transistors. Very much like the CPU chips, their technology follows to the law of Moore, which states that they double in capacity or power (for the same price) every 18 months. A RAM chip easily holds hundreds of megabytes (million characters). They are frequently pre-soldered in sets on tiny memory circuit boards called SIMMS (single in-line memory modules) or DIMMS (dual in-line memory modules) which slot directly onto the motherboard: the main circuit board that holds the CPU and other essential electronic elements. The biggest disadvantage of RAM is that its contents are lost whenever the power is switched off.

Two important types of RAM are:

(1) Cache memory is ultra-fast memory that operates at the speed of the CPU. Access to normal RAM is usually slower than the actual operating speed of the CPU. To avoid slowing the CPU down, computers usually incorporate some more expensive, faster cache RAM that sits in between the CPU and RAM. This cache holds the data and programs that are needed immediately by the CPU. Although today's CPUs already incorporate an amount of cache on the circuit itself, this on-chip cache is usually supplemented by an additional, larger, cache on the motherboard.

(2) Flash RAM or flash memory consists of special RAM chips. It fits into custom ports on many notebooks, hand-held computers and digital cameras. Unlike normal RAM, flash memory is nonvolatile. It holds its contents even without external power, so it is also useful as a secondary storage device.

4.2   Read-Only Memory (ROM)

A small but essential element of any computer, ROM also consists of electronic memory microchips but, unlike RAM, it does not lose its contents when the power is switched off. Its function is also very different from that of RAM. Since it is difficult or impossible to change the contents of ROM, it is typically used to hold program instructions that are unlikely to change during the lifetime of the computer. The main application of ROM is to store the so-called boot program. ROM chips are also found in many devices which contain programs that are unlikely to change over a significant period of time. Just like RAM, ROM comes in a number of different forms:

(1) PROM (programmable read-only memory) is initially empty and can be custom-programmed once only using special equipment. Loading or programming the contents of ROM is called burning the chip since it is the electronic equivalent of blowing tiny transistor fuses within the chip. Once programmed, ordinary PROMs cannot be modified afterwards.

(2) EPROM (erasable programmable read-only memory) is like PROM, but by using special equipment such as an ultraviolet light gun, the memory contents can be erased so that the EPROM can be re-programmed.

(3) EEPROM (electrically erasable programmable read-only memory) is similar to EPROM, but it can be re-programmed using special electronic pulses rather than ultraviolet light so no special equipment is required.

New Words

hardware	[ˈhɑːdweə]	n.计算机硬件
equipment	[ɪˈkwɪpmənt]	n.设备，装备；器材
scanner	[ˈskænə]	n.扫描设备；扫描器
printer	[ˈprɪntə]	n.打印机
capture	[ˈkæptʃə]	vt.&n.捕获，捕捉
transform	[trænsˈfɔːm]	v.转换，变换
supercomputer	[ˈsuːpəkəmpjuːtə]	n.超级计算机，巨型计算机
engine	[ˈendʒɪn]	n.发动机，引擎
application	[ˌæplɪˈkeɪʃn]	n.适用，应用，运用
mainframe	[ˈmeɪnfreɪm]	n.主机

process	[ˈprəʊses]	n.过程
		vt.加工；处理
terminal	[ˈtɜːmɪnl]	adj.终端的，末端的
		n.终端
server	[ˈsɜːvə]	n.服务器
share	[ʃeə]	v.共享，分享
file	[faɪl]	n.文件
workstation	[ˈwɜːksteɪʃn]	n.工作站
performance	[pəˈfɔːməns]	n.表现；执行
individual	[ˌɪndɪˈvɪdʒʊəl]	adj.个人的，独特的，个别的
computational	[ˌkɒmpjʊˈteɪʃənl]	adj.计算的
connect	[kəˈnekt]	vt.连接，联结；使……有联系
		vi.连接；建立关系
monitor	[ˈmɒnɪtə]	n.显示器；监测仪
		vt.监控
keyboard	[ˈkiːbɔːd]	n.键盘
independently	[ˌɪndɪˈpendəntlɪ]	adv.独立地，无关地
portability	[ˌpɔːtəˈbɪlɪtɪ]	n.可携带，轻便
connection	[kəˈnekʃn]	n.连接；联系，关系；连接点
internet	[ˈɪntənet]	n.互联网
functionality	[ˌfʌŋkʃəˈnælɪtɪ]	n.功能，功能性
text	[tekst]	n.文本
digital	[ˈdɪdʒɪtl]	adj.数字的，数据的
format	[ˈfɔːmæt]	n.格式
		vt.使格式化
enter	[ˈentə]	vt.&vi.输入，进入
model	[ˈmɒdl]	n.模型，典型
		vt.模仿
ubiquitous	[juːˈbɪkwɪtəs]	adj.无所不在的，普遍存在的
mouse	[maʊs]	n.鼠标
button	[ˈbʌtn]	n.按钮
icon	[ˈaɪkɒn]	n.光标，图标
menu	[ˈmenjuː]	n.菜单
touchscreen	[ˈtʌtʃskriːn]	n.触摸屏
sensor	[ˈsensə]	n.传感器，灵敏元件
panel	[ˈpænl]	n.面板；控制板
fancier	[ˈfænsɪə]	n.发烧友，对某事物有特别爱好的人
recognition	[ˌrekəgˈnɪʃn]	n.认识，识别
sensitive	[ˈsensətɪv]	adj.敏感的，灵敏的

infrared	[ˌɪnfrəˈred]	adj.红外线的
		n.红外线
cordless	[ˈkɔːdlɪs]	adj.不用电线与电源相连的，无电线的
three-dimensional	[θriːdɪˈmenʃənəl]	adj.三维的，立体的
sense	[sens]	n.感觉；识别力
		vt.感觉，感知，感到；理解，领会
simulator	[ˈsɪmjʊleɪtə]	n.模拟装置，模拟器
imaginary	[ɪˈmædʒɪnərɪ]	adj.想象中的，假想的，虚构的
manipulate	[məˈnɪpjʊleɪt]	vt.操作，处理
tactile	[ˈtæktaɪl]	adj.触觉的，触觉感知的
feedback	[ˈfiːdbæk]	n.反馈，反应
scan	[skæn]	vt.扫描
raster	[ˈræstə]	n.光栅
equivalent	[ɪˈkwɪvələnt]	adj.相等的，相当的，等效的
character	[ˈkærəktə]	n.字符
symbol	[ˈsɪmbl]	n.符号，记号
		vt.用符号代表
barcode	[bɑːˈkəʊd]	n.条形码
detect	[dɪˈtekt]	vt.检测
verify	[ˈverɪfaɪ]	vt.核实；证明；判定
identity	[aɪˈdentɪtɪ]	n.身份
fingerprint	[ˈfɪŋgəprɪnt]	n.指纹，指印
		vt.采指纹
iris	[ˈaɪrɪs]	n.虹膜
retinal	[ˈretɪnl]	adj.视网膜的
low-cost	[ˈləʊkɒst]	adj.价格便宜的，廉价的
component	[kəmˈpəʊnənt]	n.部件，零件
		adj.组成的，构成的
instruction	[ɪnˈstrʌkʃn]	n.指令
compare	[kəmˈpeə]	vt.&vi.比较，对照
convert	[kənˈvɜːt]	v.转换，转变
sequence	[ˈsiːkwəns]	n.序列；顺序；连续
measure	[ˈmeʒə]	n.测量，测度；措施；程度；尺寸
		v.测量；估量
chip	[tʃɪp]	n.芯片
transistor	[trænˈzɪstə]	n.晶体管
function	[ˈfʌŋkʃn]	n.功能，作用；函数
		vi.有或起作用
temporary	[ˈtemprərɪ]	adj.临时的，暂时的

program	[ˈprəʊgræm]	n.程序
		v.给……编写程序
silicon	[ˈsɪlɪkən]	n.硅
megabyte	[ˈmegəbaɪt]	n.兆字节
slot	[slɒt]	n.插槽
cache	[kæʃ]	n.高速缓冲存储区，高速缓存
supplement	[ˈsʌplɪmənt]	vt.&n.增补，补充
nonvolatile	[ˈnɒnˈvɒlətaɪl]	adj.非易失性的，不易失的
impossible	[ɪmˈpɒsəbl]	adj.不可能的
modify	[ˈmɒdɪfaɪ]	v.修改
ultraviolet	[ˌʌltrəˈvaɪələt]	adj.紫外线的
reprogram	[rɪˈprəʊgræm]	v.重新编程，改变程序
pulse	[pʌls]	n.脉冲

Phrases

information system	信息系统
peripheral device	外围设备，外部设备
application software	应用软件
personal digital assistant	个人数字助理
be responsible for ...	为……负责，形成……的原因
pointing device	点击设备
graphical user interface	图形用户界面
menu item	菜单项
touch-sensitive screen	触摸屏
handheld computer	手持式计算机
handwriting recognition interface	手写识别界面
pressure sensitive area	压力敏感区域
data glove	数字手套
virtual reality	虚拟现实
pick up	拿起，拾起
optical scanner	光学扫描仪
postal code	邮政编码
word processing software	字处理软件
magnetic card	磁卡
magnetized stripe	磁条
access control	访问控制，访问管理
hand geometry	手形，掌形
facial characteristic	面部特征

voice input device	语音输入设备
be entered into	被输入
clock speed	时钟速率
word length	字长
bus width	总线宽度
law of Moore	摩尔定律
circuit board	电路板
switch off	关闭，切断
digital camera	数码相机
external power	外部电源，外部供电
secondary storage device	辅助存储设备
boot program	引导程序
ultra-violet light gun	紫外光枪

Abbreviations

PC (personal computer)	个人计算机
CPU (central processing unit)	中央处理器
LCD (liquid crystal display)	液晶显示器
OCR (optical character recognition)	光学字符识别
ALU (arithmetic and logic unit)	算术逻辑部件
SIMMS (single in-line memory modules)	单列直插内存模块
DIMMS (dual in-line memory modules)	双列直插内存模块
PROM (programmable read-only memory)	可编程只读存储器
EPROM (erasable programmable read-only memory)	可擦可编程只读存储器
EEPROM (electrically erasable programmable read-only memory)	电可擦编程只读存储器

参考译文

计算机硬件

1 引言

硬件是任何信息系统中最容易被看见的部分：例如计算机、扫描仪和打印机之类的设备，它们用于捕获数据、对其进行转换并将其作为输出呈现给用户。尽管我们将主要关注个人计算机（PC）及其常用的外围设备，但是相同的原理也适用于所有计算机：

（1）超级计算机，用来表示在任何给定时间内可用的最快的计算引擎，用于运行要求极高的科学应用程序。

（2）大型计算机，为数百甚至数千个从终端操作的用户提供大容量数据处理能力和数据存储设施。

（3）服务器，具有大容量的数据存储，使用户可以共享文件和应用程序软件，尽管处理通常会在用户自己的计算机上进行。

（4）工作站，可在计算密集型领域（如工程）中为单个用户提供高性能的处理能力。

（5）个人计算机（包括膝上计算机/笔记本电脑），具有连接的显示器、键盘和CPU，并且已发展成为一种既方便又灵活的业务工具，它能够独立运行或作为组织网络的一部分运行。

（6）移动设备（如个人数字助理或最新一代的蜂窝电话），尽管它们不能提供 PC 的全部功能，但可提供最大的便携性及与互联网的无线连接。

2　输入设备

数据能够以各种不同的方式进入信息系统，由输入到系统中的数据类型、执行的频率及负责该活动的人员决定哪些输入设备最合适。例如，将输入的文本页面扫描到信息系统中比重新输入它的效率更高，但是，如果这种情况很少发生，并且很容易找到打字人员，那么扫描仪的成本可能就不合理了。但是，本章中描述的所有输入设备至少有一个共同点：能够将非数字数据类型（如文本、声音或图形）转换为数字格式以供计算机处理。

2.1　键盘

键盘仍然可以进行很多输入。通常，通过键盘输入的信息会显示在监视器上。大多数键盘的布局类似于原始打字机的布局。

2.2　点击设备

现在无处不在的电子鼠标是一种必不可少的输入设备，它用于任何图形用户界面。可以使用鼠标上的按钮选择图标或菜单项，或者使用光标跟踪屏幕上的图形。

触摸屏是在屏幕面板本身或其侧面装有传感器的计算机监视器。用户可以通过将手指按在监视器上来指示或选择屏幕上的区域或位置。除了使用手写笔以外，光笔和触摸笔的工作原理相似，可以进行更精细的控制。触摸笔更常用于手持计算机，如个人管理器或数字助理。它们具有基于笔的界面，主要通过勾选预定义的选项，从而在手持计算机的小型触摸屏上使用手写笔，尽管更高级的模型支持风格化字母输入数据（这类似于一种速记）或用其他更复杂的手写识别界面输入数据。

数字化仪平板电脑也叫作图形输入板，它使用带有触摸笔的压敏区域，可用于跟踪图形。

数据手套看起来像手套，但它包含大量传感器并连接了数据线，尽管数据线已被红外无线数据传输取代。数据手套不仅可以进行完整的三维运动，还可以感应单个手指的位置，然后将其转化为抓握感。该手套目前用于虚拟现实模拟器中。在该模拟器中，用户在人工渲染的环境中四处移动，这些环境被投影到安装在视觉护目镜中的微型 LCD 屏幕上。计算机生成各种虚拟对象，用户可以通过手套"拾取"并进行操作。最新的型号甚至可以通过内置于手套中的小压力袋实现触觉反馈。

2.3　光学扫描仪和阅读器

市场上有许多不同的光学扫描仪技术。

（1）光学扫描仪使用发光设备照亮纸张上的打印内容。根据反射的光量，光传感器确定纸张上标记的位置和暗度（或颜色）。邮政部门正在使用专用光学扫描仪读取和识别手写的邮政编码。通过把扫描仪与个人计算机相结合，可以扫描图像或文本。光学扫描仪的常见用途是扫描黑白或彩色图像和图片。扫描文本时，有必要加载附带的光学字符识别（OCR）软件，该软件将扫描的文本光栅图像转换为等效的字符符号，以便可以使用文字处理软件进行编辑。

（2）条形码扫描仪可检测不同宽度的垂直线序列。由于现在要求所有预包装产品的包装上都带有产品条形码，因此这些扫描仪在零售商中非常受欢迎。现在，图书馆通常也使用条形码扫描仪。条形码扫描仪更常用于跟踪大量的物品，如航空公司的行李处理。

（3）光学标记阅读器能够读取特殊设计形式的深色标记。许多教育和考试机构使用的红色的多项选择答案纸就是一个很好的例子。

2.4　其他输入设备

磁卡读取器读取信用卡大小的塑料卡背面的磁条。这些卡需要按照某些标准预先记录。尽管这些卡只能容纳极少量的信息，但它们在访问控制中非常受欢迎。

生物识别设备根据指纹、虹膜或视网膜扫描、手部几何形状、面部特征等验证个人身份。扫描设备用于捕获关键测量值并将它们与先前存储的信息的数据库进行比较。这种类型的身份验证在物理访问控制中变得越来越重要。

最后，语音输入设备已经成熟。语音识别技术最近凭借大量低成本的系统进入了市场，这些系统可与当今的个人计算机完美配合，它们允许对大多数标准应用程序进行语音控制。

3　中央处理器（CPU）

数据输入到计算机后，将由 CPU 对其进行处理，CPU 是计算机真正的大脑。

3.1　CPU 组件

CPU 有两个主要组件。

（1）算术逻辑部件（ALU）执行实际指令。它知道如何加或乘数字、比较数据或将数据转换为不同的内部格式。

（2）控制单元执行"内部处理"。它确保按时、按正确的顺序处理指令，并对正确的数据进行操作。

3.2　处理速度

可以通过检查处理一条指令所需的时间来测量 CPU 的速度。除了执行一条指令所花费的时间外，处理速度通常由1s 内 CPU 可以执行多少条指令（或计算）表示。

实际上，处理器的速度由4个不同的要素决定："时钟速度"，它表示每秒可以执行多少条简单指令；字长，即在任何时候 CPU 可以处理的位数；总线宽度，确定可以同时移入或移出 CPU 的位数；芯片的物理设计，即各个晶体管的布局。

4　主存储器

主存储器（也称为主要存储器、主存或内部存储器）的功能是在程序执行期间为指令和数据提供临时存储。主存储器通常称为 RAM，它代表随机存储器。

4.1　随机存储器（RAM）

RAM 由包含数百万个微型晶体管的标准刻写电路硅芯片组成。与 CPU 芯片非常相似，它们的技术遵循摩尔定律，该定律指出，每 18 个月它们的容量或性能就会增加一倍（以相同的价格）。一个 RAM 芯片很容易容纳数百兆字节（百万个字符）。它们通常被预先焊接在称为 SIMMS（单列直插式内存模块）或 DIMMS（双列直插式内存模块）的微型存储电路板上，这些电路板直接插入主板，主板是用于固定 CPU 和其他组件的主电路板。RAM 的最大缺点是，一旦关闭电源，其内容就会丢失。

RAM 的两种重要类型是：

（1）高速缓存是一种超快内存，它以 CPU 的速度运行。访问普通 RAM 的速度通常比 CPU 的实际运行速度慢。为了避免降低 CPU 的速度，计算机通常会在 CPU 和 RAM 之间集成一些更昂贵、速度更快的缓存 RAM。这些高速缓存保存 CPU 立即需要的数据和程序。尽管当今的 CPU 已经在电路本身上集成了一定数量的高速缓存，但通常还要在主板上增加一个更大的高速缓存以提供片载高速缓存。

（2）Flash RAM（或闪存）由特殊的 RAM 芯片组成。它适合许多笔记本电脑、手持计算机和数码相机的自定义端口。与普通 RAM 不同，闪存是非易失性的。即使没有外部电源，它也可以保存其内容，因此它也可用作辅助存储设备。

4.2　只读存储器（ROM）

ROM 是一个很小但任何计算机中必不可少的单元，它也由电子存储微芯片组成，但是与 RAM 不同，ROM 在关闭电源时不会丢失其内容。它的功能也与 RAM 完全不同。由于很难或不可能更改 ROM 的内容，因此它通常用于保存在计算机寿命期内不太可能更改的程序指令。ROM 的主要应用是存储所谓的引导程序。ROM 芯片也出现在许多设备中，这些设备包含的程序在相当长的时间内不太可能更改。就像 RAM 一样，ROM 也有多种形式：

（1）PROM（可编程只读存储器）最初为空，只能使用特殊设备进行一次自定义编程。加载或编程 ROM 的内容称为烧录芯片，因为这等效于在芯片内烧制微小的晶体管熔丝。一旦进行了编程，普通的 PROM 就无法再修改。

（2）EPROM（可擦可编程只读存储器）类似于 PROM，但是通过使用特殊设备（如紫外线枪），可以擦除存储内容，以便对 EPROM 进行重新编程。

（3）EEPROM（电可擦编程只读存储器）与 EPROM 相似，可以使用特殊的电子脉冲而不是紫外线对它进行重新编程，因此不需要特殊的设备。

Text B

扫码听课文

Different Types of Software

Software is a computer program that provides instructions and data to execute user's commands.

1　Application Software

As a user of technology, application software or "apps" are what you engage with the most. They are productive end-user programs that help you perform tasks. The following are some examples of application software that allow you to do specific work:

(1) Microsoft Excel: It is a spreadsheet software that you can use for presenting and analyzing data.

(2) Photoshop: It is a photo editing application software by Adobe. You can use it to visually enhance, catalog and share your pictures.

(3) Skype: It is an online communication app that you can use for video chat, voice calling and instant messaging.

Software applications are also referred to as non-essential software. They are installed and operated on a computer based on the user's requirement. There are plenty of application software that you can use to perform different tasks. The number of such apps keeps increasing with technological advances and the evolving needs of the users. You can categorize these software types into different groups, as shown in the following table 4-1:

Table 4-1   Application Software Type and Examples

Application Software Type	Examples
Word processing software: Tools that are used to create word sheets and type documents etc.	Microsoft Word, WordPad, AppleWorks and Notepad
Spreadsheet software: Software used to compute quantitative data	Apple Numbers, Microsoft Excel and Quattro Pro
Database software: Used to store data and sort information	Oracle, Microsoft Access and FileMaker Pro
Application Suites: A collection of related programs sold as a package	OpenOffice, Microsoft Office
Multimedia software: Tools used for a mixture of audio, video, image and text content	Real Player, Media Player
Communication Software: Tools that connect systems and allow text, audio, and video-based communication	Microsoft NetMeeting, IRC, ICQ
Internet Browsers: Used to access and view websites	Netscape Navigator, Microsoft Internet Explorer, and Google Chrome
Email Programs: Software used for emailing	Microsoft Outlook, Gmail, Apple Mail

2   System Software

System software helps the user, hardware, and application software to interact and function together. This type of computer software allows an environment or platform for other software and applications to work in. This is why system software is essential in managing the whole computer system.

When you first power up your computer, it is the system software that is initially loaded into memory. Unlike application software, the system software is not used by end-users. It only runs in the background of your device at the most basic level while you use other application software. This is why system software is also called "low-level software".

Operating systems are an example of system software. All of your computer-like devices run on an operating system, including your desktop, laptop, smartphone, and tablet, etc. Here is a list of examples of an operating system. Let's take a look and you might spot some familiar names of system software:

For desktop computers, laptops and tablets: Microsoft Windows, Mac (for Apple devices), Linux.

Other than operating systems, some people also classify programming software and driver software as types of system software.

3   Programming Software

Programming software are programs that are used to write, develop, test, and debug other software, including apps and system software. For someone who works at a bespoke software development company, for example, this type of software would make their life easier and efficient.

Programming software is used by software programmers as translator programs. They are facilitator software used to translate programming languages (i.e., Java, C++, Python, PHP, BASIC, etc.) into machine language code. Translators can be compilers, interpreters and assemblers. You can understand compilers as programs that translate the whole source code into machine code and execute it. Interpreters run the source code as the program is run line by line. And assemblers translate the basic computer instructions – assembly code – into machine code.

Different programming language editors, debuggers, compilers and integrated development environment (IDE) are an example of programming software.

4　Driver Software

Driver software is often classified as one of the types of system software. They operate and control devices and peripherals plugged into a computer. Drivers are important because they enable the devices to perform their designated tasks. They do this by translating commands of an operating system for the hardware or devices, assigning duties. Therefore, each device connected with your computer requires at least one device driver to function.

Since there are thousands of types of devices, drivers make the job of your system software easier by allowing it to communicate through a standardized language. Some examples of driver software that you may be familiar with are: printer driver, mouse driver.

Usually, the operating system comes built-in with drivers for mouse, keyboard, and printers by default. They often do not require third-party installations. But for some advanced devices, you may need to install the driver externally. Moreover, if you use multiple operating systems like Linux, Windows, and Mac, then each of these supports different variants of drivers. For them, separate drivers need to be maintained for each.

5　Another Classification of Software

Let's discuss five additional subcategories of software and understand them using examples of trendy software.

5.1　Freeware

Freeware software is any software that is available to use for free. They can be downloaded and installed over the internet without any cost. Some well-known examples of freeware are: Google Chrome, Skype, Instagram, Snapchat, Adobe reader.

Although they all fall under the category of application or end-user software, they can further be categorized as freeware because they are free for you to use.

5.2　Shareware

Shareware, on the other hand, are software applications that are paid programs, but are made available for free for a limited period of time known as "trial period". You can use the software without any charges for the trial period but you will be asked to purchase it for use after the trial ends. Shareware allows you to test drive the software before you actually invest in purchasing it. Some examples of shareware that you must be familiar with are: Adobe Photoshop, Adobe Illustrator, Netflix App, MATLAB, McAfee Antivirus.

5.3　Open Source Software

This is a type of software that has an open source code that is available to use for all users. It can be modified and shared to anyone for any purpose. Common examples of open source software used by programmers are: LibreOffice, PHP, GNU Image Manipulation Program (GIMP).

5.4　Closed Source Software

These are the types of software that are non-free for the programmers. For this software, the source code is the intellectual property of software publishers. It is also called "proprietary software" since only the original authors can copy, modify and share the software. The following are some of the most common examples of closed-source software: .Net, Java, Microsoft Office, Adobe Photoshop.

5.5　Utility Software

Utility software is considered a subgroup of system software. They manage the performance of your hardware and application software installed on your computer, to ensure they work optimally. Some features of utility software include: Antivirus and security software, File compressor, Disk cleaner, Disk defragmentation software, Data backup software.

6　Conclusion

In conclusion, there can be multiple ways to classify different types of computer software. The software can be categorized based on the function they perform such as application software, system software, programming software, and driver software. They can also be classified based on different features such as the nature of source code, accessibility, and cost of usage.

New Words

software	[ˈsɒftweə]	n.软件
end-user	[end ˈjuːzə]	n.最终用户，端用户
spreadsheet	[ˈspredʃiːt]	n.电子表格
analyze	[ˈænəlaɪz]	vt.分析
app	[æp]	n.计算机应用程序
		abbr.应用(application)
non-essential	[nɒnɪˈsenʃl]	adj.不重要的，非本质的
requirement	[rɪˈkwaɪəmənt]	n.要求，需求；必要条件
quantitative	[ˈkwɒntɪtətɪv]	adj.定量的，数量（上）的
database	[ˈdeɪtəbeɪs]	n.数据库
suite	[swiːt]	n.（软件的）套件
mixture	[ˈmɪkstʃə]	n.混合，混杂
browser	[ˈbraʊzə]	n.浏览器，浏览程序
email	[ˈiːmeɪl]	n.电子邮件
		vt.给……发电子邮件
background	[ˈbækgraʊnd]	n.后台，背景
desktop	[ˈdesktɒp]	n.桌面
tablet	[ˈtæblət]	n.平板电脑
develop	[dɪˈveləp]	v.开发
test	[test]	v.测试
debug	[ˌdiːˈbʌg]	vt.调试，排除故障
bespoke	[bɪˈspəʊk]	adj.定做的
facilitator	[fəˈsɪlɪteɪtə]	n.促进者，帮助者
compiler	[kəmˈpaɪlə]	n.编译器，编译程序
interpreter	[ɪnˈtɜːprɪtə]	n.解释器，解释程序
assembler	[əˈsemblə]	n.汇编程序
editor	[ˈedɪtə]	n.编辑器，编辑软件，编辑程序
debugger	[ˌdiːˈbʌgə]	n.调试器，调试程序
driver	[ˈdraɪvə]	n.驱动器，驱动程序
assign	[əˈsaɪn]	vt.分配
standardize	[ˈstændədaɪz]	vt.使标准化；用标准校检
third-party	[ˈθɜːdpɑːtɪ]	adj.第三方的
installation	[ˌɪnstəˈleɪʃn]	n.安装
multiple	[ˈmʌltɪpl]	adj.多重的；多个的；多功能的
variant	[ˈveərɪənt]	n.变种，变异体；变形，变量
		adj.不同的，相异的

separate	[ˈsepəreɪt]	v.（使）分开，分离；分割；划分；（使）分离，分散；隔开
subcategory	[ˈsʌbˈkætɪgərɪ]	n.亚类，子类
freeware	[ˈfriːweə]	n.免费软件
download	[ˌdaʊnˈləʊd]	v.下载
shareware	[ˈʃeəweə]	n.共享软件
trial	[ˈtraɪəl]	adj.试验的
antivirus	[ˈæntɪvaɪrəs]	n.抗病毒软件
available	[əˈveɪləbl]	adj.可利用的；可得到的；有效的
publisher	[ˈpʌblɪʃə]	n.发布者，发表者
proprietary	[prəˈpraɪətərɪ]	adj.专有的，专利的
		n.所有权，所有物
optimally	[ˈɒptəməlɪ]	adv.最佳地
compressor	[kəmˈpresə]	n.压缩程序
accessibility	[əkˌsesəˈbɪlətɪ]	n.可访问性

Phrases

engage with	接触；处理
instant messaging	即时通信
a collection of	一组，一些，一批
system software	系统软件
power up	加电，开机
low-level software	低级软件
machine language	机器语言
source code	源代码
machine code	机器代码
assembly code	汇编代码
be classified as	被归类为……，被认为……
plug into	接入（计算机系统），插入
open source software	开源软件
open source code	开源代码
closed source software	闭源软件
intellectual property	知识产权
original author	原作者
disk defragmentation software	磁盘碎片整理软件

Abbreviations

IDE (integrated development environment)　　　集成开发环境

GNU　　　GNU's Not Unix!的递归缩写

GIMP (GNU Image Manipulation Program)　　　GNU 图像处理程序

参考译文

软件的不同类型

软件是一种计算机程序，提供执行用户命令的指令和数据。

1 应用软件

作为技术用户，最常使用的是应用软件或"应用"。它们是高效的最终用户程序，可以帮助执行任务。以下是一些执行特定工作的应用程序软件示例。

（1）Microsoft Excel：这是一个电子表格软件，可用于呈现和分析数据。

（2）Photoshop：它是 Adobe 的图片编辑应用程序软件，可以使用它可视化地增强、分类和共享图片。

（3）Skype：这是一个在线通信应用程序，可用于视频聊天、语音呼叫和即时消息传递。

软件应用程序也称为非必需软件。它们可以根据用户要求在计算机上安装和操作。可以使用许多应用程序软件执行不同的任务。随着技术的进步和用户需求的不断变化，此类应用的数量持续增加。可以将这些软件类型分为不同的组，如表 4-1 所示。

表 4-1　应用软件类型和示例

应用软件类型	示　　例
文字处理软件：用于创建文字表和输入文档等的工具	Microsoft Word、WordPad、AppleWorks 和 Notepad
电子表格软件：用于计算定量数据的软件	Apple Numbers、Microsoft Excel 和 Quattro Pro
数据库软件：用于存储数据和排序信息	Oracle、Microsoft Access 和 FileMaker Pro
应用程序套件：打包出售的相关程序的集合	OpenOffice、Microsoft Office
多媒体软件：用于混合音频、视频、图像和文本内容的工具	Real Player、Media Player
通信软件：用于连接系统并允许基于文本、音频和视频通信的工具	Microsoft NetMeeting、IRC、ICQ
因特网浏览器：用于访问和查看网站	Netscape Navigator、Microsoft Internet Explorer 和 Google Chrome
电子邮件程序：用于电子邮件发送的软件	Microsoft Outlook、Gmail、Apple Mail

2 系统软件

系统软件可帮助用户、硬件和应用软件进行交互并协同工作。此类计算机软件是一个环境或平台，其他软件和应用程序运行于其上。这就是系统软件对于管理整个计算机系统至关重要的原因。

首次打开计算机电源时，系统软件就被加载到内存中。与应用程序软件不同，最终用户不会使用系统软件。当使用其他应用程序软件时，它仅在最基本级别的设备后台运行。这就是为什么系统软件也被称为"低级软件"。

操作系统是系统软件的一个示例。所有类似计算机的设备都在操作系统上运行，包括台式机、笔记本电脑、智能手机和平板电脑等。以下操作系统示例的列表，你可能会发现一些熟悉的系统软件名称：

对于台式机、笔记本电脑和平板电脑：Microsoft Windows、Mac（用于 Apple 设备）和 Linux。

除操作系统外，有些人还将编程软件和驱动程序软件归类为系统软件。

3 编程软件

编程软件是用于编写、开发、测试和调试其他软件（包括应用程序和系统软件）的程序。例如，对于在定制软件开发公司工作的人来说，这种类型的软件将使他们的生活更轻松、高效。

编程软件被软件程序员用作转换器程序。它们是用于将编程语言（即 Java、C ++、Python、PHP、BASIC 等）转换为机器语言代码的辅助软件。转换器可以是编译器、解释器和汇编器。可以将编译器理解为将整个源代码转换为机器代码并执行的程序。当程序逐行运行时，解释器将运行源代码。汇编器将基本的计算机指令（汇编代码）转换为机器代码。

不同的编程语言编辑器、调试器、编译器和集成开发环境（IDE）是编程软件的示例。

4 驱动程序软件

驱动程序软件通常被归为系统软件。它们操作和控制插入计算机的设备和外围设备。驱动程序很重要，因为它们使设备能够执行其指定的任务。它们通过为硬件或设备转换操作系统命令、分配任务实现此目的。因此，与计算机连接的每个设备都需要至少一个设备驱动程序才能运行。

由于存在数千种设备，因此驱动程序允许其通过标准化语言进行通信，从而使系统软件的工作更加轻松。你可能会熟悉的一些驱动程序软件示例包括打印机驱动程序、鼠标驱动程序。

通常，操作系统默认内置了鼠标、键盘和打印机的驱动程序，通常不需要第三方安装。但是对于某些高级设备，可能需要在外部安装驱动程序。此外，如果使用多个操作系统（如 Linux、Windows 和 Mac），则每个操作系统都支持不同的驱动程序变体，因此，需要为每个设备编制单独的驱动程序。

5 另一种软件分类

下面讨论软件的另外 5 个子类别，并使用流行的软件示例了解它们。

5.1 免费软件

免费软件是可以免费使用的任何软件，可以通过互联网免费下载和安装它们。免费软件的一些著名示例有谷歌浏览器、Skype、Instagram、Snapchat 和 Adobe Reader。

尽管它们都属于应用程序或最终用户软件的类别，但它们可以进一步归为免费软件，因为它们可以免费使用。

5.2 共享软件

共享软件是付费应用程序，但是在有限的"试用期"内免费提供。可以在试用期内免费使用该软件，但是在试用期结束后，系统会要求购买该软件以继续使用。共享软件使用户可以在实际投资购买软件之前对其进行测试。共享软件常见的一些示例包括 Adobe Photoshop、Adobe Illustrator、Netflix App、MATLAB、McAfee Antivirus。

5.3 开源软件

这是一种所有用户都可使用的开源代码软件。无论出于何种目的，任何人都可对其进行修改并分享给其他人。程序员使用的开源软件的常见示例包括 LibreOffice、PHP、GNU 图像处理程序（GIMP）。

5.4 闭源软件

程序员不可以免费获得这类软件。对于此类软件，源代码是软件发行者的知识产权。它也被称为"专有软件"，因为只有原始作者才能复制、修改和分享该软件。闭源软件的一些最常见示例有.Net、Java、Microsoft Office、Adobe Photoshop。

5.5 实用软件

实用软件被视为系统软件的子类。它们管理安装在计算机上的硬件和应用程序软件，以确保它们以最佳状态工作。实用软件的某些功能包括防病毒和安全软件、文件压缩器、磁盘清理器、磁盘碎片整理软件及数据备份软件。

6 结论

总之，可以有多种方法对不同类型的计算机软件进行分类。可以根据软件的用途对其分类，如应用程序软件、系统软件、编程软件和驱动程序软件。还可以根据不同的功能对它们进行分类，如源代码的性质、可访问性和使用成本。

Exercises

[Ex. 1] Answer the following questions according to Text A.

1. What are supercomputers?

2. What do personal computers have? What have they developed into?

3. What will the input device that is most appropriate usually depend on?

4. What are touchscreens? What can the user do by pressing a finger onto the monitor?

5. What does the data glove do? Where is the data glove currently used?

6. What are the different optical scanner technologies on the market?

7. What are the two major components the CPU has?

8. What is main memory also referred to as? What is the function of main memory?

9. What does RAM stand for? What are the two important types of RAM?

10. What does ROM stand for? What is the main application of ROM?

[Ex. 2] Answer the following questions according to Text B.

1. What are some examples of application software that allow you to do specific work?

2. What is word processing software? What are the examples?

3. What does system software do? Why is it essential in managing the whole computer system?

4. What are programming software?

5. Why are drivers important?

6. What are some examples of driver software that you may be familiar with?

7. What is freeware software? What are some well-known examples of freeware?

8. What does shareware allow you to do? What are some examples of shareware that you must be familiar with?

9. What are common examples of open source software used by programmers?

10. What are some of the most common examples of closed source software?

[Ex. 3] Translate the following terms or phrases from English into Chinese and vice versa.

1. access control	1.
2. circuit board	2.
3. clock speed	3.
4. graphical user interface	4.
5. secondary storage device	5.

6. *n.*按钮	6.
7. *vt.&n.*捕获，捕捉	7.
8. *n.*部件，零件 *adj.*组成的，构成的	8.
9. *n.*反馈，反应	9.
10. *n.*功能，功能性	10.

[Ex. 4] Translate the following passage into Chinese.

Main Components of a Computer

CPU is considered the most important component in a computer and for good reason. It handles most operations, by processing instructions and giving signals out to other components. The CPU is the main bridge between all the computer's major parts.

RAM is a computer component where data used by the operating system and software applications is stored so that the CPU can process them quickly. Everything stored on RAM is lost if the computer is shut off. Depending on the applications you use, there is typically a maximum limit of RAM you will need for the computer to function properly.

HDD – also known as hard disk drive, it is the component where photos, apps, documents and such are kept. Although they are still being used, we have much faster types of storage devices such as solid state drives (SSD) that are also more reliable.

Motherboard – there is no acronym for this component but without it, there can't be a computer. The motherboard acts as the home for all other components, allows them to communicate with each other and gives them power in order to function. There are components that don't require a physical connection to the motherboard in order to work, such as bluetooth or Wi-Fi but, if there is no connection or signal what so ever, the computer won't know it's there.

Video and sound cards – two components which help the user interact with the computer. Although one can use a computer with a missing sound card, it's not really possible to use it without a video card. The sound card is used mainly to play sound through a speaker. However, a video card is used to send images on the screen. Without it, it would be like looking at an empty monitor.

Network adapter – even though it is not actually required to operate the computer, the network adapter improves the user's experience as it provides access to the internet. Modern computers with operating systems such as Windows will not offer the user all of its features without an Internet connection.

Reading

Embedded System

An embedded system[①] is a combination of computer hardware and software designed for a specific function. Embedded systems may also function within a larger system. The systems can be programmable or have a fixed functionality. Industrial machines, consumer electronics, agricultural and processing industry devices, automobiles, medical equipment, cameras, digital watches, household appliances, airplanes, vending machines and toys as well as mobile devices are possible locations for an embedded system.

While embedded systems are computing systems, they can range from having no user interface (UI) to complex graphical user interfaces (GUIs). User interfaces can include buttons, LEDs (light-emitting diodes) and touchscreen[②] sensing. Some systems use remote user interfaces as well.

1 How Does an Embedded System Work?

Embedded systems always function as part of a complete device. They are low-cost, low-power-consuming small computers that are embedded in other mechanical or electrical systems. Generally, they comprise a processor, power supply, memory and communication ports. Embedded systems use the communication ports to transmit data between the processor and peripheral devices — often, other embedded systems — using a communication protocol. The processor interprets this data with the help of minimal software stored on the memory. The software is usually highly specific to the function that the embedded system serves.

The processor may be a microprocessor or microcontroller. Microcontrollers are simply microprocessors with peripheral interfaces and integrated memory included. Microprocessors use separate integrated circuits for memory and peripherals instead of including them on the chip. Both can be used, but microprocessors typically require more support circuitry than microcontrollers because there is less integrated into the microprocessor. The term system on chip (SoC[③]) is often used. SoCs include multiple processors and interfaces on a single chip. They are often used for high-volume embedded systems. Some example SoC types are the application-specific integrated circuit (ASIC) and the field-programmable gate array (FPGA[④]).

Often, embedded systems are used in real-time operating environments and use a real-time operating system (RTOS) to communicate with the hardware. Near-real-time approaches are

---

① embedded system: 嵌入式系统
② touchscreen [ˈtʌtʃskriːn] n.触摸屏
③ system on chip: 片载系统，片上系统
④ field-programmable gate array: 现场可编程门阵列

suitable at higher levels of chip capability, defined by designers who have increasingly decided the systems are generally fast enough and the tasks tolerant of slight variations in reaction. In these instances, stripped-down versions[①] of the Linux operating system are commonly deployed, although other OSes have been pared down to run on embedded systems.

2 Characteristics of Embedded Systems

The main characteristic of embedded systems is that they are task-specific. Additionally, embedded systems can include the following characteristics:

(1) They typically consist of hardware, software and firmware;

(2) They can be embedded in a larger system to perform a specific function, as they are built for specialized tasks within the system, not various tasks;

(3) They can be either microprocessor-based or microcontroller-based — both are integrated circuits that give the system compute power;

(4) They are often used for sensing and real-time computing in internet of things (IoT) devices, which are devices that are internet-connected and do not require a user to operate;

(5) They can vary in complexity and in function, which affects the type of software, firmware and hardware they use;

(6) They are often required to perform their function under a time constraint to keep the larger system functioning properly.

3 Structure of Embedded Systems

Embedded systems vary in complexity but, generally, consist of three main elements:

(1) Hardware. The hardware of embedded systems is based around microprocessors and microcontrollers. Microprocessors are very similar to microcontrollers and, typically, refer to a CPU (central processing unit) that is integrated with other basic computing components such as memory chips and digital signal processors (DSPs[②]). Microcontrollers have those components built into one chip.

(2) Software and firmware. Software for embedded systems can vary in complexity. However, industrial-grade microcontrollers and embedded IoT systems usually run very simple software that requires little memory.

(3) Real time operating systems. These are not always included in embedded systems, especially smaller-scale systems. RTOSes define how the system works by supervising the software and setting rules during program execution.

---

① stripped-down version: 精简版
② digital signal processor: 数字信号处理器

In terms of hardware, a basic embedded system would consist of the following elements:

(1) Sensors. They convert physical sense data into an electrical signal.

(2) Analog-to-digital (A/D) converters. They change an analog electrical signal into a digital one.

(3) Processors. They process digital signals and store them in memory.

(4) Digital-to-analog (D/A) converters. They change the digital data from the processor into analog data.

(5) Actuators. They compare actual output to memory-stored output and choose the correct one.

The sensor reads external inputs, the converters make that input readable to the processor, and the processor turns that information into useful output for the embedded system.

4　Types of Embedded Systems

There are a few basic embedded system types, which differ in their functional requirements. They are:

(1) Mobile embedded systems. They are small-sized systems that are designed to be portable. Digital cameras are an example of this.

(2) Networked embedded systems. They are connected to a network to provide output to other systems. Examples include home security systems and point of sale (POS) systems.

(3) Standalone embedded systems. They are not reliant on a host system. Like any embedded system, they perform a specialized task. However, they do not necessarily belong to a host system, unlike other embedded systems. A calculator or MP3 player is an example.

(4) Real time embedded systems. They give the required output in a defined time interval. They are often used in medical, industrial and military sectors because they are responsible for time-critical tasks. A traffic control system is an example.

Embedded systems can also be categorized by their performance requirements:

(1) Small scale embedded systems. They often use no more than an 8-bit microcontroller.

(2) Medium scale embedded systems. They use a larger microcontroller[①] (16-32 bit) and often link microcontrollers together.

(3) Sophisticated scale embedded systems. They often use several algorithms that result in software and hardware complexities and may require more complex software, a configurable processor and/or a programmable logic array.

There are several common embedded system software architectures, which become necessary as embedded systems grow and become more complex in scale. These include:

(1) Simple control loops. They call subroutines[②], which manage a specific part of the hardware or embedded programming.

---

① microcontroller [ˌmaɪkrəʊkɒnˈtrəʊlə] n.微控制器

② subroutine [ˈsʌbruːtiːn] n.子程序

(2) Interrupt① controlled systems. They have two loops: a main one and a secondary one. Interruptions in the loops trigger tasks.

(3) Cooperative multitasking. It is essentially a simple control loop located in an application programming interface (API②).

(4) Preemptive multitasking or multithreading③. It is often used with an RTOS and features synchronization and task switching strategies.

(5) Very large scale integration (VLSI) circuits. They are common features of embedded systems. Many ICs in embedded systems are VLSIs.

VLSI is a term that describes the complexity of an integrated circuit (IC). VLSI is the process of embedding hundreds of thousands of transistors into a chip, whereas LSI (large scale integration) microchips contain thousands of transistors, MSI (medium scale integration) contains hundreds of transistors, and SSI (small scale integration) contains tens of transistors. ULSI (ultra large scale integration) refers to placing millions of transistors on a chip.

5　Embedded System Trends

While some embedded systems can be relatively simple, they are becoming more complex, and more and more of them are now able to either supplant human decision-making or offer capabilities beyond what a human could provide. For instance, some aviation systems, including those used in drones④, are able to integrate sensor data and act upon that information faster than a human could, permitting new kinds of operating features.

The embedded system is expected to continue growing rapidly, driven in large part by the internet of things. Expanding IoT applications, such as wearables⑤, drones, smart homes, smart buildings, video surveillance⑥, 3D printers and smart transportation are expected to fuel embedded system growth.

---

① interrupt [ˌɪntəˈrʌpt] v.中断
② application programming interface: 应用程序设计接口
③ multithread [məltɪˈθred] n.多线程
④ drone [drəʊn] n.无人驾驶飞机
⑤ wearable [ˈweərəbl] adj.可穿用的，可佩带的
⑥ surveillance [sɜːˈveɪləns] n.监督，监视

Unit 5

扫码听课文

Text A

Classification of Sensors (I)

A sensor is a device that responds to a physical stimulus (such as heat, light, sound, pressure, magnetism, or a particular motion) and transmits a resulting impulse (as for measurement or operating a control). It converts stimuli such as heat, light, sound and motion into electrical signals. These signals are passed through an interface that converts them into a binary code and passes this on to a computer to be processed.

The advantages of sensors are as follows.

(1) They accelerate processes and make them more accurate.

(2) They collect process and asset data in real-time.

(3) They monitor processes and assets accurately, reliably, and continuously.

(4) They increase productivity and reduce the total cost of ownership.

(5) They lower energy wastage.

There are various types of sensors, and we can use different criteria to classify them, such as their conversion principles, their uses, their output signal types, and the materials and processes that make them.

1 Types of Sensors Classified by Working (Detection) Principles

The detection principle refers to the mechanism of physical, chemical and biological effects on which the sensor works. There are resistive, capacitive, inductive, piezoelectric, electromagnetic, magnetoresistive, photoelectric, piezoresistive, thermoelectric, nuclear radiation, and semiconductor sensors.

According to the principle of variable resistance, there are corresponding sensors such as a potentiometer, strain gauge, and piezoresistive. According to the principle of electromagnetic induction, there are corresponding inductive, differential pressure transmitters, eddy current, electromagnetic, and magnetic resistance sensors, etc. According to semiconductor-related theories, there are corresponding solid-state sensors such as semiconductor force-sensitive, heat-sensitive, light-sensitive, gas-sensitive, and magnetic sensitive.

The advantage of this classification method is that it is convenient for sensor professional workers to conduct inductive analysis and research on the principle and design. It avoids too many names of sensors, so it is most commonly used. The disadvantage is that users will feel inconvenient when choosing sensors.

Sometimes this method is combined with the use and principle named, such as inductive displacement sensors, piezoelectric force sensors, etc., to avoid too many sensor names.

1.1　Electrical Sensor

Electrical sensors are a kind of sensors with a wide range of applications in non-electricity measurement technology. Commonly used sensors are resistive sensors, capacitive sensors, inductive sensors, magnetoelectric sensors and eddy current sensors.

1.1.1　Resistive Sensor

The resistive sensor is made by using the principle of the varistor to convert the measured non-electricity quantity into a resistance signal. Resistive sensors generally include potentiometer type, contact variable resistance type, resistance strain gauge type and piezoresistive sensor. Resistance sensors are mainly used for the measurement of parameters such as displacement, pressure, force, strain, torque, airflow rate, liquid level and liquid flow (see Figure 5-1) .

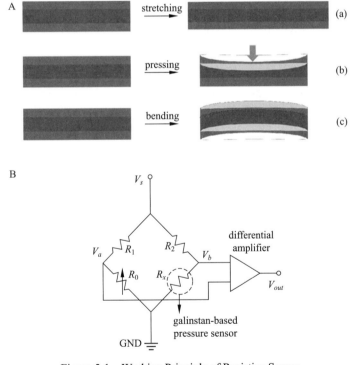

Figure 5-1　Working Principle of Resistive Sensor

1.1.2　Capacitive Sensor

Capacitive sensors are made using the principle of changing the geometric size of the capacitor or changing the nature and content of the medium, thereby changing the capacitance.

They are mainly used for the measurement of pressure, displacement, liquid level, thickness, moisture content and other parameters (see Figure 5-2).

Figure 5-2　Capacitive Sensors

1.1.3　Inductive Sensor

Inductive sensors are made by the principle of inductance or piezomagnetic effect that changes the geometric size of the magnetic circuit and the position of the magnet to change the inductance or mutual inductance. They are mainly used for the measurement of displacement, pressure, force, vibration, acceleration and other parameters.

1.1.4　Magnetoelectric Sensor

The magnetoelectric sensors are made by using the principle of electromagnetic induction to convert the measured non-electricity into electrical energy. They are mainly used for the measurement of parameters such as flow, speed and displacement.

1.1.5　Eddy Current Sensor

The eddy current sensors are made by the principle that metal chips move in the magnetic field to cut the magnetic field lines and form an eddy current in the metal chips. They are mainly used for the measurement of parameters such as displacement and thickness.

1.2　Magnetic Sensor

Magnetic sensors are made using some physical effects of ferromagnetic substances, and are mainly used for the measurement of parameters such as displacement and torque.

1.3　Photoelectric Sensor

Photoelectric sensors play an important role in non-electricity electrical measurement and automatic control technology. They are made using the photoelectric effect and optical principle of the photoelectric device, and are mainly used for the measurement of parameters such as light intensity, luminous flux, displacement, concentration, etc. (see Figure 5-3).

Figure 5-3　Photoelectric Sensors

1.4　Potential Sensor

Potential sensors are made using the principles of pyroelectric effect, photoelectric effect, and Hall effect. They are mainly used for the measurement of parameters such as temperature, magnetic flux, current, speed, light intensity, and thermal radiation.

1.5　Charge Sensor

The charge sensor is made using the principle of the piezoelectric effect and is mainly used for force and acceleration measurement.

1.6　Semiconductor Sensor

Semiconductor sensors are made using the principles of semiconductor piezoresistive effect, internal photoelectric effect, magnetoelectric effect, and substance change caused by the contact between semiconductor and gas. They are mainly used for temperature, humidity, pressure, acceleration, magnetic field and harmful gas measurement.

1.7　Resonant Sensor

The resonant sensor is made by the principle of changing the inherent parameters of electricity or machinery to change the resonant frequency, which is mainly used to measure pressure.

1.8　Electrochemical Sensor

Electrochemical sensors are made based on ion conductivity. According to the formation of different electrical characteristics, electrochemical sensors can be divided into potentiometric sensors, conductivity sensors, electric quantity sensors, polarographic sensors, and electrolytic sensors. Electrochemical sensors are mainly used to analyze the measurement of gas, liquid or solid components dissolved in liquid, the PH of the liquid, electrical conductivity and redox potential.

2 Types of Sensors Classified by Energy Relationship

Sensors can be divided into the following two types according to the energy relationship between the sensitive element and the measured object.

2.1 Energy Conversion Type (Active Type, Self-Sourced Type, Power Generation Type)

In this type of sensor, no additional energy is required when performing the signal conversion. The energy is directly input from the measured object, and the input signal energy is converted into another form of energy output to make it work. The active sensor is similar to a micro-generator, which can convert the input non-electric energy into electrical energy output. The sensor itself does not need an external power supply, and the signal energy is directly obtained from the measured object. Therefore, as long as it is equipped with the necessary amplifier, it can promote the display and recording capabilities of the instrument. Such as piezoelectric (see Figure 5-4), piezoelectric magnetic, electromagnetic, electric, thermocouple, photovoltaic, Hall element, magnetostrictive, electrostrictive, electrostatic and other sensors.

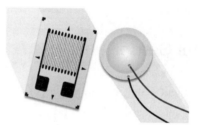

Figure 5-4   Piezoelectric Sensors

In this type of sensor, part of the energy conversion is reversible, and it can also convert electrical energy into mechanical energy or other non-electricity. Such as piezoelectric, piezoelectric magnetic, electric sensors, etc.

2.2 Energy Control Type (Passive Type, Other Source Types, Parametric Type)

When performing the signal conversion, it is necessary to supply energy first, that is, to supply auxiliary energy from the outside to make the sensor work, and the change of external energy supply is controlled by the measured objects. For passive sensors, the measured non-electric quantity only controls or modulates the energy in the sensor. It must be converted into voltage or current through the measurement circuit, and then converted and amplified to promote the indication or recording capabilities of the instrument. The matching measurement circuit is usually a bridge circuit or a resonance circuit. Such as resistance type, capacitance type, inductance type, differential transformer type, eddy current type, thermistor, photocell, photoresistor, humidity-sensitive resistor, magnetoresistive resistor, etc.

New Words

magnetism	[ˈmægnətɪzəm]	n.磁性，磁力
measurement	[ˈmeʒəmənt]	n.量度；尺寸；测量法
motion	[ˈməʊʃn]	n.运动
wastage	[ˈweɪstɪdʒ]	n.消耗
criterion	[kraɪˈtɪərɪən]	n.（判定的）标准，准则
mechanism	[ˈmekənɪzəm]	n.机制，机能
resistive	[rɪˈzɪstɪv]	adj.电阻的
piezoelectric	[paɪˌiːzəʊˈlektrɪk]	adj.压电的
magnetoresistive	[ˌmægniːtɔːˈsɪstɪv]	adj.磁阻的
photoelectric	[ˌfəʊtəʊˈlektrɪk]	adj.光电的
piezoresistive	[paɪiːzəʊˈzɪstɪv]	n.压阻的
thermoelectric	[ˈθɜːməʊˈlektrɪk]	adj.热电的
heat-sensitive	[ˈhiːtˈsensətɪv]	adj.热敏的
inconvenient	[ˌɪnkənˈviːnɪənt]	adj.不方便的，麻烦的
varistor	[væeɪrɪstə]	n.变阻器
parameter	[pəˈræmɪtə]	n.参数
strain	[streɪn]	n.应变
torque	[tɔːk]	n.扭矩，扭转力
thickness	[ˈθɪknəs]	n.厚度
inductance	[ɪnˈdʌktəns]	n.电感，感应系数
displacement	[dɪsˈpleɪsmənt]	n.位移
ferromagnetic	[ˌferəʊmægˈnetɪk]	adj.铁磁的，铁磁体的
humidity	[hjuːˈmɪdətɪ]	n.湿度
resonant	[ˈrezənənt]	adj.谐振的，共振的
ion	[ˈaɪən]	n.离子
conductivity	[ˌkɒndʌkˈtɪvətɪ]	n.导电性；电导率
redox	[ˈredɒks]	n.氧化还原作用
thermocouple	[ˈθɜːməˈkʌpl]	n.热电偶
photovoltaic	[ˌfəʊtəʊvɒlˈteɪk]	adj.光电池的；光伏的
magnetostrictive	[mægniːtəʊˈstrɪktɪv]	adj.磁致伸缩的，磁力控制的
electrostrictive	[ˈelektrɒstrɪktɪv]	adj.电致伸缩的，电力控制的
electrostatic	[ɪˌlektrəʊˈstætɪk]	adj.静电的
reversible	[rɪˈvɜːsəbl]	adj.可逆的

auxiliary	[ɔːgˈzɪlɪərɪ]	adj.辅助的；备用的
modulate	[ˈmɒdjuleɪt]	v.调整；调制；调节
thermistor	[θɜːˈmɪstə]	n.电热调节器
photocell	[ˈfəʊtəʊsel]	n.光电池
photoresistor	[fəʊtəʊrɪˈzɪstə]	n.光敏电阻（器）；光电导管

Phrases

physical stimulus	物理刺激
total cost of ownership	总拥有成本
nuclear radiation	核辐射
strain gauge	应变仪，应变规
differential pressure transmitter	差压变送器
eddy current	涡流，涡电流
be combined with	与……结合,与……组合
inductive displacement sensor	电感式位移传感器
resistive sensor	电阻传感器
capacitive sensor	电容传感器
inductive sensor	电感传感器
magnetoelectric sensor	磁电传感器
airflow rate	空气流量，气流速率
geometric size	几何尺寸
moisture content	含水量
piezomagnetic effect	压磁效应，压磁性
magnetic field	磁场
light intensity	光强度；亮度
luminous flux	光通量
pyroelectric effect	热电效应
Hall effect	霍尔效应
thermal radiation	热辐射
charge sensor	电荷传感器
harmful gas	有害气体
resonant sensor	谐振传感器
electrochemical sensor	电化学传感器
potentiometric sensor	电位传感器
electric quantity sensor	电量传感器
polarographic sensor	极谱传感器
dissolved in	溶解于

energy conversion	能量转换
be converted into	转化为
power supply	电源；供电
electrical energy	电能
mechanical energy	机械能
bridge circuit	桥接电路；桥路
resonance circuit	共振回路
humidity-sensitive resistor	湿度敏感电阻器
magnetoresistive resistor	磁阻电阻器

参考译文

传感器的类型(一)

传感器是一种对物理刺激（如热、光、声、压、磁或特定运动）做出响应并传输产生的脉冲（用于测量或操作控制装置）的装置。它将热、光、声音和运动等刺激转换为电信号。这些信号通过一个接口传递，该接口将其转换为二进制代码，然后传递给计算机进行处理。

传感器的优点如下。

（1）它们会加速处理过程并使其更加准确。

（2）它们实时收集过程和资产的数据。

（3）它们准确、可靠、持续地监控过程和资产。

（4）它们提高了生产率，降低了总拥有成本。

（5）它们降低了能源消耗。

传感器有各种类型，可以使用不同的标准对它们进行分类，如按照它们的转换原理、用途、输出信号类型及制造它们的材料和工艺来分类。

1 按工作（检测）原理分类的传感器类型

检测原理是指传感器工作的物理、化学和生物效应机制。有电阻传感器、电容传感器、电感传感器、压电传感器、电磁传感器、磁阻传感器、光电传感器、压阻传感器、热电传感器、核辐射传感器和半导体传感器。

根据可变电阻原理，有相应的传感器，如电位计传感器、应变仪传感器和压阻传感器。根据电磁感应原理，有相应的电感传感器、差压变送器、涡流传感器、电磁传感器和磁阻传感器等。根据半导体相关理论，有相应的固态传感器，如半导体力敏传感器、热敏传感器、光敏传感器、气敏传感器和磁敏传感器。

这种分类方法的优点是便于传感器专业人员对原理和设计进行归纳分析和研究。它避免了太多的传感器名称，所以它是最常用的。缺点是用户在选择传感器时会感到不方便。

有时，这种方法与命名的用途和原理相结合，如电感位移传感器、压电力传感器等，以避免传感器名称过多。

1.1　电传感器

电传感器是一种在非电量测量技术中有着广泛应用的传感器。常用的传感器有电阻传感器、电容传感器、电感传感器、磁电传感器和涡流传感器。

1.1.1　电阻传感器

电阻传感器是利用变阻器原理制成的，它将被测非电量转换成电阻信号。电阻传感器一般包括电位计型、接触式可变电阻型、电阻应变计型和压阻传感器。电阻传感器主要用于测量位移、压力、力、应变、扭矩、气流速度、液位和液体流量等参数，如图 5-1 所示。

（图略）

1.1.2　电容传感器

电容传感器的原理是改变电容器的几何尺寸或改变介质的性质和内容，从而改变电容。主要用于压力、位移、液位、厚度、含水量等参数的测量，如图 5-2 所示。

（图略）

1.1.3　电感传感器

电感传感器根据电感或压磁效应原理制成，通过改变磁路的几何尺寸和磁铁的位置以改变电感或互感。它主要用于位移、压力、力、振动、加速度等参数的测量。

1.1.4　磁电传感器

磁电传感器是利用电磁感应原理制成的，它将被测非电能转换为电能。它主要用于测量流量、速度和位移等参数。

1.1.5　涡流传感器

涡流传感器的原理是，金属片在磁场中移动，切割磁场线，在金属片中形成涡流。它主要用于测量位移和厚度等参数。

1.2　磁传感器

磁传感器是利用铁磁性物质的某些物理效应制成的，主要用于测量位移和扭矩等参数。

1.3　光电传感器

光电传感器在非电量电气测量和自动控制技术中发挥着重要作用。它们利用光电器件的光电效应和光学原理制成，主要用于测量光强、光通量、位移、浓度等参数，如图 5-3 所示。

（图略）

1.4　电位传感器

电位传感器利用热电效应、光电效应和霍尔效应原理制成，主要用于测量温度、磁通量、电流、速度、光强和热辐射等参数。

1.5 电荷传感器

电荷传感器采用压电效应原理制成,主要用于测量力和加速度。

1.6 半导体传感器

半导体传感器利用半导体压阻效应、内部光电效应、磁电效应和半导体与气体接触引起的物质变化的原理制成,主要用于测量温度、湿度、压力、加速度、磁场和有害气体。

1.7 谐振传感器

谐振传感器利用改变电或机械的固有参数以改变谐振频率的原理制成,主要用于测量压力。

1.8 电化学传感器

电化学传感器基于离子导电性制成。根据形成的不同的电学特性,电化学传感器可分为电位传感器、电导传感器、电量传感器、极谱传感器和电解传感器。电化学传感器主要用于分析溶解在液体中的气体、液体或固体成分,液体的 pH 值,电导率和氧化还原电位的测量。

2 按能量关系分类的传感器类型

根据敏感元件与被测物体之间的能量关系,传感器可分为以下两种类型。

2.1 能量转换型(有源型、自供电型、发电型)

在这种类型的传感器中,执行信号转换时不需要额外的能量。能量直接从被测对象输入,输入信号能量转换为另一种形式的能量输出,使其工作。有源传感器类似于微型发电机,可以将输入的非电能转换为电能输出。传感器本身不需要外部电源,信号能量直接从被测对象获得。因此,只要配备必要的放大器,就可以提升仪器的显示和记录性能,如压电传感器(见图 5-4)、压电磁传感器、电磁传感器、电传感器、热电偶传感器、光伏传感器、霍尔元件传感器、磁致伸缩传感器、电致伸缩传感器、静电传感器等。

(图略)

在这种类型的传感器中,部分能量转换是可逆的,它还可以将电能转换为机械能或其他非电能,如压电传感器、压电磁传感器、电传感器等。

2.2 能量控制型(无源型、其他电源类型、参数型)

在进行信号转换时,需要首先提供能量,即从外部提供辅助能量使传感器工作,外部能量供应的变化由被测对象控制。对于无源传感器,测量的非电量仅控制或调节传感器中的能量。必须通过测量电路将其转换为电压或电流,然后进行转换和放大,以提升仪器的指示或记录性能。匹配的测量电路通常是桥式电路或谐振电路。如电阻型、电容型、电感型、差动变压器型、涡流型、热敏电阻、光电池、光敏电阻、湿敏电阻、磁阻电阻等。

Text B

Classification of Sensors (II)

1   Types of Sensors Classified by Input Quantity

If the input quantities are temperature, pressure, displacement, speed, humidity, light, gas and other non-electricity, the corresponding sensors are called temperature sensors, pressure sensors, weighing sensors, etc.

This classification method clearly explains the purpose of the sensor and provides convenience to the user. It is easy to select the required sensor according to the measurement object. The disadvantage is that this classification method classifies sensors with different principles into one category. It is difficult to find out the commonalities and differences in the conversion mechanism of each sensor. It is unfavorable to grasp some basic principles and analysis methods of the sensor because the same type of sensor, such as a piezoelectric sensor, can be used to measure acceleration, velocity, and amplitude in mechanical vibration as well as impact and force, but the working principle is the same.

This classification method divides most types of physical quantities into two categories: basic quantities and derived quantities. For example, the force can be regarded as a basic physical quantity, and pressure, weight, stress, moment, etc. can be derived from the force. When we need to measure the above physical quantities, we only need to use force sensors. So understanding the relationship between basic physical quantities and derived physical quantities is very helpful for what kind of sensors the system uses.

2   Physical Sensor and Structural Sensor

2.1   Physical Sensor

During the signal conversion process, the structural parameters are basically unchanged, but the change of the physical or chemical properties of some materials (sensitive components) is used to realize the signal conversion.

This kind of sensor generally has no movable structure and is easy to be miniaturized, so it is also called a solid-state sensor. It is a solid-state device that uses semiconductors, dielectrics, ferroelectrics and other sensitive materials. Such as thermocouple, piezoelectric quartz crystal, thermal resistance and various semiconductor sensors such as force sensitive, heat-sensitive, humidity sensitive, gas-sensitive, light-sensitive elements, etc.

2.2 Structural Sensor

Structural sensor relies on the change of the geometric shape or size of the sensor mechanical structure (that is, the structural parameter) to convert the external measured parameters into corresponding changes in physical quantities such as resistance, inductance, capacitance, etc., to achieve signal conversion and thus detect signal under test. Such as capacitive, inductive, strain gauge, potentiometer, etc.

3 Analog Sensor and Digital Sensor

According to the nature of the output signal, sensors can be divided into the following two types.

3.1 Analog Sensor

Analog sensor converts the non-electricity to be measured into a continuously changing voltage or current. If it is required to cooperate with a digital display or digital computer, it needs to be equipped with an analog-to-digital (A / D) conversion device.

3.2 Digital Sensor

Digital sensor can directly convert non-electricity to digital quantity. It can be directly used for digital display and calculation. It can directly cooperate with computers, and it has the advantages of strong anti-interference ability and is suitable for distance transmission.

At present, this type of sensor can be divided into three categories: pulse, frequency and digital output. Such as grating sensors.

4 Contact and Non-contact Type Sensor

4.1 Contact Type

Potentiometer type, strain type, capacitive type, inductive type, etc. all belong to contact type. The advantage of the contact type is that the sensor and the measured object are regarded as one, and the calibration of the sensor does not need to be performed on the site. The disadvantage is that the contact between the sensor and the measured object will inevitably affect the state or characteristics of the measured object.

4.2   Non-contact Type

Non-contact measurement can eliminate the influence of the sensor intervention. It can improve the accuracy of the measurement, and at the same time, it can increase the service life of the sensor. However, the output of the non-contact sensor will be affected by the medium or environment between the measured object and the sensor. Therefore, the sensor calibration must be carried out on site. Such as infrared sensors (see Figure 5-5) .

Figure 5-5   Infrared Sensor

5   Types of Sensors Classified by Composition

Basic sensor: It is a most basic single conversion device.

Combined sensor: It is a sensor composed of different single conversion devices.

Applied sensor: It is a sensor composed of a basic sensor or combination sensor combined with other mechanisms.

For example, a thermocouple is a basic sensor. It is combined with a heat absorber that converts infrared radiation into heat to form an infrared radiation sensor, that is, a combined sensor; applying this combined sensor to infrared scanning equipment is an application sensor.

6   Special Types of Sensors

The classification introduced above is the basic type of sensor, which can be divided into the following types according to particularity:

(1) According to the detection function, sensors can be divided into sensors that detect temperature, pressure, flowmeter, flow rate, acceleration, magnetic field, luminous flux, etc.

(2) According to the physical basis of sensors work, sensors can be divided into mechanical, electrical, optical, liquid, etc.

(3) According to the scope of the conversion phenomenon, sensors can be divided into chemical sensors, electromagnetic sensors, mechanical sensors and optical sensors.

(4) According to the material, sensors can be divided into metals, ceramics, organic polymer materials, semiconductor sensors, etc.

(5) According to the application field, sensors are divided into industrial, civil, scientific research, medical, agricultural, military and other sensors.

(6) According to functional purposes, sensors are divided into sensors for measurement, monitoring, inspection, diagnosis, control, analysis, etc.

New Words

convenience	[kənˈviːnɪəns]	n.方便；便利
amplitude	[ˈæmplɪtjuːd]	n.振幅
movable	[ˈmuːvəbl]	adj.可移动的
dielectric	[ˌdaɪˈlektrɪk]	n.电介质，绝缘体
		adj.非传导性的
display	[dɪˈspleɪ]	v.显示
		n.显示器
anti-interference	[ˈæntɪ ɪntəˈfɪərəns]	n.抗干扰；反干扰
calibration	[ˌkælɪˈbreɪʃn]	n.校准
inevitably	[ɪnˈevɪtəblɪ]	adv.不可避免地；必然地
radiation	[ˌreɪdɪˈeɪʃn]	n.辐射
flowmeter	[ˈfləʊmiːtə]	n.流量计
ceramic	[səˈræmɪk]	n.陶瓷
inspection	[ɪnˈspekʃn]	n.检查；检验

Phrases

derived quantity	导出量
be regarded as	被认为，被看作
solid-state sensor	固态传感器
geometric shape	几何形状
output signal	输出信号
analog sensor	模拟传感器
cooperate with ...	与……协作，与……合作
digital sensor	数字传感器
service life	使用寿命
heat absorber	吸热器
infrared scanning equipment	红外扫描设备
organic polymer material	有机聚合物材料

参考译文

传感器的类型(二)

1　按输入量分类的传感器类型

如果输入量为温度、压力、位移、速度、湿度、光照、气体和其他非电量，则相应的传感器称为温度传感器、压力传感器、称重传感器等。

这种分类方法清楚地解释了传感器的用途，并为用户提供了方便，可以很容易地根据测量对象选择所需的传感器。缺点是，这种分类方法将具有不同原理的传感器分为一个类别，很难找出每个传感器转换机制的共性和区别。这不利于掌握传感器的一些基本原理和分析方法，因为相同类型的传感器（如压电传感器）可以用来测量机械振动中的加速度、速度和振幅，以及冲击和力，但工作原理是相同的。

这种分类方法将大多数类型的物理量分为两类：基本量和导出量。例如，力可以被视为一个基本的物理量，压力、重量、应力、力矩等可以从力中导出。当需要测量上述物理量时，只需要使用力传感器。因此，了解基本物理量和导出物理量之间的关系对于系统使用何种传感器非常有帮助。

2　物理传感器和结构传感器

2.1　物理传感器

在信号转换过程中，结构参数基本不变，只是利用了一些材料（敏感元件）的物理或化学性质的变化来实现信号转换。

这种传感器一般没有可移动的结构，易于小型化，因此也被称为固态传感器。它是一种使用半导体、电介质、铁电体和其他敏感材料的固态器件。如热电偶传感器、压电石英晶体传感器、热电阻传感器，以及如力敏、热敏、湿敏、气敏、光敏元件等各种半导体传感器。

2.2　结构传感器

结构传感器依靠传感器机械结构（结构参数）的几何形状或尺寸的变化，将外部测量参数转换为电阻、电感、电容等物理量的相应变化，实现信号转换，从而检测被测信号，如电容传感器、电感传感器、应变仪传感器、电位计传感器等。

3　模拟传感器和数字传感器

根据输出信号的性质，传感器可分为以下两种类型。

3.1　模拟传感器

模拟传感器将要测量的非电量转换为持续变化的电压或电流。如果需要与数字显示器或数字计算机配合，则需要配备模数（A/D）转换装置。

3.2　数字传感器

数字传感器可以直接将非电量转换为数字量。它可以直接用于数字显示和计算。它可以直接与计算机配合，其优点是抗干扰能力强，适合远距离传输数据。

目前，这种传感器可分为三类：脉冲、频率和数字输出，如光栅传感器。

4　接触式和非接触式传感器

4.1　接触式传感器

电位计式、应变式、电容式、电感式等都属于接触式。接触式传感器的优点是将传感器和被测对象视为一个整体，无须在现场进行传感器校准。缺点是传感器与被测物体之间的接触不可避免地会影响被测物体的状态或特性。

4.2　非接触式传感器

非接触测量可以消除传感器干预的影响。它可以提高测量的精度，同时可以延长传感器的使用寿命。然而，非接触式传感器的输出会受到被测对象和传感器之间的介质或环境的影响。因此，传感器校准必须在现场进行，如红外传感器，见图5-5。

（图略）

5　按组成分类的传感器类型

基本传感器：它是最基本的单一转换设备。

组合传感器：由不同的单个转换设备组成的传感器。

应用传感器：由基本传感器或组合传感器与其他机构组合而成的传感器。

例如，热电偶是一种基本的传感器。它与将红外辐射转化为热量的吸热器组合，形成红外辐射传感器，即组合传感器，将这种组合传感器应用于红外扫描设备就是一种应用传感器。

6　特殊类型的传感器

以上介绍的分类是传感器的基本类型，根据其特殊性可分为以下类型：

（1）根据检测功能，可以分为检测温度、压力、流量计、流量、加速度、磁场、光通量等的传感器。

（2）根据传感器工作的物理基础，可以分为机械、电、光学、液体等传感器。

（3）根据转换现象的范围，可以分为化学传感器、电磁传感器、机械传感器和光学传感器。

（4）根据材料，可以分为金属、陶瓷、有机高分子材料、半导体等传感器。

（5）根据应用领域，可以分为工业、民用、科研、医疗、农业、军事等传感器。

（6）根据功能目的，可以分为测量、监控、检查、诊断、控制、分析等传感器。

Exercises

[Ex. 1] Answer the following questions according to Text A.

1. What is a sensor?

2. What does the detection principle refer to?

3. What is the advantage of types of sensors classified by working (detection) principles?

4. What is the resistive sensor?

5. What are inductive sensors mainly used for?

6. How are magnetic sensors made? What are they mainly used for?

7. How are photoelectric sensors made? What are they mainly used for?

8. What can electrochemical sensors be divided into according to the formation of different electrical characteristics?

9. What are the two types sensors can be divided into according to the energy relationship between the sensitive element and the measured object?

10. What is it necessary when performing the signal conversion?

[Ex. 2] Answer the following questions according to Text B.

1. What does the classification method of sensors by input quantity do?

2. Why is it unfavorable to grasp some basic principles and analysis methods of the sensor?

3. Why is physical sensor also called a solid-state sensor?

4. What are the two types that sensors can be divided into according to the nature of the output signal?

5. How many categories can digital sensors be divided into? What are they?

6. What is the advantage of the contact type?

7. What can non-contact measurement do?

8. What are the types of sensors classified by composition?

9. What can sensors be divided into according to the detection function?

10. What are sensors divided into according to the application field?

[Ex. 3] Translate the following terms or phrases from English into Chinese and vice versa.

1. bridge circuit	1.
2. electric quantity sensor	2.
3. inductive sensor	3.
4. magnetic field	4.
5. pyroelectric effect	5.
6. *n.*参数	6.
7. *n.*位移	7.
8. *adj.*静电的	8.
9. *n.*电感，感应系数	9.
10. *adj.*磁阻的	10.

[Ex. 4] Translate the following passage into Chinese.

Questions Related to Sensors

1 What Are the Types of Sensors?

All types of sensors can be basically classified into analog sensors and digital sensors. But, there are a few types of sensors such as temperature sensors, IR sensors, ultrasonic sensors, pressure sensors, proximity sensors, and touch sensors that are frequently used in most electronics applications.

2 What Are the Characteristics of Sensors?

Important static characteristics of sensors include sensitivity, resolution, linearity, zero drift and full-scale drift, range, repeatability and reproducibility. Sensitivity is a measure of the change in output of the sensor relative to the change in the input (the measured quantity).

3 What Is the Difference Between Active and Passive Sensors?

Active sensors have their own source of light or illumination. In particular, it actively sends a pulse and measures the backscatter reflected in the sensor. But passive sensors measure reflected sunlight emitted from the sun. When the sun shines, passive sensors measure this energy.

4 How Do Sensors Work in General?

Simply put, a sensor converts stimuli such as heat, light, sound and motion into electrical signals. These signals are passed through an interface that converts them into a binary code and passes this on to a computer to be processed.

5　What Is the Repeatability of a Sensor?

Repeatability—this is the ability of a sensor to repeat a measurement when put back in the same environment. It is often directly related to the accuracy, but a sensor can be inaccurate, yet be repeatable in making observations.

Reading

Wireless Sensor Network

1　What Is Wireless Sensor Network?

Wireless sensor network[①] (WSN) can be defined as a self-configured[②] and infrastructureless[③] wireless network to observe physical or environmental conditions, like temperature, pressure, motion, sound, vibration, or pollutants[④], and to directly pass their data or information through the network to a sink which is also called the main location where the information is often observed and analyzed.

A base station or sink seems like an interface between the users and the network. It can convert back some required information from the network by injecting[⑤] some queries[⑥] and gathering results from the sink. Typically, a wireless sensor network contains thousands of sensor nodes.

The sensory nodes can communicate with each other by using radio signals. The wireless sensor nodes are equipped with sensing and radio transceivers[⑦], computing devices, and power components.

A sensor node in a wireless sensor network is inherently resource-constrained. It also has limited processing speed, storage capacity, and communication bandwidth. After the sensor nodes are installed[⑧], they're responsible for self-organizing[⑨] an appropriate network infrastructure often with multi-hop communication with them. Then the onboard sensors begin to collect information of their interest. And then the specifically designed devices of wireless sensor networks reply to those queries sent from a "control site" to perform specific instructions or provide sensing samples.

---

① wireless sensor network：无线传感器网络
② self-configured [self kən'fɪɡəd] *adj.*自配置的
③ infrastructureless ['ɪnfrəstrʌktʃəlɪs] *adj.*无基础设施的
④ pollutant [pə'lu:tənt] *n.*污染物
⑤ inject [ɪn'dʒekt] *vt.*（给……）注入；（给……）添加
⑥ query ['kwɪərɪ] *n.*查询
⑦ transceiver [træn'si:və] *n.*无线电收发机，收发器
⑧ install [ɪn'stɔ:l] *vt.*安装
⑨ self-organizing ['self'ɔ:gənaɪzɪŋ] *n.*自组织的

The working mode of the sensor nodes can also be either continuous or event-driven. GPS (global positioning system) and LPA (local positioning algorithms[①]) can be used to obtain location and positioning information.

Wireless sensor devices are often equipped with actuators to "act" upon certain conditions. These networks are sometimes or normally called wireless sensor network and actuator network.

2 Types of Wireless Sensor Networks

2.1 Terrestrial Wireless Sensor Networks

Terrestrial[②] WSNs are used for communicating base stations efficiently, and they comprise thousands of wireless sensor nodes deployed either in an unstructured[③] (ad hoc) or structured (pre-planned) manner.

In an unstructured (ad hoc) mode, the sensor nodes are randomly distributed within the target area that's dropped from a set plane.

In WSNs, the battery power is limited, however, the battery is provided with solar cells[④] as a secondary power source. The conservation[⑤] of energy of the WSNs is achieved by using low duty cycle operations, optimal routing, minimizing delays, and so on.

2.2 Underground[⑥] Wireless Sensor Networks

In terms of deployment, maintenance, equipment cost considerations[⑦], and careful planning, underground wireless sensor networks are more expensive than terrestrial WSNs.

The underground wireless sensor networks comprise several sensory nodes that are hidden in the ground to observe underground conditions.

Additional sink nodes[⑧] are located above the bottom to transfer information from the sensor nodes to the base station, These underground WSNs deployed into the ground are difficult to recharge[⑨].

The sensor battery nodes equipped with limited battery power are also difficult to recharge. Additionally, the underground environment makes wireless communication a challenge because of

---

① local positioning algorithms：局部定位算法，本地定位算法
② terrestrial [təˈrestriəl] adj.陆地的，地面的
③ unstructured [ʌnˈstrʌktʃəd] adj.非结构化的
④ solar cell：太阳能电池
⑤ conservation [ˌkɒnsəˈveɪʃn] n.保护；节约
⑥ underground [ˌʌndəˈɡraʊnd] adj.地下的
⑦ consideration [kənˌsɪdəˈreɪʃn] n.仔细考虑
⑧ sink node：汇聚节点
⑨ recharge [ˌriːˈtʃɑːdʒ] vt.再充电

the high attenuation[①] and signal loss level.

2.3　Underwater Wireless Sensor Networks

About more than 70% of the earth's planet is covered with water. These networks contain several sensor nodes and vehicles deployed underwater[②]. Autonomous[③] underwater devices and vehicles are used to collect data from these sensor nodes.

A challenge of underwater communication may be a long propagation delay, bandwidth and sensor failures. Underwater WSNs are equipped with a limited battery that can't be recharged or replaced[④].

The difficulty of energy conservation for underwater WSNs involves the development of underwater communication and networking techniques.

2.4　Multimedia Wireless Sensor Networks

Multimedia wireless sensor networks[⑤] are proposed to enable tracking and monitoring of events in the sort of multimedia, like video, imaging, and audio.

These networks contain low-cost sensor nodes equipped with cameras and microphones[⑥]. These sensory nodes of multimedia WSNs are interconnected together over a wireless connection for data retrieval, data compression, and correlation.

The challenges with the multimedia WSNs include high bandwidth requirements, high energy consumption, processing, and compressing techniques. Additionally, multimedia contents need high bandwidth for the content to be delivered properly and easily.

2.5　Mobile Wireless Sensor Networks

Mobile WSNs comprise a group of sensor nodes that can be moved on their own and can be interacted with the physical environment. The mobile nodes can also compute sense and communicate respectively[⑦].

Mobile wireless sensor networks are more versatile than static[⑧] sensor networks. The benefits of mobile WSNs over static WSNs include better and improved coverage[⑨], superior channel capacity, better energy efficiency, and so on.

---

① attenuation [əˌtenjʊˈeɪʃn] *n.*衰减

② underwater [ˌʌndəˈwɔːtə] *adj.*在水中的；水面下的

③ autonomous [ɔːˈtɒnəməs] *adj.*自主的；自治的

④ replace [rɪˈpleɪs] *v.*替换；以……取代；更新

⑤ multimedia wireless sensor network：多媒体无线传感器网络

⑥ microphone [ˈmaɪkrəfəʊn] *n.*麦克风，话筒

⑦ respectively [rɪˈspektɪvlɪ] *adv.*各自地，分别地

⑧ static [ˈstætɪk] *adj.*静止的，静态的

⑨ coverage [ˈkʌvərɪdʒ] *n.*覆盖范围

3 Characteristics of Wireless Sensor Network

Some basic characteristics of wireless sensor networks are as follows:

(1) Power consumption constraints for nodes using energy harvesting① or mainly batteries are used.

(2) Having the ability to deal with node failures.

(3) Having some mobility② of nodes.

(4) Scalability to the large scale of deployment.

(5) Ability to resist harsh③ environmental conditions.

(6) Heterogeneity④ of nodes.

(7) Homogeneity⑤ of nodes.

(8) Easy to use.

(9) Cross-layer optimization.

4 The Advantages and Disadvantages of Wireless Sensor Networks

The advantages of wireless sensor networks are as follows:

(1) It is suitable for non-reachable places like over the sea, in mountains, rural areas, or deep forests.

(2) It avoids lots of wiring.

(3) It may accommodate⑥ new devices at any time.

(4) It can also be accessed by using a centralized⑦ monitor.

(5) It is flexible if there's a random situation when the additional workstation is required.

(6) The implementation pricing is affordable.

(7) It's flexible to undergo physical partitions.

The disadvantages of wireless sensor networks are as follows:

(1) It is less secure because hackers⑧ can enter the access point and obtain all the data.

(2) It has lower speed when compared with a wired network.

(3) It's easy for hackers to hack if we couldn't control the propagation of waves.

---

① energy harvesting：能量收集

② mobility [məʊˈbɪlətɪ] n.移动性

③ harsh [hɑːʃ] adj.恶劣的

④ heterogeneity [ˌhetərəˈdʒəˈniːətɪ] n.异质性

⑤ homogeneity [ˌhɒmədʒəˈniːətɪ] n.同质性

⑥ accommodate [əˈkɒmədeɪt] v.容纳，接纳

⑦ centralized [ˈsentrəlaɪzd] adj.集中的

⑧ hacker [ˈhækə] n.黑客

(4) It is even more complicated① compared with a wired network.

(5) It is easily troubled by surroundings② (walls, microwave, large distances because of signal attenuation, etc.).

(6) It has comparatively low speed of communication.

(7) It gets distracted by various elements like bluetooth.

(8) It is still costly (most importantly).

① complicate ['kɒmplɪkeɪt] v.使复杂化
② surrounding [sə'raʊndɪŋ] adj.周围的，附近的

Unit 6

Text A
Digital Signal Processing

扫码听课文

Digital signal processing (DSP) is an exciting area and it provides a world of possibilities for engineers to design new embedded system products. DSP technology uses specially designed programs and algorithms to manipulate analog signals and produce a signal that is of higher-quality, less prone to degradation and easier to transmit.

1 What Is Digital Signal Processing?

Digital signal processing is a powerful technology with applications in many areas of science, engineering, health care, and communications. DSP technology enables the processing and manipulation of data obtained from a variety of real-world sources. Visual images, sound waves, and even seismic waves can all act as inputs for digital signal processing.

The general function of a DSP is to measure, compress, or filter an analog signal. This typically requires the DSP to perform a large number of simple mathematical functions (addition, subtraction, multiplication, division, and the like) within a fixed or constrained time frame. To achieve this, companies like Texas Instruments have developed specialized microprocessor chips that are optimized for the task of digital signal processing.

The development of DSP began in the late 1960s and early 1970s. At that time, the application of DSP technology was focused on the military and government sectors, in areas like radar and sonar, space and oil exploration, and medical imaging. As personal computing became commonplace through the 1980s and onward, digital signal processing saw a wider range of commercial and consumer-focused applications. Mobile phones, movie special effects, and MP3 files all depend on DSP technology.

2 Components of Digital Signal Processing

A typical digital signal processing system follows a basic architecture that facilitates the digital conversion and manipulation of an analog signal. The first requirement for DSP is always a signal source. There must be a signal to filter, measure, or compress. The first step in processing the signal is to convert the analog signal into a digital signal using an analog-to-digital converter

(ADC). An ADC converts an input analog voltage into a digital measurement of that voltage.

Following the conversion of the signal to the digital format, the data can be passed through a DSP microprocessor chip where the signal may be filtered, compressed or otherwise manipulated according to application-specific requirements. Once the digital signal has been suitably modified, it may be converted back into an analog format with the use of a digital-to-analog converter (DAC). The end result will be a new analog signal that represents a digital modification of the original input signal.

A digital signal processing chip contains four main components:

(1) Program Memory — DSP chips contain two types of memory. The first type, the program memory, stores the programs and algorithms that the chip will use to process data. Programming for DSP chips varies significantly by application.

(2) Data Memory — the second type of memory used in DSP chips is known as data memory. This is where the chip stores the data it receives and that will be processed on the chip. Data is typically received as a digital signal that was previously converted from an analog signal.

(3) Compute Engine — the compute engine is the central processing unit of the DSP chip. This is where the computational power for the chip lives and where the algorithms from program memory will be applied to process data.

(4) Input/Output — a DSP chip may possess a number of different types of ports, including serial ports, timers, host ports, external ports, link ports, and other types. Ports are used to implement the data transmission between DSP and other devices, such as ADC or DAC converters. A DSP may also be incorporated into a larger system by port connections.

3   How Is DSP Different from Analog Signals?

Now that we've shed some light on how digital signal processing works, you might be wondering about various applications of DSP and the real value of converting analog signals into a digital format. To address this question, we need to understand more about the definitions and differences between analog and digital signals.

An analog signal is a continuous signal whose time variable is analogous to some physical quantity that changes over time, such as tone, voltage, or pressure. An analog signal depicting changes in voltage over time might reflect an amplitude of $+/-120$ V, with the signal expressing all values within that range. In contrast, a digital signal would represent the same voltage as a sequence of discrete values, often coded using the binary number system.

Analog and digital signals contain the same information, but are formatted in different ways. Analog signals reflect the reality that we live in a world where we can see an infinite number of different colors, hear an infinite number of tones and even smell an infinite number of smells. We can convert these data into a digital format that expresses each color, smell or sound as a combination of ones and zeroes. Then, we can write programs that manipulate the data in different and useful ways with the help of digital signal processing. As a final step, we can convert the digitally manipulated data back out of binary codes and into an analog form where we can hear or see the results.

4　Applications of Digital Signal Processing

To demonstrate the versatility and usefulness of DSP, we can briefly explore just a few of the many applications of digital signal processing technology.

4.1　DSP in Audio Processing

Digital signal processing technology plays a major role in processing audio signals.

The process of recording music depends on DSP to produce a final mix that is optimally pleasing to the human ear. In the recording studio, the various components of a track are recorded in analog and converted into a digital format where they can be manipulated for volume, tonality, and a range of other features. DSP can assist with filtering, signal addition and subtraction (adding new sounds or subtracting unwanted sounds), editing, and more.

DSP is used in computer-generated speech applications, which combine digital recording technology and vocal tract simulation to replicate human speech patterns using a computer.

4.2　DSP in Echo Location

Digital signal processing plays a significant role in the functioning of modern radar systems. DSP can be used to compress a pulsed radio frequency, increasing the accuracy of distance determination for objects detected on radar. A DSP chip can also increase the effective range of radar systems by filtering noise, and it may allow the operator to transmit radio waves pulses of varying shapes and lengths, enabling pulse optimization on a per-case basis.

New Words

embed	[ɪmˈbed]	v. (使) 嵌入，融入
degradation	[ˌdegrəˈdeɪʃn]	n.衰减，衰退；恶化
enable	[ɪˈneɪbl]	v.使能够；使可行
visual	[ˈvɪʒuəl]	adj.视觉的，可视的
compress	[kəmˈpres]	v.压缩；精简
mathematical	[ˌmæθəˈmætɪkl]	adj.数学的；精确的
multiplication	[ˌmʌltɪplɪˈkeɪʃn]	n.乘法，乘法运算
constrain	[kənˈstreɪn]	v.约束，限制
radar	[ˈreɪdɑː]	n.雷达

sonar	[ˈsəʊnɑː]	n.声呐装置，声呐系统
commonplace	[ˈkɒmənpleɪs]	adj.平常的，普遍的
		n.平常的事；老生常谈
suitably	[ˈsuːtəblɪ]	adv.适当地，合适地
definition	[ˌdefɪˈnɪʃn]	n.定义，释义；清晰（度）
reflect	[rɪˈflekt]	v.反映；反射
reality	[rɪˈæləti]	n.现实，事实
tone	[təʊn]	n.音色；色调
demonstrate	[ˈdemənstreɪt]	v.证明；说明
usefulness	[ˈjuːsfəlnəs]	n.有用，有益，有效
mix	[mɪks]	v.混合；调制混录
		n.混合；混音
track	[træk]	n.音轨
tonality	[təʊˈnæləti]	n.（音乐）音调；色调
subtraction	[səbˈtrækʃn]	n.除去，减去
noise	[nɔɪz]	n.噪声；干扰信息

Phrases

embedded system	嵌入式系统
sound wave	音波
oil exploration	石油勘探
personal computing	个人计算
movie special effect	电影特效
digital format	数字格式
compute engine	计算引擎
central processing unit	中央处理器
serial port	串行端口
be incorporated into	被纳入，被整合到
binary code	二进制代码
audio processing	音频处理
computer-generated speech	计算机生成的语音
vocal tract simulation	声道模拟

Abbreviations

DSP (digital signal processing)	数字信号处理

数字信号处理

数字信号处理（DSP）是一个令人兴奋的领域，它为工程师设计新的嵌入式系统产品提供了无限可能。DSP 技术使用专门设计的程序和算法处理模拟信号，并产生质量更高、不易衰减和更容易传输的信号。

1 什么是 DSP?

DSP 是一项功能强大的技术，在科学、工程、医疗和通信等许多领域都有应用。DSP 技术能够处理和操作从各种真实世界来源获得的数据。视觉图像、声波甚至地震波都可以作为 DSP 的输入。

DSP 的一般功能是测量、压缩或滤波模拟信号，这通常要求 DSP 在固定或受限的期限内执行大量简单的数学函数（加法、减法、乘法、除法等）。为了实现这一目标，德州仪器等公司已经开发了专门针对 DSP 任务进行优化的微处理器芯片。

DSP 的开发始于 20 世纪 60 年代末和 20 世纪 70 年代初。当时，DSP 技术的应用主要集中在军事和政府部门，如雷达和声呐、太空和石油勘探及医学成像等领域。随着个人计算在 20 世纪 80 年代及以后变得普遍，DSP 见证了更广泛的商业和以消费者为中心的应用。手机、电影特效和 MP3 文件处理都依赖于 DSP 技术。

2 DSP 组件

典型的 DSP 系统遵循一种基本的体系结构，该体系结构有助于模拟信号的数字转换和操作。DSP 的第一个要求始终是信号源，必须有一个要进行滤波、测量或压缩的信号。处理信号的第一步是使用模数转换器（ADC）将模拟信号转换为数字信号。ADC 将输入模拟电压转换为该电压的数字测量值。

在将信号转换为数字格式后，数据可以通过 DSP 微处理器芯片传递。在该芯片中，可以根据特定应用要求对信号进行滤波、压缩或其他操作。一旦数字信号经过适当修改，就可以使用数模转换器（DAC）将其转换回模拟格式。最终结果将是一个新的模拟信号，它代表对原始输入信号的数字化修改。

DSP 芯片包含 4 个主要组件：

（1）程序存储器——DSP 芯片包含两种类型的存储器。第一种类型是程序存储器，其存储芯片用于处理数据的程序和算法。DSP 芯片的编程因应用而异。

（2）数据存储器——DSP 芯片中使用的第二种存储器称为数据存储器。芯片在这里存储接收到的数据，这些数据将在芯片上处理。接收到的数据是之前从模拟信号转换而来的数字信号。

（3）计算引擎——计算引擎是 DSP 芯片的中央处理器。这是芯片的计算能力所在，程序存储器中的算法将用于处理数据。

（4）输入/输出——DSP 芯片可能拥有多种不同类型的端口，包括串行端口、定时器、主机端口、外部端口、链路端口等。端口用来实现 DSP 与其他设备（如 ADC 或 DAC 转换器）之间的数据传输。DSP 也可以通过端口连接集成到更大的系统中。

3　DSP 与模拟信号有何不同？

现在已经了解了 DSP 的工作原理，你可能想知道 DSP 的各种应用，以及将模拟信号转换为数字格式的真正价值。为了解决这个问题，需要更多地了解模拟信号和数字信号之间的定义与区别。

模拟信号是一种连续信号，其时间变量类似于随时间变化的物理量，如音调、电压或压力。描述电压随时间变化的模拟信号可能反映+/−120 V 的振幅，该信号表示该范围内的所有值。相比之下，数字信号将相同的电压表示为离散值序列，这些离散值通常使用二进制数字系统进行编码。

模拟信号和数字信号包含相同的信息，但格式不同。模拟信号反映了这样一个现实：人们生活在一个可以看到无数种不同颜色、听到无数种音调甚至闻到无数种气味的世界。可以将这些数据转换成数字格式，将每种颜色、气味或声音表示为 1 和 0 的组合。然后，可以编写程序，在 DSP 的帮助下，以不同且有用的方式处理数据。最后一步，可以将经过数字处理的数据从二进制代码转换回模拟形式，就可以听到或看到结果。

4　DSP 的应用

为了展示 DSP 的多功能性和实用性，可以简单地探讨 DSP 技术的众多应用的一部分。

4.1　音频处理中的 DSP

DSP 技术在处理音频信号方面发挥着重要作用。

录制音乐的过程依赖 DSP，以产生最适合人耳的最终混音。在录音室中，音轨的各个组成部分以模拟方式录制，并转换成数字格式，可以对其进行音量、音调和一系列其他功能的操作。DSP 可以协助滤波、信号加减（添加新声音或减去不需要的声音）、编辑等。

DSP 可用于计算机生成的语音应用，它结合了数字记录技术和声道模拟，以便使用计算机复制人类的语音模式。

4.2　回波定位中的 DSP

DSP 在现代雷达系统的运行中起着重要作用。DSP 可用于压缩脉冲射频，从而提高雷达检测到的物体的距离确定精度。DSP 芯片还可以通过滤波噪声扩大雷达系统的有效范围，并允许操作员发射不同形状和长度的无线电波脉冲，从而根据具体情况对脉冲进行优化。

扫码听课文

Text B

Digital Image Processing

1   What Is Digital Image Processing?

Digital image processing is an advanced technology that enables you to manipulate digital images through computer software. It is the subfield of signal processing, which focuses primarily on images. Digital image processing allows the user to take the digital image as an input and perform the different algorithms on it to generate an output. These algorithms may vary from image to image according to the desired output image. Adobe Photoshop is the most popular software that uses digital image processing to edit or manipulate images.

The three primary phases that constitute image processing are:

(1) Importing the image using picture acquisition tools.

(2) Picture processing.

(3) Changing the output of the image or report based on image analysis.

2   Types of Image

An image is a 2D array of numeric values called pixels. These pixels carry a value that indicates the amount of light for that particular pixel. The pixel value represents information about the number of intensities present in the image. The value 0 represents the color black, the value 1 represents the color white. The images are further characterized in two types.

2.1   Greyscale Image

The color grey lies within the white and black range. The images with pixel values between 0 to 1 are characterized as greyscale images.

2.2   RGB Image

RGB stands for red, green, and blue. Any other color can be derived from these three primary colors. Each pixel of a colored image carries different 16 or 24-bit color values. These 16 or 24 bits are further divided into three values that correspond to the RGB values. The combination of the RGB forms the exact colors of the pixel (see Figure 6-1).

Figure 6-1　RGB Image and Greyscale Image

3　Basic Functions of Digital Image Processing

Here are some basic functions that can be performed on an image, which will change the characteristics of the image.

3.1　Image Enhancement

The image enhancement function uses its algorithms to improve image features. It adjusts the image in such a form that all the results are more suitable for further analysis. Also, this helps the user to extract hidden features by using techniques like sharpening, curves, etc. The function improves the visualization, removes the unwanted parts, deblurrs the image, and much more.

3.2　Noise Addition

Noise is the unwanted parts of the image. It is added to an image for testing purposes. It helps the user to test the efficiency of the noise removal filters. There are different types of noises, some of which are listed as follows.

3.2.1　Salt and Pepper Noise

Massive and abrupt fluctuations in the image signal may cause this noise. This type of noise consists of white with black pixels. The white pixels are termed as salt pixels and pepper as black pixels in the image (see Figure 6-2) .

Figure 6-2　Salt and Pepper Noise

3.2.2 Gaussian Noise

Gaussian noise is the statistical noise with a probability density function (PDF). This type of noise is used to mimic many random natural processes like high temperature, transmission, and poor illumination.

3.2.3 Motion Blur

Motion blur is the most well-known type of noise. It is caused in the image due to the scattering of pixels because of camera motion while taking the picture. This blur can also be added to an image using the image processing techniques.

3.3 Filtering

In digital image processing filtering is very important. Filters are usually used to perform a different function on the image, such as removing noise, enhancing the image, detecting edges, and much more. There are different types of noises, and they require different filters to remove them, some of them are as follows.

3.3.1 Median Filter

Median filters are handy for removing random noise from the image. This filter is very effective for the noise. Unlike low pass filters and high pass filters, the median filter does not require a mask. This filter solely depends upon the mathematical concept of the median.

In order to apply the median filter, a window slides throughout the image. After that, the median of all the pixels is calculated using the standard mathematical formula of the median. The calculated median replaces the pixel at the center of the sliding window. This process is repeated on the whole image to obtain the median filtered image.

3.3.2 Laplacian Filter

The Laplacian filter is a second derivative filter which is used to find the edges in an image. The Laplacian image highlights rapid intensity-change in images; these areas are usually the edges. These kinds of filters are susceptible to the noise, so in order to apply this filter, one must smoothen the image. In most cases, the smoothing of the image is done using the Gaussian filter, and after that, the Laplacian filter is applied.

3.3.3 Gaussian Filter

A Gaussian filter is a filter whose impulse response gives you an approximation of a Gaussian function. Gaussian filters have the potential to neglect a phase feature while reducing the noise. It is a linear filter which is also used for preprocessing in the edge detection. It is even faster than the median filter due to the less complexity in the equation.

4 Applications

Image processing is playing a key role in many industries like medical, computer vision, and AI. Advanced image processing techniques, including image recovery, analysis, and enhancing, have helped a lot in the evolution of medical imaging.

In computer vision and AI, image processing techniques are used to extract the hidden features of the image. This is very effective in processes like image recognition and facial recognition.

New Words

subfield	['sʌbfi:ld]	n.子域；分支
generate	['dʒenəreɪt]	vt.产生，形成，造成
constitute	['kɒnstɪtju:t]	v.组成，构成
array	[ə'reɪ]	n.数组，数列
pixel	['pɪksl]	n.像素
intensity	[ɪn'tensətɪ]	n.强度
greyscale	['greskel]	adj.灰度的；灰色调的
enhancement	[ɪn'hɑ:nsmənt]	n.增强，增加，提高
extract	['ekstrækt]	v.提取，选取
hidden	['hɪdn]	adj.隐藏的
sharpen	['ʃɑ:pən]	v.锐化
curve	[kɜ:v]	n.曲线；(使)呈曲线形
visualization	[ˌvɪʒʊəlaɪ'zeɪʃn]	n.可视化，形象化
deblur	[dɪ'blɜ:]	vt.去模糊，使变清晰
abrupt	[ə'brʌpt]	adj.突然的，意外的
fluctuation	[ˌflʌktʃʊ'eɪʃn]	n.波动，涨落，起伏
statistical	[stə'tɪstɪkl]	adj.统计的，统计学的
mimic	['mɪmɪk]	vt.模仿，摹拟
random	['rændəm]	adj.随机的；任意的
illumination	[ɪˌlu:mɪ'neɪʃn]	n.照明；照度
scatter	['skætə]	v.散射
blur	[blɜ:]	v.（使）变得模糊不清；（使）看不清楚
handy	['hændɪ]	adj.容易做的；便利的
formula	['fɔ:mjələ]	n.公式，方程式
derivative	[dɪ'rɪvətɪv]	n.导数
smoothen	['smu:ðən]	v.使平滑
potential	[pə'tenʃl]	adj.潜在的
		n.潜力；可能性
neglect	[nɪ'glekt]	v.疏忽；忽视
preprocess	[pri:'prəʊses]	vt.预处理，预加工

Phrases

image processing	图像处理，图像加工
picture acquisition tool	图像采集工具
image analysis	图像分析
greyscale image	灰度图像
be characterized as	被描述为
be derived from ...	从……得到，源自……
pepper noise	胡椒噪声
Gaussian noise	高斯噪声
median filter	中值滤波器
low pass filter	低通滤波器
high pass filter	高通滤波器
Laplacian filter	拉普拉斯滤波器
derivative filter	导数滤波器
Gaussian filter	高斯滤波器
impulse response	脉冲响应
computer vision	计算机视觉
image recovery	图像恢复
facial recognition	面部识别

Abbreviations

2D (2-Dimensional)	二维
RGB (Red, Green, Blue)	三原色
PDF (probability density function)	概率密度函数

参考译文

数字图像处理

1 什么是数字图像处理?

数字图像处理是一种先进的技术，使用户能够通过计算机软件处理数字图像。它是信号处理的子领域，主要关注图像。数字图像处理允许用户将数字图像作为输入，并对其执行不同的算法以生成输出。这些算法可能因所需的输出图像而异。Adobe Photoshop 是最流行的软件，它使用数字图像处理编辑或处理图像。

构成图像处理的三个主要阶段是:

(1) 使用图片采集工具导入图像。

(2) 处理图像。

(3) 根据图像分析更改图像或报告的输出。

2 图像类型

图像是一个称为像素的二维数值数组。这些像素带有一个值,该值表示特定像素的光量。像素值表示图像中强度的数量信息。值 0 代表黑色,值 1 代表白色。这些图像进一步分为以下两种类型。

2.1 灰度图像

灰色介于白色和黑色之间。像素值在 0~1 的图像被描述为灰度图像。

2.2 RGB 图像

RGB 代表三原色,即红色、绿色和蓝色。任何其他颜色都可以从这三种原色中衍生出来。彩色图像的每个像素具有不同的 16 位或 24 位颜色值。这 16 位或 24 位颜色值被进一步划分为与 RGB 值相对应的三个值。RGB 的组合形成了该像素的精确颜色,如图 6-1 所示。

3 数字图像处理的基本功能

下面是一些可以在图像上执行的基本功能,这些功能将改变图像的特征。

3.1 图像增强

图像增强功能使用其算法改善图像特征。它调整图像,使所有结果更适合进一步分析。此外,这有助于用户通过使用锐化、曲线等技术提取隐藏的特征。该功能可以改善可视化效果、删除不需要的部分、消除图像的模糊等。

3.2 增加噪声

噪声是图像中不被需要的部分。给图像添加噪声是为了测试。它可以帮助用户测试去噪滤波器的效率。下面列出一些不同类型的噪声。

3.2.1 椒盐噪声

图像信号中的巨大而突然的波动可能会导致这种噪声。这种类型的噪声由白色和黑色像素组成。在图像中,白色像素被称为盐像素,而黑色像素被称为胡椒像素,如图 6-2 所示。

3.2.2 高斯噪声

高斯噪声是具有概率密度函数(PDF)的统计噪声。这种类型的噪声被用来模拟许多随机的自然过程，如高温、传输和照明不良。

3.2.3　运动模糊

运动模糊是最知名的噪声类型。它是由于拍照时相机运动导致像素散射而在图像中造成的。这种模糊也可以使用图像处理技术添加到图像中。

3.3　滤波

在数字图像处理中，滤波非常重要。通常使用滤波器对图像进行不同的处理，如去除噪声、增强图像、检测边缘等。有不同类型的噪声，需要不同的滤波器消除它们，列举如下。

3.3.1　中值滤波器

中值滤波器可以方便地去除图像中的随机噪声。该滤波器对噪声非常有效。与低通滤波器和高通滤波器不同，中值滤波器不需要遮罩。该滤波器完全依赖中值的数学概念。

为了应用中值滤波器，一个窗口在整个图像中滑动。然后，使用中值的标准数学公式计算所有像素的中值。计算出的中值将替换滑动窗口中心的像素。在整个图像上重复该过程以获得中值滤波图像。

3.3.2　拉普拉斯滤波器

拉普拉斯滤波器是一种二阶导数滤波器，用于寻找图像中的边缘。拉普拉斯图像突出显示图像中的快速强度变化，这些区域通常是边缘。这种滤波器容易受到噪声的影响，因此为了应用它，必须对图像进行平滑处理。在大多数情况下，使用高斯滤波器对图像进行平滑处理，再用拉普拉斯滤波器。

3.3.3　高斯滤波器

高斯滤波器的脉冲响应提供高斯函数的近似值。高斯滤波器有可能在减少噪声的同时忽略相位特征。它是一种线性滤波器，也用于边缘检测的预处理。由于方程的复杂性更低，它甚至比中值滤波器更快。

4　应用

图像处理在医疗、计算机视觉和人工智能等许多行业中发挥着关键作用。先进的图像处理技术，包括图像恢复、分析和增强，对医学成像的发展起到了很大的帮助。

在计算机视觉和人工智能中，图像处理技术用于提取图像的隐藏特征。这在图像识别和面部识别等过程中非常有效。

Exercises

[Ex. 1] Answer the following questions according to Text A.

1. What does DSP technology do?

2. What is digital signal processing?

3. What is the general function of a DSP?

4. What is the first step in processing the signal?

5. How many main components does a digital signal processing chip contain? What are they?

6. What does the program memory do?

7. What is the compute engine?

8. What do analog signals do?

9. What is the role DSP plays in the process of recording music?

10. In the functioning of modern radar systems, what can DSP be used to do?

[Ex. 2] **Answer the following questions according to Text B.**

1. What is digital image processing?

2. What is Adobe Photoshop?

3. What are the three primary phases that constitute image processing?

4. What are characterized as greyscale images?

5. What does RGB stand for? What does its combination do?

6. What are some basic functions that can be performed on an image?

7. What are the different types of noises mentioned in the passage?

8. What are the different types of filters mentioned in the passage?

9. What is the Laplacian filter?

10. What are image processing techniques used to in computer vision and AI?

[Ex. 3] **Translate the following terms or phrases from English into Chinese and vice versa.**

1. digital format	1.
2. embedded system	2.
3. serial port	3.
4. central processing unit	4.
5. computer vision	5.
6. *n.*噪声；干扰信息	6.
7. *adj.*视觉的，可视的	7.
8. *n.*数组，数列	8.
9. *vt.*去模糊，使变清晰	9.
10. *n.*增强，增加，提高	10.

[Ex. 4] Translate the following passage into Chinese.

Video and Image Processing

The different video and image processing methods are often grouped into the categories listed below.

1   Image Processing

Image processing originates from the more general field of signal processing and covers methods used to segment the object of interest. Segmentation here refers to methods which in some way enhance the object while suppressing the rest of the image (for example the edges in an image).

2   Video Processing

Video processing covers most of the image processing methods, but also includes methods where the temporal nature of video data is exploited. Image analysis is to analyze the image, first to find the objects of interest and then extract some parameters of these objects. For example, finding an object's position and size.

3   Machine Vision

When applying video processing, image processing or image analysis in production industries it is normally referred to as machine vision.

4   Computer Vision

Humans have human vision and similarly a computer has computer vision. Computer vision is the subcategory of artificial intelligence (AI) that focuses on building and using digital systems to process, analyze and interpret visual data.

Computer vision enables computers to see, identify and process images in the same way that human vision does, and then provide appropriate output. It is like imparting human intelligence and instincts to a computer. The computer must interpret what it sees, and then perform appropriate analysis or act accordingly. The aim of computer vision is to enable computers to perform the same kind of tasks as humans with the same efficiency.

Reading

Text Processing

Computing has the power to do some of the things that the human brain can do, thanks to the advances in artificial intelligence. One of those advances is text processing[①], which also relates to natural language processing[②](NLP). This article is a deep dive into what text processing is and how it can generate value for an enterprise.

---

① text processing：文本处理
② natural language processing：自然语言处理

1   What Is Text Processing?

The term text processing refers to the automation of analyzing electronic text. This allows machine learning models to get structured[①] information about the text and use it to analyze, manipulate the text, or to generate new text.

Text processing is one of the most common tasks used in machine learning applications such as language translation, sentiment analysis[②], spam filtering[③], and many others.

2   What Is the Difference Between Text Processing and Natural Language Processing?

Text processing only refers to the analysis, manipulation, and generation of text, while natural language processing refers to the ability of a computer to understand human language in a valuable way. Basically, natural language processing is the next step after text processing.

For example, a simple sentiment analysis would require a machine learning model to look for instances of positive[④] or negative[⑤] sentiment words, which could be provided to the model beforehand. This would be text processing, since the model isn't understanding the words, it's just looking for words that it is programmed to look for.

A natural language processing model would be translating full sentences into another language. Since syntax varies from one language to another, the computer has to understand the meaning of the sentences in order to accurately translate them. But while NLP is more advanced than text processing, it always has text processing involved as a step in the process.

3   Why Is Text Processing Important?

Since text processing is one of the machine learning uses, average technology consumers don't even realize they're using. However, most people use apps daily that are using text processing behind the scenes.

Since our interactions with companies have become increasingly online and text-based, text data is one of the most important ways for companies to derive business insights[⑥]. Text data can show a business how their customers search, buy products, and interact with competitors[⑦] online.

---

① structured ['strʌktʃəd] *adj.*结构化的
② sentiment analysis：情感分析
③ spam filtering：垃圾邮件过滤
④ positive ['pɒzətɪv] *adj.*积极的
⑤ negative ['negətɪv] *adj.*消极的
⑥ insight ['ɪnsaɪt] *n.*洞察力，见解
⑦ competitor [kəm'petɪtə] *n.*竞争者

Text processing with machine learning allows enterprises to handle these large amounts of text data.

4　How Is Text Processing Used?

Topic analysis — This technique interprets and categorizes large collections of text into topics or themes.

Sentiment analysis — This function automatically detects the emotional undertones of text and classifies them as positive, negative, or neutral[①].

Intent[②] detection — This classification model detects the intent, purpose, or goal of the text. For example, it may determine whether the intent is to gain information, make a purchase, or unsubscribe[③] from the company.

Language classification — This classifies text based on which language it's written in.

5　How Can Text Processing Generate Business Value?

Text processing allows businesses to automate processes that provide valuable insights, leading to more informed decision making[④]. Customer experience can be greatly improved using automated text processing.

5.1　Surveys[⑤] and Reviews

With text processing, a company can analyze their customer surveys or product reviews to classify customers as promoters[⑥], passives, or detractors[⑦] based on their answers to open-ended questions about the product. This can help determine the health of the company's customer retention rate[⑧], and also determine what offers or information they will receive from the company via email or elsewhere.

Survey data could be analyzed using keyword extractors[⑨] to look for a certain word or words in customer answers, using topic classification to determine which topics are common among

---

① neutral [ˈnjuːtrəl] *adj.*中立的
② intent [ɪnˈtent] *n.*意图，目的；意思
③ unsubscribe [ˌʌnsəbˈskraɪb] *v.*取消订阅
④ decision making：决策
⑤ survey [ˈsɜːveɪ] *n. & v.*调查，审察
⑥ promoter [prəˈməʊtə] *n.*发起人
⑦ detractor [dɪˈtræktə] *n.*批评者，贬低者
⑧ customer retention rate：客户保留率
⑨ keyword extractor：关键字提取器

customers, and using sentiment analysis to understand what portions of customers feel positive, negative, or neutral about the brand.

5.2　Support Tickets

Businesses often allow customers to submit[①] customer service support tickets online. This is common for large companies that operate worldwide, and text processing can help make customer support easier to handle. Text processing can determine the topic of the ticket, the urgency[②] of the ticket, and route the ticket to a customer service representative that speaks the same language as the customer. Without machine learning, this would be a time-consuming process to conduct manually.

Data and customer experience are the lifeblood[③] of a company, and they go hand in hand[④] with the help of text processing and other machine learning models. Automating analyses with machine learning improves the accuracy and amount of valuable data a company has, which is crucial when making big decisions. There is no excuse to be making uninformed[⑤] decisions when you can get accurate data insights about almost anything.

---

① submit [səbˈmɪt] v.提交
② urgency [ˈɜːdʒənsɪ] n.紧迫，急迫
③ lifeblood [ˈlaɪfblʌd] n.命脉，命根子，生命线
④ hand in hand：手拉手，携手；密切合作
⑤ uninformed [ˌʌnɪnˈfɔːmd] adj.信息不足的，情况不明的

Computer Network

扫码听课文

1　What Is a Computer Network?

Computer network is a group of computers connected with each other through wires, optical fiber or optical links so that various devices can interact with each other through a network. The aim of computer network is to share resources among various devices.

2　Components of Computer Network

2.1　NIC

NIC is a device that helps the computer to communicate with another device. The network interface card contains the hardware addresses. The data link layer protocol uses this address to identify the system on the network so that it transfers the data to the correct destination.

There are two types of NIC: wireless NIC and wired NIC.

Wireless NIC: All the modern laptops use the wireless NIC. In wireless NIC, a connection is made using the antenna that employs the radio wave technology.

Wired NIC: Cables use the wired NIC to transfer the data over the medium.

2.2　Hub

Hub is a central device that splits the network connection into multiple devices. When a computer requests for information from another computer, it sends the request to the hub. Hub distributes this request to all the interconnected computers.

2.3　Switch

Switch is a networking device that groups all the devices over the network to transfer the data to another device. A switch is better than a hub as it does not broadcast the message over the network, i.e., it sends the message to the device for which it belongs to. Therefore, we can say that switch sends the message directly from source to the destination (see Figure 7-1).

Figure 7-1   Switch

2.4   Cable

Cable is a transmission media that transmits the communication signals. There are three types of cables:

(1) Twisted pair cable: it is a high-speed cable that transmits the data over 1Gbps or more.

(2) Coaxial cable: it resembles like a TV installation cable. It is more expensive than twisted pair cable, but it provides the high data transmission speed.

(3) Fiber optic cable: it is a high-speed cable that transmits the data using light beams. It provides higher data transmission speed as compared to other cables. It is more expensive as compared to other cables.

2.5   Router

Router is a device that connects the LAN to the internet. The router is mainly used to connect the distinct networks or connect the internet to multiple computers.

3   Uses of Computer Network

(1) Resource sharing: it is the sharing of resources such as programs, printers, and data among the users on the network without the requirement of the physical location of the resource and user.

(2) Server-client model: computer networking is used in the server-client model. A server is a central computer used to store the information and maintained by the system administrator. Clients are the machines used to access the information stored in the server remotely.

(3) Communication medium: computer network behaves as a communication medium among the users. For example, a company contains more than one computer and has an email system which the employees use for daily communication.

(4) E-commerce: computer network is also important in businesses. People can do business over the internet. For example, amazon.com is doing their business over the internet.

4　Computer Network Architecture

Computer network architecture is defined as the physical and logical design of the software, hardware, protocols, and media of the transmission of data. There are two types of network architectures used: peer-to-peer network and client/server network.

4.1　Peer-to-Peer Network

Peer-to-peer network is a network in which all the computers are linked together with equal privilege and responsibilities for processing the data. It is useful for small environments, usually up to 10 computers. It has no dedicated server. Special permissions are assigned to each computer for sharing the resources, but this can lead to a problem if the computer with the resource is down.

Advantages of peer-to-peer network:

(1) It is less costly as it does not contain any dedicated server.

(2) It is easy to set up and maintain as each computer manages itself.

Disadvantages of peer-to-peer network:

(1) In the case of peer-to-peer network, it does not contain the centralized system . Therefore, it cannot back up the data as the data is different in different locations.

(2) It has a security issue as the device is managed itself.

4.2　Client/Server Network

Client/server network is a network model designed for the end users called clients to access the resources from a central computer known as server.

The central controller is known as a server while all other computers in the network are called clients. A server performs all the major operations such as security and network management. It is responsible for managing all the resources such as files, directories, printer, etc. All the clients communicate with each other through a server. For example, if client 1 wants to send some data to client 2, then it first sends the request to the server for the permission. The server sends the response to the client 1 to initiate its communication with the client 2.

Advantages of client/server network:

(1) It contains the centralized system. Therefore, we can back up the data easily.

(2) It has a dedicated server that improves the overall performance of the whole system.

(3) Security is better in client/server network as a single server administers the shared resources.

(4) It also increases the speed of the sharing resources.

Disadvantages of client/server network:

(1) It is expensive as it requires the server with large memory.

(2) A server has a network operating system (NOS) to provide the resources to the clients, but the cost of NOS is very high.

(3) It requires a dedicated network administrator to manage all the resources.

5   Features of Computer Network

5.1   Communication Speed

Network allows us to communicate over the network in a fast and efficient manner. For example, we can do video conferencing, email messaging, etc. over the internet. Therefore, the computer network is a great way to share our knowledge and ideas.

5.2   File Sharing

File sharing is one of the major advantage of the computer network. Computer network allows us to share the files with each other.

5.3   Easy Back up

Since the files are stored in the main server which is centrally located, it is easy to take the back up from the main server.

5.4   Software and Hardware Sharing

We can install the applications on the main server, so the user can access the applications centrally. We do not need to install the software on every machine. Similarly, hardware can also be shared.

5.5   Security

Network offers the security by ensuring that the user has the right to access the certain files and applications.

5.6   Scalability

Scalability means that we can add new components on the network. Network must be scalable so that we can extend the network by adding new devices. But, it decreases the speed of the connection and data of the transmission speed also decreases. This increases the chances of error occurring. This problem can be overcome by using the routing or switching devices.

5.7   Reliability

Computer network can use the alternative source for the data communication in case of any hardware failure.

6 Computer Network Types

6.1 LAN (local area network)

Local area network is a group of computers connected to each other in a small area such as building, office. It is used for connecting two or more personal computers through a communication medium such as twisted pair, coaxial cable, etc. It is less costly as it is built with inexpensive hardware such as hubs, network adapters, and Ethernet cables. The data is transferred at an extremely fast rate in local area network. Local area network provides higher security (see Figure 7-2) .

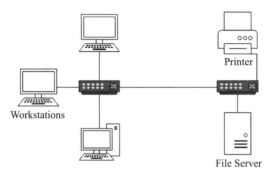

Figure 7-2   Local Area Network

6.2 MAN (metropolitan area network)

A metropolitan area network is a network that covers a larger geographic area by interconnecting a different LAN to form a larger network. Government agencies use MAN to connect to the citizens and private industries. In MAN, various LANs are connected to each other through a telephone exchange line. It has a higher range than LAN (see Figure 7-3).

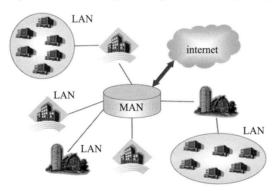

Figure 7-3   Metropolitan Area Network

Uses of metropolitan area network:
(1) MAN is used in communication between the banks in a city.

(2) It can be used in an airline reservation.

(3) It can be used in a college within a city.

6.3　WAN (wide area network)

A wide area network is a network that extends over a large geographical area such as states or countries. It is quite bigger network than the LAN. It is not limited to a single location, but it spans over a large geographical area through a telephone line, fiber optic cable or satellite links. The internet is one of the biggest WAN in the world. A wide area network is widely used in the field of business, government, and education.

Examples of wide area network:

(1) Mobile broadband: a 4G network is widely used across a region or country.

(2) Last mile: a telecom company provides the internet services to the customers in hundreds of cities by connecting their home with fiber.

(3) Private network: a bank provides a private network that connects lots of offices. This network is made by using the telephone leased line provided by the telecom company.

Advantages of wide area network:

(1) Geographical area: a wide area network provides a large geographical area. Suppose if the branch of our office is in a different city then we can connect with them through WAN. The internet provides a leased line through which we can connect with another branch.

(2) Centralized data: in case of WAN network, data is centralized. Therefore, we do not need to buy the emails, files or back up servers.

(3) Get updated files: software companies work on the live server. Therefore, the programmers get the updated files within seconds.

(4) Exchange messages: in a WAN network, messages are transmitted fast. The web application like Facebook, WhatsApp, Skype allows you to communicate with friends.

(5) Sharing of software and resources: in WAN network, we can share the software and other resources like a hard drive, RAM.

(6) Global business: we can do the business over the internet globally.

Disadvantages of wide area network:

(1) Security issue: a WAN network has more security issues as compared to LAN and MAN network, as all the technologies are combined together and that creates the security problem.

(2) Need of firewall and antivirus software: the data is transferred on the internet which can be changed or hacked by the hackers, so firewall needs to be used. Some people can inject the virus in our system so antivirus is needed .

(3) High setup cost: an installation cost of the WAN network is high as it involves the purchasing of routers, switches.

(4) Troubleshooting problems: it covers a large area so fixing the problem is difficult.

6.4 Internetwork

An internetwork is defined as two or more LANs or WANs or computer network segments which are connected using devices and they are configured by a local addressing scheme. An interconnection between public, private, commercial, industrial, or government computer networks can be defined as internetworking. An internetworking uses the internet protocol. The reference model used for internetworking is open system interconnection (OSI).

There are two types of internetwork. They are extranet and intranet.

An extranet is a communication network based on the internet protocol. It is used for information sharing. The access to the extranet is restricted to only those users who have login credentials. An extranet is the lowest level of internetworking. It can be categorized as MAN, WAN or other computer networks. An extranet cannot have a single LAN. It must have at least one connection to the external network.

An intranet is a private network based on the internet protocol. An intranet belongs to an organization which is only accessible by the organization's employee or members. The main aim of the intranet is to share the information and resources among the organization employees. An intranet provides the facility to work in groups and for teleconferences.

New Words

network	['netwɜːk]	n.网络
		v.将……连接成网络
wire	['waɪə]	n.电线
address	[əˈdres]	n.地址
protocol	['prəʊtəkɒl]	n.协议
medium	['miːdɪəm]	n.介质，媒介物
		adj.中等的，中级的
hub	[hʌb]	n.集线器
split	[splɪt]	vt.分开；分担
		n.划分
request	[rɪˈkwest]	n.&vt.请求
distribute	[dɪˈstrɪbjuːt]	vt.分配，散发，分发
switch	[swɪtʃ]	n.交换机
broadcast	['brɔːdkɑːst]	vt.广播
resemble	[rɪˈzembl]	vt.与……相像，类似于
router	['ruːtə]	n.路由器
administrator	[ədˈmɪnɪstreɪtə]	n.管理员，管理者

E-commerce	[iˈkɒmɜːs]	n.电子商务
logical	[ˈlɒdʒɪkl]	adj.逻辑的
privilege	[ˈprɪvəlɪdʒ]	n.特权
permission	[pəˈmɪʃn]	n.允许；批准
initiate	[ɪˈnɪʃɪeɪt]	vt.开始，发起
dedicated	[ˈdedɪkeɪtɪd]	adj.专用的
scalable	[ˈskeɪləbl]	adj.可升级的
decrease	[dɪˈkriːs]	v.降低；减少，减小
overcome	[ˌəʊvəˈkʌm]	v.战胜，克服
alternative	[ɔːlˈtɜːnətɪv]	adj.替代的；备选的
		n.可供选择的事物
adapter	[əˈdæptə]	n.适配器
geographic	[ˌdʒiːəˈɡræfɪk]	adj.地理的
satellite	[ˈsætəlaɪt]	n.卫星；人造卫星
broadband	[ˈbrɔːdbænd]	n.宽带
antivirus	[ˈæntɪvaɪrəs]	adj.抗病毒的，防病毒的
inject	[ɪnˈdʒekt]	vt.引入；（给……）添加
internetwork	[ˈɪntənetwɜːk]	n.互联网络
segment	[ˈseɡmənt]	n.部分，段落
		v.分割，划分
extranet	[ˈekstrənet]	n.外联网
intranet	[ˈɪntrənet]	n.内联网
teleconference	[ˈtelɪkɒnfərəns]	n.远程电信会议

Phrases

optical fiber	光纤，光缆
data link layer	数据链路层
networking device	连网设备
twisted pair	双绞线
data transmission speed	数据传输速度
fiber optic cable	光缆
light beam	光束
physical location	物理位置
peer-to-peer network	对等网
set up	建立；准备；安排
end user	终端用户

video conferencing	视频会议
file sharing	文件共享，文件分享
communication medium	通信介质
last mile	最后路程，最后一英里
antivirus software	防病毒软件
be restricted to	仅限于，局限于
be categorized as	归类为

Abbreviations

NIC (network interface controller)	网络接口卡
bps (bits per second)	位每秒
NOS (network operating system)	网络操作系统
LAN (local area network)	局域网
MAN (metropolitan area network)	城域网
WAN (wide area network)	广域网
OSI (open system interconnection)	开放系统互联

参考译文

计算机网络

1 什么是计算机网络?

计算机网络是一组通过电线、光纤或光链路相互连接的计算机，以便各种设备可以通过网络相互交互。计算机网络的目的是在各种设备之间共享资源。

2 计算机网络的组成部分

2.1 NIC

NIC 是帮助计算机与另一台设备通信的设备。NIC 包含硬件地址。数据链路层协议使用该地址标识网络上的系统，以便将数据传输到正确的目的地。

NIC 有两种类型：无线 NIC 和有线 NIC。

无线 NIC：所有现代笔记本电脑都使用无线 NIC。在无线 NIC 中，以采用无线电波技术的天线进行连接。

有线 NIC：电缆使用有线 NIC 在介质上传输数据。

2.2 集线器

集线器是将网络连接拆分为多个设备的中央设备。当计算机向另一个计算机请求信息时，它将请求发送到集线器。集线器将此请求分发给所有互连的计算机。

2.3 交换机

交换机是一种联网设备，它将网络上的所有设备分组以将数据传输到另一台设备。交换机比集线器更好，因为它不通过网络广播消息，即它将消息发送到它所属的设备。因此，我们可以说交换机将消息直接从源发送到目的地，如图 7-1 所示。

（图略）

2.4 电缆

电缆是传输通信信号的传输介质。电缆分为三种：

（1）双绞线电缆：这是一种高速电缆，用于以 1Gbps 或更高的速率传输数据。

（2）同轴电缆：同轴电缆类似电视安装的电缆。同轴电缆比双绞线电缆价格高，但是它提供高的数据传输速度。

（3）光纤电缆：光纤电缆是使用光束传输数据的高速电缆。与其他电缆相比，它提供了更高的数据传输速率，它也比其他电缆价格高。

2.5 路由器

路由器是将局域网连接到互联网的设备。路由器主要用于连接不同的网络或将互联网连接到多台计算机。

3 计算机网络的用途

（1）资源共享：资源共享是指网络上的用户之间共享程序、打印机和数据之类的资源，而不必管资源和用户的物理位置。

（2）服务器、客户机模式：使用在服务器-客户机模式中的计算机网络。服务器是用于存储信息并由系统管理员维护的中央计算机。客户机是用于远程访问服务器中存储信息的计算机。

（3）通信介质：计算机网络充当用户之间的通信介质。例如，一家公司拥有一台以上的计算机和一个电子邮件系统，员工可以使用该电子邮件系统进行日常通信。

（4）电子商务：计算机网络在企业中也很重要。人们可以通过互联网开展业务，如 amazon.com。

4 计算机网络体系结构

计算机网络体系结构被定义为软件、硬件、协议和数据传输介质的物理和逻辑设计。有两类网络体系结构：对等网络和客户机/服务器网络。

4.1 对等网络

对等网络中的所有计算机都以相同的优先权和责任连接在一起，以处理数据。它通常用于小型环境，最多有 10 台计算机。它没有专用服务器。每台计算机都分配了特殊权限以共享资源，但是如果资源所在的计算机关闭，则可能会引发问题。

对等网络的优点：

（1）它不包含任何专用服务器，因此成本较低。

（2）由于每台计算机都可以自我管理，因此易于设置和维护。

对等网络的缺点：

（1）它不包含集中式系统。因此，由于不同位置的数据不同，它无法备份数据。

（2）由于设备自我管理，因此存在安全问题。

4.2 客户机/服务器网络

客户机/服务器网络是为终端用户（称为客户）设计的网络模型，可从称为服务器的中央计算机访问资源。

中央控制器称为服务器，而网络中的所有其他计算机称为客户机。服务器执行所有的主要操作，如安全性和网络管理。它负责管理所有资源，如文件、目录、打印机等。所有客户机都通过服务器相互通信。例如，如果客户机 1 要向客户机 2 发送一些数据，则它首先将请求发送到服务器以获取许可。服务器将响应发送到客户机 1，以启动与客户机 2 的通信。

客户机/服务器网络的优点如下：

（1）它包含集中式系统。因此，可以轻松地备份数据。

（2）它具有专用的服务器，可以提高整个系统的整体性能。

（3）它的安全性更高，因为由一台服务器管理共享资源。

（4）它还可以提高共享资源的速度。

客户机/服务器网络的缺点如下：

（1）它价格昂贵，因为它要求服务器具有大内存。

（2）服务器具有网络操作系统（NOS）为客户提供资源，但是 NOS 的成本很高。

（3）需要专门的网络管理员管理所有资源。

5 计算机网络的特点

5.1 通信速度

网络使用户能够快速有效地进行通信。例如，可以通过互联网进行视频会议、用电子邮件传递消息等。因此，计算机网络是共享知识和思想的好方法。

5.2　文件共享

文件共享是计算机网络的主要优势之一。计算机网络使用户可以相互共享文件。

5.3　易于备份

由于文件存储在位于中央的主服务器上。因此，很容易从主服务器上进行备份。

5.4　软件和硬件共享

可以在主服务器上安装应用程序，这样，用户可以集中访问应用程序，不需要在每台机器上都安装软件。同样地，硬件也可以共享。

5.5　安全性

网络通过确保用户有权访问某些文件和应用程序来提供安全性。

5.6　可扩展性

可扩展性意味着可以在网络上添加新组件。网络必须具有可扩展性，以便可以通过添加新设备扩展网络。但是，它降低了连接速度和数据的传输速度，这增加了发生错误的机会，通过使用路由或交换设备可以解决此问题。

5.7　可靠性

万一发生任何硬件故障，计算机网络可以使用备用源进行数据通信。

6　计算机网络类型

6.1　局域网

局域网是指在建筑物、办公室等较小区域内相互连接的一组计算机。它通过通信介质(如双绞线电缆、同轴电缆等)连接两个及以上的个人计算机。它由廉价的硬件（如集线器、网络适配器和以太网电缆）构建，因此成本较低。数据在局域网中的传输速度非常快。局域网可以提供更高的安全性，如图 7-2 所示。

（图略）

6.2 城域网

城域网是指通过连接不同的局域网组成的覆盖区域更大的网络。政府机构使用城域网连接到公民和私营企业。在城域网中，各种局域网通过电话交换线路相互连接。它具有比局域网更大的范围，如图7-3所示。

（图略）

城域网的用途如下：

（1）城域网用于城市中银行之间的通信。

（2）可用于航空公司的订票系统。

（3）可用于城市中的大学。

6.3 广域网

广域网是延伸到很大的地理区域（如州或国家/地区）的网络。广域网是比局域网更大的网络。广域网不限于单个位置，而是通过电话线、光纤电缆或卫星链路跨越很大的地理区域。互联网是世界上最大的广域网之一。广域网广泛用于商业、政府和教育领域。

广域网的例子包括：

（1）移动宽带：4G网络在一个地区或国家广泛使用。

（2）最后一英里：一家电信公司将房屋与光纤连接起来，为数百个城市的客户提供互联网服务。

（3）专用网络：银行提供连接多个办公室的专用网络。该网络使用电信公司提供的电话租用线路建立。

广域网的优点如下：

（1）地理区域：广域网提供很大的地理区域。假设办公室的分支机构位于其他城市，则可以通过广域网与之连接。互联网提供了一条专线，可以通过它与另一个分支机构连接。

（2）集中数据：在广域网中，数据是集中的。因此，不需要购买电子邮件、文件或备份服务器。

（3）获取更新的文件：软件公司在实时服务器上工作。因此，程序员可以在几秒内获得更新的文件。

（4）交换消息：在广域网中，消息可以快速传输。Facebook、WhatsApp、Skype等网络应用程序使用户可以与朋友交流。

（5）软件和资源共享：在广域网中，可以共享软件和其他资源，如硬盘驱动器、RAM。

（6）全球业务：可以在全球范围内通过互联网开展业务。

广域网的缺点如下：

（1）安全问题：与局域网和城域网相比，广域网存在更多的安全问题，因为所有技术组合在一起就产生了安全问题。

（2）需要防火墙和防病毒软件：数据在互联网上传输，可以被黑客更改或入侵，因此需要使用防火墙。某些人可以将病毒注入我们的系统中，因此需要防病毒。

（3）高昂的安装成本：由于需要购买路由器和交换机，因此广域网的安装成本很高。

（4）故障排除问题：它覆盖的区域很大，因此解决问题很难。

6.4　互联网络

把两个或多个局域网或广域网或计算机网段用设备连接起来就被定义为互联网络，通过本地编址方案进行配置。公共、私有、商业、工业或政府计算机网络之间的互联也可以定义为互联网络。互联网络使用网际协议。用于互联网络的参考模型是开放系统互联（OSI）。

互联网有两类：外联网和内联网。

外联网是基于网际协议的通信网络，它用于信息共享。只有拥有登录凭据的用户才能访问外联网。外联网是最低级别的互联网络。它可以归类为城域网、广域网或其他计算机网络。一个外联网不能只有一个局域网，它必须至少与外部网络建立一个连接。

内联网是基于网际协议的专用网络。内联网属于某个组织，只允许组织的员工或成员访问。内联网的主要目的是在组织的员工之间共享信息和资源。内联网提供了用于分组工作和远程电信会议的功能。

扫码听课文

Text B
Computer Network Topology

1　Bus Topology

Bus topology is designed in such a way that all the stations are connected through a single cable known as a backbone cable. Each node is either connected to the backbone cable by drop cable or directly connected to the backbone cable. When a node wants to send a message over the network, it puts a message over the network. All the stations available in the network will receive the message whether it has been addressed or not. The bus topology is mainly used in 802.3 (Ethernet) and 802.4 standard networks. The configuration of a bus topology is quite simpler as compared to other topologies. The backbone cable is considered as a "single lane" through which the message is broadcast to all the stations. The most common access method of the bus topologies is CSMA (carrier sense multiple access).

Advantages of bus topology:

(1) Low-cost cable: in bus topology, nodes are directly connected to the cable without passing through a hub. Therefore, the initial cost of installation is low.

(2) Moderate data speeds: coaxial or twisted pair cables are mainly used in bus-based networks that support up to 10Mbps.

(3) Familiar technology: bus topology is a familiar technology as the installation and troubleshooting techniques are well known, and hardware components are easily available.

(4) Limited failure: a failure in one node will not have any effect on other nodes.

Disadvantages of bus topology:

(1) Extensive cabling: a bus topology is quite simple, but still it requires a lot of cabling.

(2) Difficult troubleshooting: it requires specialized test equipment to determine the cable faults. If any fault occurs in the cable, then it would disrupt the communication for all the nodes.

(3) Signal interference: if two nodes send the messages simultaneously, then the signals of both the nodes collide with each other.

(4) Reconfiguration difficult: adding new devices to the network would slow down the network.

(5) Attenuation: attenuation is a loss of signal which leads to communication issues. Repeaters are used to regenerate the signal.

2   Ring Topology

Ring topology is like a bus topology, but with connected ends. The node that receives the message from the previous computer will retransmit it to the next node. The data flows in one direction, i.e., it is unidirectional. The data flows in a single loop continuously known as an endless loop. It has no terminated ends, i.e., each node is connected to other node and having no termination point. The data in a ring topology flow in a clockwise direction (see Figure 7-4).

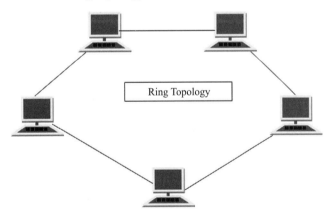

Figure 7-4   Ring Topology

The most common access method of the ring topology is token passing. It is a network access method in which token is passed from one node to another node. Token is a frame that circulates around the network.

Advantages of ring topology:

(1) Network management: faulty devices can be removed from the network without bringing the network down.

(2) Product availability: many hardware and software tools for network operation and monitoring are available.

(3) Cost: twisted pair cabling is inexpensive and easily available. Therefore, the installation cost is very low.

(4) Reliable: it is a more reliable network because the communication system is not dependent on the single host computer.

Disadvantages of ring topology:

(1) Difficult troubleshooting: it requires specialized test equipment to determine the cable faults. If any fault occurs in the cable, then it would disrupt the communication for all the nodes.

(2) Failure: the breakdown in one station leads to the failure of the overall network.

(3) Difficult reconfiguration: adding new devices to the network would slow down the network.

(4) Delay: communication delay is directly proportional to the number of nodes. Adding new devices increases the communication delay.

3　Star Topology

Star topology is an arrangement of the network in which every node is connected to the central hub, switch or a central computer. The central computer is known as a server, and the peripheral devices attached to the server are known as clients. Coaxial cable or RJ-45 cables are used to connect the computers. Hubs or switches are mainly used as connection devices in a physical star topology. Star topology is the most popular topology in network implementation (see Figure 7-5).

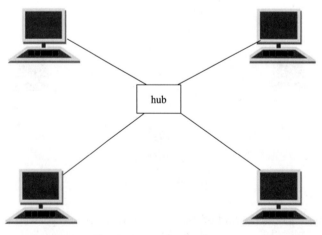

Figure 7-5　Star Topology

Advantages of star topology:

(1) Efficient troubleshooting: troubleshooting is quite efficient in a star topology as compared to bus topology. In a bus topology, the manager has to inspect kilometers of cable to troubleshoot a

problem. In a star topology, all the stations are connected to the centralized network. Therefore, the network administrator only goes to the single station to troubleshoot the problem.

(2) Network control: complex network control features can be easily implemented in the star topology. Any changes made in the star topology are automatically accommodated.

(3) Limited failure: as each station is connected to the central hub with its own cable, failure in one cable will not affect the entire network.

(4) Familiar technology: star topology is a familiar technology .

(5) Easily expandable: it is easily expandable as new stations can be added to the open ports on the hub.

(6) Cost effective: star topology networks are cost-effective as it uses inexpensive cable.

(7) High data speeds: it supports a bandwidth of approx 100Mbps. Ethernet 100BaseT is one of the most popular Star topology networks.

Disadvantages of star topology:

A central point of failure: If the central hub or switch goes down, then all the connected nodes will not be able to communicate with each other.

4　Tree topology

A tree topology is a type of structure in which all the computers are connected with each other in hierarchical fashion. The top-most node in tree topology is known as a root node, and all other nodes are the descendants of the root node. There is only one path exists between two nodes for the data transmission. Thus, it forms a parent-child hierarchy.

Advantages of tree topology:

(1) Support for broadband transmission: tree topology is mainly used to provide broadband transmission, i.e., signals are sent over long distances without being attenuated.

(2) Easily expandable: we can add the new device to the existing network. Therefore, we can say that tree topology is easily expandable.

(3) Easily manageable: in tree topology, the whole network is divided into segments known as star networks which can be easily managed and maintained.

(4) Error detection: error detection and error correction are very easy in a tree topology.

(5) Limited failure: the breakdown in one station does not affect the entire network.

(6) Point-to-point wiring: it has point-to-point wiring for individual segments.

Disadvantages of tree topology:

(1) Difficult troubleshooting: if any fault occurs in the node, then it becomes difficult to troubleshoot the problem.

(2) High cost: devices required for broadband transmission are very costly.

(3) Failure: a tree topology mainly relies on main bus cable and failure in main bus cable will damage the overall network.

(4) Difficult reconfiguration: if new devices are added, it becomes difficult to reconfigure.

5 Mesh Topology

Mesh topology is an arrangement of the network in which computers are interconnected with each other through various redundant connections. There are multiple paths from one computer to another computer. It does not contain the switch, hub or any central computer which acts as a central point of communication. The Internet is an example of the mesh topology.

Mesh topology is mainly used for WAN implementations where communication failures are a critical concern. It is mainly used for wireless networks. It can be formed by using the formula: Number of cables = $(n \times (n-1)) / 2$; Where n is the number of nodes that represents the network.

Mesh topology is divided into two categories:

(1) Full mesh topology: in a full mesh topology, each computer is connected to all the computers available in the network.

(2) Partial mesh topology: in a partial mesh topology, not all but certain computers are connected to those computers with which they communicate frequently.

Advantages of mesh topology:

(1) Reliable: the mesh topology networks are very reliable. No link breakdown will affect the communication between connected computers.

(2) Fast Communication: communication is very fast between the nodes.

(3) Easier Reconfiguration: adding new devices would not disrupt the communication between other devices.

Disadvantages of mesh topology:

(1) Cost: a mesh topology contains a large number of connected devices such as a router and more transmission media than other topologies.

(2) Management: mesh topology networks are very large and very difficult to maintain and manage. If the network is not monitored carefully, then the communication link failure goes undetected.

(3) Efficiency: in this topology, redundant connections are high, which reduces the efficiency of the network.

6 Hybrid Topology

When two or more different topologies are combined together it is known as a hybrid topology. For example, if there exists a ring topology in one branch of ABC bank and bus topology in another branch of ABC bank, connecting these two topologies will result in a hybrid topology.

Advantages of hybrid topology:

(1) Reliable: if a fault occurs in any part of the network it will not affect the functioning of the

rest of the network.

(2) Scalable: size of the network can be easily expanded by adding new devices without affecting the functionality of the existing network.

(3) Flexible: this topology is very flexible as it can be designed according to the requirements of the organization.

(4) Effective: hybrid topology is very effective as it can be designed in such a way that the strength of the network is maximized and weakness of the network is minimized.

Disadvantages of hybrid topology:

(1) Complex design: the major drawback of the hybrid topology is the design of the hybrid network. It is very difficult to design the architecture of the hybrid network.

(2) Costly hub: the hubs used in the hybrid topology are very expensive as these hubs are different from usual hubs used in other topologies.

(3) Costly infrastructure: the infrastructure cost is very high as a hybrid network requires a lot of cabling, network devices, etc.

New Words

topology	[təˈpɒlədʒɪ]	n.拓扑
backbone	[ˈbækbəʊn]	n.主干，骨干；脊椎
Ethernet	[ˈiːθənet]	n.以太网
station	[ˈsteɪʃn]	n.站点
		vt.配置，安置
moderate	[ˈmɒdərət]	adj.中等的；稳健的；适度的
fault	[fɔːlt]	n.故障
disrupt	[dɪsˈrʌpt]	vt.使中断；破坏
		adj.中断的
simultaneously	[ˌsɪməlˈteɪnɪəslɪ]	adv.同时地
reconfiguration	[ˈriːkənfɪgjʊˈreɪʃn]	n.重新配置；再配置；再组合
attenuation	[əˌtenjʊˈeɪʃn]	n.衰减
repeater	[rɪˈpiːtə]	n.中继器，转发器
regenerate	[rɪˈdʒenəreɪt]	v.使再生
transmit	[trænsˈmɪt]	vt.传输；传送，传递；发射
		vi.发送信号
continuously	[kənˈtɪnjʊəslɪ]	adv.连续不断地，接连地
endless	[ˈendlɪs]	adj.无尽的，永久的
termination	[ˌtɜːmɪˈneɪʃn]	n.结束；终止处
clockwise	[ˈklɒkwaɪz]	adj.顺时针方向的
token	[ˈtəʊkən]	n.令牌

frame	[freɪm]	n.框架；构架
breakdown	[ˈbreɪkdaʊn]	n.崩溃；损坏，故障
proportional	[prəˈpɔːʃənl]	adj.比例的，成比例的；相称的
arrangement	[əˈreɪndʒmənt]	n.安排；排列
accommodate	[əˈkɒmədeɪt]	v.容纳；适应
cost-effective	[kɔst-ɪˈfektɪv]	adj.有成本效益的，划算的
expandable	[ɪkˈspændəbl]	adj.可扩展的
hierarchical	[ˌhaɪəˈrɑːkɪkl]	adj.分层的
descendant	[dɪˈsendənt]	n.后代；后裔
redundant	[rɪˈdʌndənt]	adj.冗余的，多余的
partial	[ˈpɑːʃl]	adj.部分的
undetected	[ˌʌndɪˈtektɪd]	adj.未被发现的，未探测到的
infrastructure	[ˈɪnfrəstrʌktʃə]	n.基础设施；基础建设

Phrases

bus topology	总线拓扑
drop cable	分支电缆
single lane	单通道，单行道
a lot of	许多的
collide with...	与……相撞，与……相碰
slow down	（使）慢下来；（使）生产缓慢
ring topology	环状拓扑
data flow	数据流
star topology	星状拓扑
tree topology	树状拓扑
root node	根节点
be divided into	被分为
point-to-point wiring	点对点连线
mesh topology	网状拓扑
be formed by ...	由……组成
transmission media	传输介质
hybrid topology	混合拓扑
the rest of	其余的，剩下的

Abbreviations

| CSMA (carrier sense multiple access) | 载波侦听多路访问 |

计算机网络拓扑

1　总线拓扑

　　总线拓扑的设计方式是，所有站点都通过一条称为主干电缆的电缆连接。每个节点要么通过引入电缆连接到主干电缆，要么直接连接到主干电缆。当节点想要通过网络发送消息时，它把消息发布到网络。无论是否已寻址，网络中所有可用的站都将收到该消息。总线拓扑主要用于 802.3（以太网）和 802.4 标准网络。与其他拓扑相比，总线拓扑的配置要简单得多。主干电缆被认为是一条"单通道"，通过该通道将消息广播到所有站点。总线拓扑中最常见的访问方法是 CSMA（载波侦听多路访问）。

　　总线拓扑的优点如下：

　　（1）低成本电缆：在总线拓扑中，节点直接连接到电缆，无须通过集线器。因此，初始安装成本低。

　　（2）中等数据传输速率：同轴电缆或双绞线电缆主要用于支持速度高达 10Mbps 的基于总线的网络。

　　（3）熟悉的技术：总线拓扑是一种读者熟悉的技术，因为它的安装和故障排除技术众所周知，并且很容易获得硬件组件。

　　（4）有限的故障：一个节点中的故障不会对其他节点产生任何影响。

　　总线拓扑的缺点如下：

　　（1）广泛的布线：总线拓扑结构相当简单，但是仍然需要大量的布线。

　　（2）难以排除故障：需要专门的测试设备确定电缆故障。如果电缆发生任何故障，则将中断所有节点的通信。

　　（3）信号干扰：如果两个节点同时发送消息，则两个节点的信号会相互冲突。

　　（4）重新配置困难：将新设备添加到网络会降低网络速度。

　　（5）衰减：衰减指信号丢失，这会导致通信问题。中继器用来重新生成信号。

2　环状拓扑

　　环状拓扑很像总线拓扑，但它的两端是连接的。从上一台计算机接收消息的节点将把信息转发到下一个节点。数据沿一个方向流动，即单向流动。数据在一个循环中连续流动，称为无限循环。它没有终点，即每个节点都连接到另一个节点并且没有端接点。环状拓扑中的数据沿顺时针方向流动。

　　环状拓扑最常见的访问方法是令牌传递。它是一种网络访问方法，其中令牌从一个节点传递到另一节点。令牌是在网络中流动的框架，如图 7-4 所示。

　　（图略）

环状拓扑的优点如下：

（1）网络管理：可以从网络中删除故障设备，而不必关闭网络。

（2）产品可用性：提供了许多用于网络运行和监管的硬件和软件工具。

（3）成本：双绞线电缆价格便宜且易于获得。因此，安装成本非常低。

（4）可靠：因为通信系统不依赖于单个主机，所以它是一个更可靠的网络。

环状拓扑的缺点如下：

（1）难以排除故障：需要专门的测试设备确定电缆故障。如果电缆发生任何故障，则将中断所有节点的通信。

（2）失效：一个站点的故障会导致整个网络的故障。

（3）重新配置困难：将新设备添加到网络会降低网络速度。

（4）延迟：通信延迟与节点数成正比。添加新设备会增加通信延迟。

3　星状拓扑

星状拓扑是网络的一种布置方法，其中每个节点都连接到中央集线器、交换机或中央计算机。中央计算机称为服务器，连接到服务器的外围设备称为客户。同轴电缆或 RJ-45 电缆用于连接计算机。集线器或交换机主要用作物理星状拓扑中的连接设备。星状拓扑是网络实施中最流行的拓扑，如图 7-5 所示。

（图略）

星状拓扑的优点如下：

（1）高效的故障排除：与总线拓扑相比，星状拓扑中的故障排除效率很高。在总线拓扑中，管理者必须检查数公里的电缆以排除故障。在星状拓扑中，所有站点都连接到集中式网络。因此，网络管理员只要到单个工作站去解决问题。

（2）网络控制：复杂的网络控制功能可以在星状拓扑中轻松实现。星状拓扑中所做的任何更改都将自动调节。

（3）有限的故障：由于每个站点都使用自己的电缆连接到中央集线器，因此一根电缆的故障不会影响整个网络。

（4）熟悉的技术：星状拓扑是一种熟悉的技术。

（5）易于扩展：它可以轻松扩展，因为可以将新工作站添加到集线器上的开放端口。

（6）经济高效：星状拓扑网络由于使用廉价的电缆而具有成本效益。

（7）高速数据：它支持大约 100Mbps 的带宽。以太网 100BaseT 是最流行的星状拓扑网络之一。

星状拓扑的缺点如下：

中心故障点：如果中心集线器或交换机出现故障，则所有连接的节点将无法相互通信。

4　树状拓扑

树状拓扑中的所有计算机都以分层方式相互连接。树状拓扑中最顶层的节点称为根节点，所有其他节点都是根节点的后代。在两个节点之间只有一条路径可用于数据传输。因此，它形成了父-子层次结构。

树状拓扑的优点如下：

（1）支持宽带传输：树状拓扑主要用于提供宽带传输，即信号在不衰减的情况下长距离发送。

（2）易于扩展：可以将新设备添加到现有网络。因此，可以说树状拓扑很容易扩展。

（3）易于管理：在树状拓扑中，整个网络被划分为称为星状网络的网段，可以轻松地进行管理和维护。

（4）错误检测：在树状拓扑中，错误检测和错误纠正都非常容易。

（5）有限的故障：一个站点的故障不会影响整个网络。

（6）点对点布线：它具有用于各个段的点对点布线。

树状拓扑的缺点如下：

（1）难以排除故障：如果节点中发生任何故障，则很难排除。

（2）高成本：宽带传输所需的设备非常昂贵。

（3）失效：树状拓扑主要依赖主总线电缆，主总线电缆发生故障会损坏整个网络。

（4）难以重新配置：如果添加了新设备，将很难重新配置。

5　网状拓扑

网状拓扑是网络的一种布置，其中计算机通过各种冗余实现互连。从一台计算机到另一台计算机有多种路径。它不包含用作通信中心的交换机、集线器或任何中央计算机。互联网是网状拓扑的一个例子。

网状拓扑结构主要用于 WAN 实施，在此，通信故障是人们关注的一个焦点。它主要用于无线网络。其构成符合公式：电缆数量$=(n \times (n-1))/2$，其中 n 是代表网络的节点数。

网状拓扑分为以下两类：

（1）全网状拓扑：在全网状拓扑中，每台计算机都连接到网络中所有可用的计算机。

（2）局部网状拓扑：在局部网状拓扑中，除了某些计算机之外，不是所有计算机都连接到它们经常通信的计算机。

网状拓扑的优点如下：

（1）可靠：网状拓扑网络非常可靠，任何链路故障都不会影响所连接计算机之间的通信。

（2）快速通信：节点之间的通信非常快。

（3）重新配置更容易：添加新设备不会中断其他设备之间的通信。

网状拓扑的缺点如下：

（1）成本：网状拓扑包含大量的连接设备（如路由器），并且传输介质比其他拓扑更多。

（2）管理：网状拓扑网络非常大，很难维护和管理。如果未仔细监管网络，则无法检测到通信链路故障。

（3）效率：在这种拓扑中，冗余连接数很高，从而降低了网络效率。

6 混合拓扑

将两个或多个不同的拓扑组合在一起即为混合拓扑。例如，如果 ABC 银行的一个分行中用环状拓扑，而 ABC 银行的另一个分行用总线拓扑，则将这两个拓扑连接起来就是混合拓扑。

混合拓扑的优点如下：

（1）可靠：如果网络的任何部分发生故障，则不会影响网络其余部分的功能。

（2）可扩展：可通过添加新设备轻松扩展网络规模，而不会影响现有网络的功能。

（3）灵活：此拓扑非常灵活，因为可以根据组织的要求进行设计。

（4）有效：混合拓扑非常有效，因为它可以通过设计使网络的性能最优而弱点最小。

混合拓扑的缺点如下：

（1）设计复杂：混合拓扑的主要缺点是混合网络的设计。设计混合网络的架构非常困难。

（2）昂贵的集线器：混合拓扑中使用的集线器非常昂贵，因为这些集线器不同于其他拓扑中使用的常规集线器。

（3）昂贵的基础架构：基础架构成本很高，因为混合网络需要大量的电缆、网络设备等。

Exercises

[Ex. 1] Answer the following questions according to Text A.

1. What is computer network? What is the aim of computer network?

2. What is NIC? How many types of NIC are there? What are they?

3. What is switch？ Why is a switch better than a hub?

4. How many types of cables are there? What are they?

5. What are the uses of computer network?

6. What is peer-to-peer network? What are the advantages of peer-to-peer network?

7. What is a client/server network? What are the disadvantages of client/server network?

8. What are the features of computer network?

9. What is local area network?

10. What are example of wide area network?

[Ex.2] Answer the following questions according to Text B.

1. How is bus topology designed?

2. What are the advantages of bus topology?

3. What is the most common access method of the ring topology? What are the disadvantages of ring topology?

4. What is star topology? What are hubs or switches mainly used as?

5. What is a tree topology?

6. What are the disadvantages of tree topology?

7. What is mesh topology?

8. What are the advantages of mesh topology?

9. What is hybrid topology? What are the advantages of hybrid topology?

10. What are the disadvantages of hybrid topology?

[Ex. 3] Translate the following terms or phrases from English into Chinese and vice versa.

1. communication medium	1.
2. data link layer	2.
3. optical fiber	3.
4. twisted pair	4.
5. hybrid topology	5.
6. *n.*适配器	6.
7. *n.*宽带	7.
8. *vt.*广播	8.
9. *n.*协议	9.
10. *n.*路由器	10.

[Ex. 4] Translate the following passage into Chinese.

Communication Technologies Terminologies

1 Channel

Physical medium like cables over which information is exchanged is called channel. Transmission channel may be analog or digital. As the name suggests, analog channels transmit data using analog signals while digital channels transmit data using digital signals.

In popular network terminology, path over which data is sent or received is called data channel. This data channel may be a tangible medium like copper wire cables or broadcast medium like radio waves.

2 Data Transfer Rate

The speed of data transferred or received over transmission channel, measured per unit time, is called data transfer rate. The smallest unit of measurement is bits per second (bps). 1 bps means 1 bit (0 or 1) of data is transferred in 1 second.

3　Bandwidth

Data transfer rates that can be supported by a network is called its bandwidth. It is measured in bits per second (bps). Modern day networks provide bandwidth in Kbps, Mbps and Gbps. Some of the factors affecting a network's bandwidth include: network devices used, protocols used, number of users connected, network overheads like collision, errors, etc.

4　Throughput

Throughput is the actual speed with which data gets transferred over the network. Besides transmitting the actual data, network bandwidth is used for transmitting error messages, acknowledgement frames, etc.

Throughput is a better measurement of network speed, efficiency and capacity utilization rather than bandwidth.

5　Protocol

Protocol is a set of rules and regulations used by devices to communicate over the network. Just like humans, computers also need rules to ensure successful communication. Similarly, devices connected on the network need to follow some rules like when and how to transmit data, when to receive data, how to give error-free message, etc.

Reading

Transmission Media[①]

For any networking to be effective, raw stream of data is to be transported from one device to other over some medium. Various transmission media can be used for transfer of data. These transmission media may be of two types:

(1) Guided — in guided media, transmitted data travels through cabling system that has a fixed path. For example, copper wires, fiber optic wires, etc.

(2) Unguided — in unguided media[②], transmitted data travels through free space in the form of electromagnetic signal. For example, radio waves, lasers, etc.

Each transmission media has its own advantages and disadvantages in terms of bandwidth, speed, delay, cost per bit, ease of installation and maintenance, etc.

1　Twisted Pair Cables[③]

Copper wires are the most common wires used for transmitting signals because of good performance at low costs. They are most commonly used in telephone lines. However, if two or

---

① transmission media：传输介质
② unguided media：无导线介质
③ twisted pair cable：双绞线电缆

more wires are lying together, they can interfere with each other's signals. To reduce this electromagnetic interference[①], pairs of copper wires are twisted together in helical shape[②] like a DNA molecule. Such twisted copper wires are called twisted pair. To reduce interference between nearby twisted pairs, the twist rates are different for each pair.

Twisted pair cables are the oldest and most popular cables all over the world. This is due to the many advantages that they offer:

(1) They can be used for both analog and digital transmissions.

(2) They are least expensive for short distances.

With its many advantages, twisted pair cables offer some disadvantages too:

(1) Signals cannot travel long distances without repeaters.

(2) They have high error rate for distances greater than 100m.

(3) They are very thin and hence break easily.

(4) They are not suitable for broadband connections.

2　Shielding[③] Twisted Pair Cables

To counter the tendency of twisted pair cables to pick up noise signals, wires are shielded in the following three ways:

(1) Each twisted pair is shielded.

(2) Set of multiple twisted pairs in the cable is shielded.

(3) Each twisted pair is shielded first and then all the pairs are shielded.

Such twisted pairs are called shielded twisted pair[④] (STP) cables. The wires that are not shielded but simply bundled together in a protective sheath are called unshielded twisted pair[⑤] (UTP) cables. These cables can have maximum length of 100 meters.

Shielding makes the cable bulky, so UTP are more popular than STP. UTP cables are used as the last mile network connection in homes and offices.

3　Coaxial Cables

Coaxial cables are copper cables with better shielding than twisted pair cables, so that transmitted signals may travel longer distances at higher speeds. A coaxial cable consists of these layers, starting from the innermost:

(1) Stiff copper wire as core.

(2) Insulating material surrounding the core.

---

① electromagnetic interference：电磁干扰

② helical shape：螺旋形

③ shielding [ʃiːldɪŋ] adj.屏蔽的，防护的

④ shielded twisted pair：屏蔽双绞线

⑤ unshielded twisted pair：非屏蔽双绞线

(3) Closely woven braided mesh[①] of conducting material surrounding the insulator.

(4) Protective plastic sheath[②] encasing the wire.

Coaxial cables are widely used for cable TV connections and LANs (see Figure 7-6).

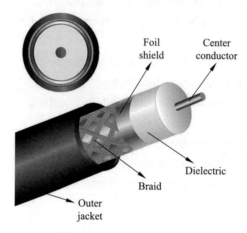

Figure 7-6　Coaxial Cable

These are the advantages of coaxial cables:

(1) They have excellent noise immunity[③].

(2) Signals can travel longer distances at higher speeds, e.g. 1 to 2Gbps for 1km cable.

(3) They can be used for both analog and digital signals.

(4) They are inexpensive as compared with fiber optic cables[④].

(5) They are easy to install and maintain.

These are some of the disadvantages of coaxial cables:

(1) They are expensive as compared with twisted pair cables.

(2) They are not compatible with twisted pair cables.

4　Optical Fiber

Thin glass or plastic threads used to transmit data using light waves are called optical fiber. Light emitting diodes (LEDs) or laser diodes (LDs) emit light waves at the source, which is read by a detector at the other end. Optical fiber cable has a bundle of such threads or fibers bundled together in a protective covering. Each fiber is made up of these three layers, starting with the innermost layer:

(1) Core made of high quality silica glass[⑤] or plastic.

---

① braided mesh：编织网

② sheath [ʃiːθ] *n.*护套

③ immunity [ɪˈmjuːnətɪ] *n.*免除，免疫

④ fiber optic cable：光纤电缆

⑤ silica glass：石英玻璃，二氧化硅玻璃

(2) Cladding made of high quality silica glass or plastic, with a lower refractive index[①] than the core.

(3) Protective outer covering called coating.

See Figure 7-7.

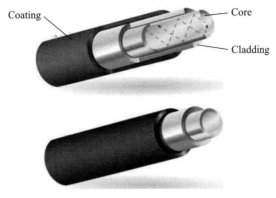

Coating   Core

Cladding

Figure 7-7   Optical Fiber

Optical fiber is fast replacing copper wires because of these advantages that it offers:

(1) High bandwidth.

(2) Immune to electromagnetic interference.

(3) Suitable for industrial and noisy areas.

(4) Signals carrying data can travel long distances without weakening.

Despite long segment lengths and high bandwidth, using optical fiber may not be a viable option for every one due to these disadvantages:

(1) Optical fiber cables are expensive.

(2) Sophisticated[②] technology is required for manufacturing, installing and maintaining optical fiber cables.

(3) Light waves are unidirectional[③], so two frequencies are required for full duplex[④] transmission.

5   Infrared

Low frequency infrared waves[⑤] are used for very short distance communication like TV remote, wireless speakers, automatic doors, hand held devices[⑥] etc. Infrared signals can propagate

---

① refractive index：折射率

② sophisticated [sə'fistɪkeɪtɪd] *adj.*复杂的；精致的

③ unidirectional [ˌjuːnɪdɪ'rekʃənəl] *adj.*单向的，单向性的

④ full duplex：全双工通信

⑤ low frequency infrared wave：低频红外波

⑥ hand held device：手持装置

within a room but cannot penetrate① walls. However, due to such short range, it is considered to be one of the most secure transmission modes.

6 Radio Wave

Transmission of data using radio frequencies is called radio-wave transmission. We all are familiar with radio channels that broadcast entertainment programs. Radio stations transmit radio waves using transmitters, which are received by the receiver installed in our devices.

Both transmitters and receivers use antennas to radiate or capture radio signals. These radio frequencies can also be used for direct voice communication within the allocated range. This range is usually 10 miles.

These are some of the advantages of radio wave transmissions:

(1) They are an inexpensive mode of information exchange.

(2) No land needs to be acquired for laying cables.

(3) The installation and maintenance of devices is cheap.

These are some of the disadvantages of radio wave transmissions:

(1) Insecure② communication medium.

(2) Prone to weather changes like rain, thunderstorms, etc.

---

① penetrate ['penətreɪt] v.穿透
② insecure [ˌɪnsɪ'kjʊə] adj.不安全的

Unit 8

Text A

扫码听课文

Control Systems

1   What Is a Control System?

A control system can be described as a system that can control the output quantity. Basically, it is a device or a set of devices which can manage, command, and regulate the operation of the other device or a system that uses control loops. So this system can control and regulate the operation of another system. A system consists of different elements and devices that are interconnected to do a process. The control system is formed by the component interconnection and thus a system configuration is achieved. The major components of a control system are actuators, sensors, reference input, and actual output. The system is the process or plant which needs to be controlled and the actuator would convert the control signal to a power signal. The sensor would measure the system output and the actual output represents the required output (see Figure 8-1).

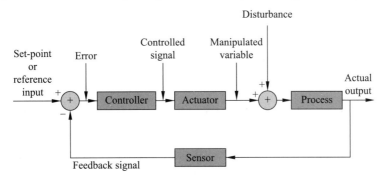

Figure 8-1   A Control System

2   Why Is a Control System Needed?

A control system is needed to maintain a process at the required operating conditions safely and effectively. The control system is able to maintain product quality. We will be able to get high-value products and also increase yield with the help of a control system. It can meet environmental safety regulations such as reducing pollution and ensuring safety.

3 What Is a Set Point Change and Disturbance Change?

A set point is the predetermined value for the control variable, so if there is a change in the set point, certain adjustments will be done in order to achieve the new operating conditions.

Disturbance change is the change in the process because of a disturbance, so the control system must be capable of returning the controlled variable to the set point.

4 What Are the Hardwares of a Control System?

4.1 Sensor

The sensor will measure the system variable. In the automatic control this would act as a signal source.

4.2 Controller

The controller will do the comparison and the computation process.

4.3 Control Element

The control element is the equipment to do the control action in a process. It will receive signals from the controller and according to that, it will perform certain actions. In most cases, the control element will be the control valve.

5 What Are the Major Functions of a Control System?

The control system must be capable of doing the measurement, and it compares the measured value with the required value. The control system should be able to compute the difference between the required value and the measured value. So while comparing the measured value with the desired value, if the measured value is not close to the desired value then correction must be done.

6 What Are the Requirements of a Control System?

(1) It should be accurate.
(2) It must be really sensitive.
(3) It should not be sensitive to external noise but it must be sensitive to the input commands.
(4) It must be stable.

(5) It should have a good frequency response.

(6) It must operate very quickly.

7 What Are the Disturbances in a Control System?

In a control system, the disturbance is a signal which will affect the system output value. There are two types of disturbance: one is the internal disturbance that is generated within the system, the other is the external disturbance which is generated outside the system.

8 What Are the Different Types of Control System?

8.1 Open Loop Control System

This is also known as a non-feedback system, in which the control action is not dependent on the output of the system. In this type of control system, there is no feedback and it is really difficult to get the required output from this type of system. These systems are not capable of taking the disturbances into account. So it can only make changes in the output by making changes in the input.

Advantages of an open loop control system: simple construction, economical, easy to maintain, stable.

Disadvantages of an open loop control system:

(1) It is not accurate.

(2) It is no reliable.

(3) Any change in the output cannot be corrected automatically.

8.2 Closed Loop Control System

In this type of control system, there is a sensor that will measure the output and it uses feedback of the sensed value to influence the control input variable. In this type of control system, the output will have an effect on the input quantity in a way that it can maintain the required output value. So with the help of the feedback, a closed-loop control system is able to correct the changes in the output that occur due to the disturbances. The feedback feature of a closed-loop system makes it an automatic control system. In this system, the output is checked all the time so that it can be compared with the desired output and if it is not close to the desired output, then there will be an error signal. So by checking the error signal the control elements in the system will do the required actions and thus the required output can be achieved.

Advantages of a closed loop control system:

(1) It is accurate.

(2) It is very accurate even in the presence of non-linearity.

(3) Stability is increased by decreasing the sensitivity.

(4) The system is not affected by noise.

Disadvantages of a closed loop control system:

(1) It is more expensive.

(2) The design is complicated.

(3) More maintenance is needed.

9　What Is a Feedback and Feedforward Control?

The feedback control takes the system output to the controller and the controller will compare this output with the required value. The feedforward control will detect the disturbances directly and it will take proper actions to remove the effect of this disturbance from the output.

Advantages of a feedback control:

(1) It will measure the controlled variable.

(2) It will take proper actions regardless of the disturbance source.

(3) It will decrease the sensitivity of the controlled variable to the disturbances and also to the change in process.

Disadvantages of a feedback control:

(1) Corrective action will only take place after the disturbance.

(2) The response is not stable.

Advantages of a feedforward control:

(1) Feedforward control is adjusted in advance and the speed is fast.

(2) It will correct the disturbance before it makes any changes in the process.

Disadvantages of a feedforward control:

(1) It is not really sensitive so sometimes it can't measure the disturbance.

(2) There won't be any corrective action for the unmeasured disturbances.

New Words

quantity	[ˈkwɒntətɪ]	n.数量；大量，众多
command	[kəˈmɑːnd]	n.&v.命令；控制
operation	[ˌɒpəˈreɪʃn]	n.运行；活动；运算
loop	[luːp]	n.循环；回路
interconnect	[ˌɪntəkəˈnekt]	vi.互相连接，互相联系
		vt.使互相连接；使互相联系
configuration	[kənˌfɪgəˈreɪʃn]	n.配置；构造，布局

actuator	[ˈæktʃʊeɪtə]	n.执行器，执行机构
actual	[ˈæktʃʊəl]	adj.真实的，实际的
maintain	[meɪnˈteɪn]	v.维持，保持
condition	[kənˈdɪʃn]	n.条件；状况；环境，处境
environmental	[ɪnˌvaɪrənˈmentl]	adj.环境的
predetermine	[ˌpriːdɪˈtɜːmɪn]	v.预先设定，预定
adjustment	[əˈdʒʌstmənt]	n.调整，调节
disturbance	[dɪˈstɜːbəns]	n.干扰
automatic	[ˌɔːtəˈmætɪk]	adj.自动的，自动化的
controller	[kənˈtrəʊlə]	n.控制器
comparison	[kəmˈpærɪsn]	n.比较，对照
computation	[ˌkɒmpjuˈteɪʃn]	n.计算
correction	[kəˈrekʃn]	n.纠正，校正
stable	[ˈsteɪbl]	adj.稳定的；牢固的
economical	[ˌiːkəˈnɒmɪkl]	adj.经济的；节约的
automatically	[ˌɔːtəˈmætɪklɪ]	adv.自动地；机械地
influence	[ˈɪnfluəns]	v.影响；支配
stability	[stəˈbɪlətɪ]	n.稳定性
feedforward	[ˈfiːdfɔːwəd]	n.前馈

Phrases

control system	控制系统
control loop	控制循环
control signal	控制信号
power signal	动力信号，电力信号
set point	设定点，设定值
control variable	控制变量
be capable of	有能力
system variable	系统变量
automatic control	自动控制；自控
control element	控制元件
control valve	控制阀，调节阀
external noise	外部噪声
frequency response	频率响应，频率特性
internal disturbance	内部干扰
external disturbance	外部干扰

open loop	开环
non-feedback system	无反馈系统
closed loop	闭环
feedback control	反馈控制

参考译文

控 制 系 统

1 什么是控制系统?

控制系统可以被描述为能够控制输出量的系统。基本上，它是一个或一组设备，可以管理、命令和调节另一个设备或使用控制回路的系统的运行。因此，该系统可以控制和调节另一个系统的运行。一个系统由不同的元件和设备组成，这些元件和设备相互连接以执行一个过程。这些组成部分的互连构成控制系统，从而实现系统配置。控制系统的主要组成部分是执行器、传感器、参考输入和实际输出。系统是需要控制的过程或设备。执行器将控制信号转换为动力信号。传感器将测量系统的输出，实际输出代表所需的输出，如图 8-1 所示。

（图略）

2 为什么需要控制系统?

需要一个控制系统将过程安全有效地保持在所需的运行条件下。控制系统能够保持产品质量。在控制系统的帮助下，能够获得高价值的产品，并提高产量。它可以满足如减少污染、确保安全等环境安全法规的要求。

3 什么是设定值改变和干扰改变?

设定值是控制变量的预定值，因此，如果设定值发生变化，将进行某些调整，以达到新的运行条件。

干扰变化是过程中由于干扰而发生的变化，因此控制系统必须能够将受控变量返回到设定值。

4 控制系统有哪些硬件?

4.1 传感器

传感器将测量系统变量。在自动控制中，它将充当信号源。

4.2 控制器

控制器将执行比较和计算过程。

4.3 控制元件

控制元件是在过程中执行控制的设备。它将接收来自控制器的信号，并据此执行某些操作。在大多数情况下，控制元件是控制阀。

5 控制系统的主要功能是什么？

控制系统必须能够进行测量，并将测量值与要求值进行比较，计算要求值和测量值之间的差值。因此，在将测量值与期望值进行比较时，如果测量值不接近期望值，则必须进行校正。

6 控制系统的要求是什么？

（1）它应该是准确的。
（2）它必须很灵敏。
（3）它不应该对外部噪声灵敏，但必须对输入命令灵敏。
（4）它必须是稳定的。
（5）它应该有良好的频率响应。
（6）它必须运行得非常快。

7 什么是控制系统中的干扰？

在控制系统中，干扰是影响系统输出值的信号。有两种类型的干扰：一种是系统内部产生的内部干扰，另一种是系统外部产生的外部干扰。

8 控制系统有几种不同的类型？

8.1 开环控制系统

这也被称为非反馈系统，其中控制动作不依赖系统的输出。在这种类型的控制系统中，因为没有反馈，所以要从中获得所需的输出很困难。这些系统无法考虑干扰，所以只能通过改变输入来改变输出。

开环控制系统的优点包括：构造简单、经济、易于维护、稳定。

开环控制系统的缺点包括：

（1）它并不精确。

（2）它不可靠。

（3）输出中的任何更改都无法自动更正。

8.2 闭环控制系统

在此类控制系统中，有一个传感器测量输出，并使用感测值的反馈来影响控制输入变量。输出将对输入量产生影响，从而保持所需的输出值。因此，在反馈的帮助下，闭环控制系统能够校正因干扰而产生的输出变化。闭环系统的反馈特性使其成为自动控制系统。在该系统中，始终检查输出，以便将其与所需输出进行比较，如果不接近所需输出，则会出现错误信号。因此，通过检查错误信号，系统中的控制元件将执行所需的操作，从而实现所需的输出。

闭环控制系统的优点如下：

（1）它是精确的。

（2）即使存在非线性，它也非常精确。

（3）可通过降低灵敏度提高稳定性。

（4）系统不受噪声影响。

闭环控制系统的缺点如下：

（1）它更贵。

（2）设计很复杂。

（3）需要更多的维护。

9 什么是反馈控制和前馈控制？

反馈控制将系统输出带到控制器，控制器将此输出与所需值进行比较。前馈控制将直接检测干扰，并采取适当措施消除输出中干扰的影响。

反馈控制的优点如下：

（1）它将测量受控变量。

（2）无论干扰源是什么，它都会采取适当的措施。

（3）这将降低受控变量对干扰和过程变化的灵敏度。

反馈控制的缺点如下：

（1）只有在干扰发生后才能采取纠正措施。

（2）响应并不稳定。

前馈控制的优点如下：

（1）前馈控制是提前进行调整，速度快。

（2）它将在对过程进行任何更改之前纠正干扰。

前馈控制的缺点如下：

（1）它不是很灵敏，所以有时无法测量干扰。

（2）对于未测量到的干扰，不会采取任何纠正措施。

Text B

扫码听课文

Programmable Logic Controller

At present, we rely on automated machinery to perform many of our most critical industrial processes. Automation technology has brought our production and innovation to a new level. However, our current level of automation wouldn't have been reached but for a critical invention called the programmable logic controller (PLC).

1 What Is a Programmable Logic Controller?

A programmable logic controller is a type of tiny computer that can receive data through its inputs and send operating instructions through its outputs. Fundamentally, a PLC's job is to control a system's functions using the internal logic programmed into it.

A PLC takes in inputs, whether from automated data capture points or from human input points such as switches or buttons. Based on its programming, the PLC then decides whether or not to change the output. A PLC's outputs can control a huge variety of equipment, including motors, solenoid valves, lights, switchgear, safety shut-offs and many others.

The physical location of PLCs can vary widely from one system to another. Usually, however, PLCs are located in the general vicinity of the systems they operate, and they're typically protected by an electrical box.

2 Advantages of Using PLCs

PLCs have been a standard element of industrial machinery design for many decades. What advantages do PLCs offer that make them such a popular choice?

(1) PLCs are fairly intuitive to program. Their programming languages are simple compared with other industrial control systems, which makes PLCs great for businesses that want to minimize complexity and costs.

(2) PLCs are a mature technology with years of testing and analysis backing them up. It's easy to find robust research about many different PLC types and comprehensive tutorials for programming and integrating them.

(3) PLCs are available at a wide range of price points, including many extremely affordable basic models that small businesses and startups often use.

(4) PLCs are extremely versatile, and most PLC models are suitable for controlling a wide variety of processes and systems.

(5) PLCs are completely solid-state devices, which means they have no moving parts. That makes them exceptionally reliable and more able to survive the challenging conditions present in many industrial facilities.

(6) PLCs have relatively few components, which makes them easier to troubleshoot and helps reduce maintenance downtime.

(7) PLCs are efficient and don't consume very much electrical power. This helps conserve energy and may simplify wiring considerations.

3   Drawbacks of Using PLCs

No technology is perfect for every scenario, and there are some applications for which PLCs aren't the best choice. Let's look at some of the most significant potential drawbacks of using PLCs.

(1) PLCs have less capacity to handle extremely complex data or large numbers of processes that involve analog rather than discrete inputs. As manufacturing facilities become more integrated, increasing numbers of them may shift toward a distributed control system or another alternative industrial control method.

(2) PLCs from different manufacturers often use proprietary programming software. This makes PLC programming interfaces less interoperable.

(3) PLCs, like many other types of electronic equipment, are vulnerable to electromagnetic interference (EMI). They can also experience other kinds of common electronics malfunctions such as corrupted memory and communication failures.

4   How Does a Programmable Logic Controller Work?

Now let's take a look at what's going on inside a programmable logic controller. Remember that a PLC is an input-output system, which means that each unit both accepts inputs and controls outputs. Between inputs and outputs is the third element of the system: logic programming, which happens in the CPU and controls the relationship between the inputs and outputs (see Figure 8-2).

Here's how each element works:

(1) Input monitoring: the PLC monitors relevant data inputs and sends the data to the CPU. Some PLCs only use data inputs with discrete (on/off) inputs, but PLCs with analog capabilities can accept analog inputs for continuous variables. Inputs may come from IoT devices, robots, safety sensors, human-machine interfaces, or almost any other type of data entry point.

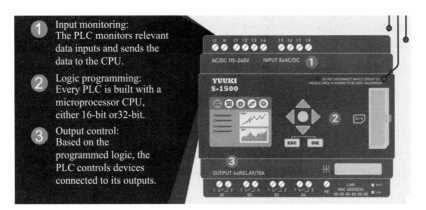

Figure 8-2   How a PLC Works

(2) Logic programming: every PLC is built with a microprocessor CPU, either 16-bit or 32-bit. Engineers and technicians program the PLC's CPU to recognize certain conditions and values and to make changes in the outputs based on its programmed rules. The CPU is constantly checking the state of variables and making decisions based on programmed conditions. This simple premise allows a wide variety of designs and functions.

(3) Output control: based on the programmed logic, the PLC controls various switches, motor starters, relays, and other devices connected to its outputs. This allows the PLCs to take control of mechanical processes such as the operation of a machine. Engineers can also link multiple system parts by programming PLCs to send their output signal to another PLC in a chain.

Compact PLC units generally include the CPU, inputs, and outputs in the same unit. In the rack-mount modular PLC systems that many industrial facilities use, the PLC's inputs and outputs are located together in the I/O module, while the logic operations happen in a separate CPU module. I/O modules may be located close to the CPU, but they can also be quite distant — sometimes even in different buildings.

5   Choosing a PLC

Many factors will influence your choice when it comes to specifying a PLC model for your application. Some key considerations include:

(1) Electrical capacity: PLCs have different voltage requirements for their power supplies, so check to ensure that your selection is compatible with your electrical system.

(2) Processing speed: check a PLC model's CPU speed to determine whether it meets your application's needs.

(3) Compatibility: ensure that your PLC model is compatible with any new or existing system hardware.

(4) Temperature tolerance: most PLCs are designed for safe operation within the range of 0 to 60°C. However, some specialized PLC models can operate at extreme temperatures, which is

important for facilities with unusually hot or cold manufacturing conditions.

(5) Memory: a PLC needs sufficient ROM and RAM to execute the processes it's intended to automate. The controller uses ROM to store its operating system and instructions and uses RAM to execute its functions.

(6) Connectivity: make sure your PLC has enough input and output ports, and make sure it's able to be connected to the type of peripherals that your system requires.

(7) Analog I/O: although PLCs are primarily used for discrete functions, some models also have analog inputs and outputs that can control processes with continuous variables.

See Figure 8-3.

Figure 8-3　Key Considerations When Choosing a PLC

6　Programming a PLC

Most PLCs can be programmed using a standard computer and PLC programming software. The International Electrical Code's IEC 61131-3 standard defines five languages for PLC programming. Three of those languages use graphical interfaces for programming, while the other two use text interfaces.

Ladder logic has traditionally been the most commonly used programming language for PLCs. It's one of the most intuitive languages available because it uses a graphic interface that's designed to resemble electrical diagrams, even using many of the same symbols for contacts and relays. Ladder logic uses a series of "rungs" to represent a controller's I/O channels, each of which can be programmed with conditions and rules.

However, other PLC programming languages offer more sophisticated tools. For example, structured text (ST) allows programmers to quickly create complex, scalable programs using text commands. For the most complex tasks, there's a sequential function chart (SFC), which allows programmers to connect multiple systems and subroutines in other programming languages.

As we mentioned earlier, it's common for PLCs to use proprietary software. However, although it might feel unfamiliar to navigate a new PLC programming application, remember that each still operates under the basic principles of IEC 61131-3.

New Words

machinery	[məˈʃiːnərɪ]	n.机器；机械装置
switch	[swɪtʃ]	n.开关
switchgear	[ˈswɪtʃgɪə]	n.开关设备；接电装置
intuitive	[ɪnˈtjuːɪtɪv]	adj.直观的；直觉的
robust	[rəʊˈbʌst]	adj.健壮的，可靠的
affordable	[əˈfɔːdəbl]	adj.价格合理的，买得起的
startup	[ˈstɑːtʌp]	n.启动；新兴公司
versatile	[ˈvɜːsətaɪl]	adj.多用途的；多功能的
exceptionally	[ɪkˈsepʃənəlɪ]	adv.异常地
downtime	[ˈdaʊntaɪm]	n.停工期
scenario	[səˈnɑːrɪəʊ]	n.情景；设想
malfunction	[ˌmælˈfʌŋkʃn]	vi.失灵；发生故障
		n.故障；功能障碍
corrupt	[kəˈrʌpt]	adj.损坏的，有错误的
chain	[tʃeɪn]	n.链，链条
compact	[kəmˈpækt]	adj.紧凑的，小型的
modular	[ˈmɒdjələ]	adj.模块化的
compatibility	[kəmˌpætəˈbɪlətɪ]	n.兼容性
extreme	[ɪkˈstriːm]	adj.极端的
sufficient	[səˈfɪʃnt]	adj.足够的；充足的
connectivity	[ˌkɒnekˈtɪvɪtɪ]	n.连通性
peripheral	[pəˈrɪfərəl]	n.外部设备
contact	[ˈkɒntækt]	n.触点，接触器
rung	[rʌŋ]	n.阶梯，梯级
subroutine	[ˈsʌbruːtiːn]	n.子程序
principle	[ˈprɪnsəpl]	n.原则，法则

Phrases

operating instruction	操作指令
solenoid valve	电磁阀
electrical box	电气箱
industrial control system	工业控制系统
conserve energy	节能
distributed control system	分布式控制系统，分散型控制系统
human-machine interface	人机接口
be compatible with ...	与……兼容，适合于

graphical interface	图形界面
text interface	文本界面
ladder logic	梯形逻辑
electrical diagram	电气图
a series of	一系列；一连串
structured text	结构化文本

Abbreviations

PLC (programmable logic controller)	可编程逻辑控制器
EMI (electromagnetic interference)	电磁干扰
I/O (input/output)	输入/输出
IEC (International Electrical Code)	国际电气规范
SFC (sequential function chart)	顺序功能图

参考译文

可编程逻辑控制器

目前，人们依靠自动化机械执行许多最关键的工业过程。自动化技术将生产和创新提升到了一个新的水平。然而，如果没有一项叫作可编程逻辑控制器（PLC）的关键发明，那么目前的自动化水平是无法达到的。

1 什么是 PLC？

PLC 是一种微型计算机，可以通过其输入接收数据，并通过其输出发送操作指令。从根本上说，PLC 的工作是使用在系统内编程的内部逻辑控制系统的功能。

PLC 接收输入，无论这些输入是来自自动数据采集点还是来自开关或按钮等人工输入点。然后，PLC 根据其编程决定是否改变输出。PLC 的输出可以控制各种各样的设备，包括电机、电磁阀、灯、开关设备、安全切断装置和许多其他设备。

PLC 的物理位置可能因系统而异。通常情况下，PLC 位于它们运行的系统附近，由电气箱保护。

2 使用 PLC 的优点

几十年来，PLC 一直是工业机械设计的标准元素。PLC 有哪些优势使其成为如此受欢迎的选择？

（1）PLC 的编程相当直观。与其他工业控制系统相比，它的编程语言很简单，这使 PLC 非常适合希望将复杂性和成本降至最低的企业。

（2）PLC 是一项成熟的技术，经过了多年的测试和分析支持。很容易找到关于不同类型 PLC 的可靠研究及进行编程和集成的综合教程。

（3）PLC 的价格范围很广，包括许多小企业和初创企业经常使用的价格非常低廉的基本型号。

（4）PLC 的用途非常广泛，大多数 PLC 型号适用于控制各种过程和系统。

（5）PLC 是完全固态的设备，意味着它没有运动部件，这使它格外可靠，更能在许多工业设施中面临的具有挑战性的条件下生存。

（6）PLC 的组件相对较少，这使它更容易排除故障，并有助于减少维护停机时间。

（7）PLC 的效率高，并且不会消耗太多电能。这有助于节约能源，并可以简化布线。

3　使用 PLC 的缺点

没有哪种技术可以完美适用于所有场景，在一些应用中 PLC 并不是最佳选择。下面分析一些使用 PLC 的最重要的潜在缺点。

（1）PLC 处理极其复杂的数据或涉及模拟而非离散输入的大量过程的能力较弱。随着制造设施变得更加集成化，越来越多的设施可能会转向分布式控制系统或其他工业控制方法。

（2）来自不同制造商的 PLC 通常使用专有编程软件，这使 PLC 编程接口的互操作性更差。

（3）PLC 和许多其他类型的电子设备一样，容易受到电磁干扰（EMI）的影响。它还可能遇到其他类型常见的电子故障，如内存损坏和通信故障。

4　PLC 如何工作？

下面介绍 PLC 内部发生了什么。PLC 是一个输入输出系统，这意味着每个单元都接受输入并控制输出。输入和输出之间是系统的第三个元素：逻辑编程，它发生在 CPU 中并控制输入和输出之间的关系，如图 8-2 所示。

（图略）

以下是每个元素的工作原理：

（1）输入监控：PLC 监控相关数据输入，并将数据发送到 CPU。一些 PLC 仅使用离散（开/关）输入的数据输入，但具有模拟功能的 PLC 可以接受连续变量的模拟输入。输入可能来自物联网设备、机器人、安全传感器、人机界面或几乎所有其他类型的数据输入点。

（2）逻辑编程：每个 PLC 都内置有一个 16 位或 32 位的微处理器 CPU。工程师和技术人员对 PLC 的 CPU 进行编程，以识别特定条件和值，并根据其编程规则改变输出。CPU 不断检查变量的状态，并根据编程条件做出决策。这为进行多种设计和实现不同的功能奠定了基础。

（3）输出控制：根据编程逻辑，PLC 控制各种开关、电机起动器、继电器和其他与其输出相连的设备。这允许 PLC 控制机械过程，如机器的操作。工程师还可以通过对 PLC 进行编程将多个系统部件连接起来，将其输出信号发送到链中的另一个 PLC。

紧凑型 PLC 单元通常包括同一单元中的 CPU、输入和输出。在许多工业设施中使用的机架式模块化 PLC 系统中，PLC 的输入和输出都位于 I/O 模块中，而逻辑操作发生在单独的 CPU 模块中。I/O 模块可能靠近 CPU，但它们也可能相距遥远——有时甚至在不同的建筑中。

5 选择 PLC

在为应用程序指定 PLC 型号时，许多因素会影响选择。要考虑的关键因素包括:

（1）电气容量：PLC 对其电源有不同的电压要求，因此请检查以确保选择的 PLC 与电气系统兼容。

（2）处理速度：检查 PLC 型号的 CPU 速度，以确定其是否满足应用程序的需要。

（3）兼容性：确保 PLC 型号与任何新的或现有的系统硬件兼容。

（4）温度容限：大多数 PLC 被设计在 0~60℃ 范围内安全运行。然而，一些专用 PLC 型号可以在极端温度下运行，这对于异常高温或低温条件下运行的设施非常重要。

（5）内存：PLC 需要足够的 ROM 和 RAM 执行自动化的过程。控制器使用 ROM 存储其操作系统和指令，并使用 RAM 执行其功能。

（6）连接：确保 PLC 有足够的输入和输出端口，并确保它能够连接到系统所需的外部设备类型。

（7）模拟 I/O：虽然 PLC 主要用于离散功能，但一些型号也有模拟输入和输出，可以控制具有连续变量的过程。

如图 8-3 所示。

（图略）

6 对 PLC 编程

大多数 PLC 可以使用标准计算机和 PLC 编程软件进行编程。《国际电气规范》的 IEC 61131-3 标准定义了 5 种 PLC 编程语言。其中，3 种语言使用图形界面进行编程，另外两种语言使用文本界面。

传统上，PLC 最常用的编程语言一直是梯形逻辑。它是最直观的语言之一，因为它使用的图形界面设计类似于电气图，甚至接触器和继电器使用的符号也一样。梯形逻辑使用一系列"阶梯"表示控制器的 I/O 通道，每个通道都可以通过条件和规则进行编程。

然而，其他 PLC 编程语言提供了更先进的工具。例如，结构化文本（ST）允许程序员使用文本命令快速创建复杂、可扩展的程序。对于最复杂的任务，有一个顺序功能图（SFC），它允许程序员用其他编程语言连接多个系统和子例程。

正如前面提到的，PLC 使用专有软件是很常见的。尽管浏览一个新的 PLC 编程应用程序可能会感到不熟悉，但每个应用程序仍然按照 IEC 61131-3 的基本原则运行。

Exercises

[Ex. 1] Answer the following questions according to Text A.

1. What can a control system be described as? What is it basically?

2. What are the major components of a control system?

3. What is a control system needed to do?

4. What is a set point? What is disturbance change?

5. What are the hardwares of a control system?

6. What should the control system be able to do?

7. What are the requirements of a control system?

8. How many types of disturbance are there? What are they?

9. What are the different types of control system?

10. What are the advantages of a feedback control?

[Ex. 2] Answer the following questions according to Text B.

1. What is a programmable logic controller?

2. Where are PLCs usually located? How are they protected?

3. What makes PLCs great for businesses that want to minimize complexity and costs?

4. What are PLCs? What does that mean?

5. What are PLCs are vulnerable to? What can they also experience?

6. What do engineers and technicians program the PLC's CPU to do?

7. What does the PLC do based on the programmed logic?

8. When it comes to specifying a PLC model for your application, what are some of your key considerations?

9. What has ladder logic has traditionally been? Why is it one of the most intuitive languages available?

10. What does structured text (ST) allow programmers to do?

[Ex. 3] Translate the following terms or phrases from English into Chinese and vice versa.

1. automatic control	1.
2. frequency response	2.
3. open loop	3.
4. electrical diagram	4.
5. operating instruction	5.
6. *adv.*自动地；机械地	6.

7. *n.*配置；构造，布局	7.
8. *n.*前馈	8.
9. *n.*稳定性	9.
10. *n.*兼容性	10.

[Ex. 4] Translate the following passage into Chinese.

Open Loop Control Systems and Closed Loop Control Systems

1 Open Loop Control Systems

A system in which the output has no effect on the control action is known as an open loop control system. For a given input the system produces a certain output. If there are any disturbances, the output changes and there is no adjustment of the input to bring back the output to the original value. A perfect calibration is required to get good accuracy and the system should be free from any external disturbances. No measurements are made at the output.

A traffic control system is a good example of an open loop system. The signals change according to a preset time and are not affected by the density of traffic on any road. A washing machine is another example of an open loop control system. The quality of wash is not measured, every cycle like wash, rinse and dry' cycle goes according to a preset timing.

2 Closed Loop Control Systems

Closed loop control systems are also known as feedback control systems. A system which maintains a prescribed relationship between the controlled variable and the reference input, and uses the difference between them as a signal to activate the control is known as a feedback control system. The output or the controlled variable is measured and compared with the reference input and an error signal is generated. This is the activating signal to the controller which, by its action, tries to reduce the error. Thus the controlled variable is continuously feedback and compared with the input signal. If the error is reduced to zero, the output is the desired output.

Reading

Industrial Robots[①]

In the 1960s, Silicon Valley company SRI International introduced the first alert, mobile robot. The robot, Shakey, was able to navigate a complex environment. While it was awkward and slow,

---

① robot [ˈrəʊbɒt] *n.*机器人

Shakey set the standard for what was to follow, which is a groundbreaking sector of industrial robots[①] that is making waves in the world of technology each day.

Better algorithms and stronger processors are allowing robots to become more efficient. As a result, many grueling, tedious[②], dangerous, and monotonous[③] human jobs are being replaced by robotic machines. Intelligent, physically embodied machines, robots are becoming more and more integrated into the many aspects of our world every day.

1　What Are Industrial Robots?

Industrial robots are mechanical devices that are programmable. They are used in replacement of humans as they can perform repetitive or dangerous[④] tasks with extreme accuracy.

Many parts go into making industrial robots. Cables, small parts, grippers, guarding, and many other components are used to make these robots.

2　What Are the Different Types of Industrial Robots?

While there are many different types of industrial robots, there are a few main types that are used by many different manufacturers.

2.1　Cartesian Robots

Cartesian robots[⑤], which are also called linear robots or gantry robots[⑥], are industrial robots that work on three linear axes that use the Cartesian coordinate[⑦] system (x, y, and z), meaning they move in straight lines on 3-axis (up and down, in and out, and side to side). Cartesian robots are a popular choice due to being highly flexible in their configurations, giving users the ability to adjust the robot's speed, precision, stroke length, and size. Cartesian robots are one of the most commonly used robot types for industrial applications and are often used for CNC machines and 3D printing (see Figure 8-4).

Figure 8-4　Cartesian Robots

---

① industrial robot：工业机器人
② tedious ['tiːdɪəs] *adj.*乏味的
③ monotonous [mə'nɒtənəs] *adj.*单调的
④ dangerous ['deɪndʒərəs] *adj.*危险的
⑤ Cartesian robot：直角坐标型机器人
⑥ gantry robot：桁架式机器人
⑦ coordinate [kəʊ'ɔːdɪneɪt] *adj.*坐标的

2.2　SCARA Robots

SCARA is an acronym that stands for selective compliance assembly robot arm[①] or selective compliance articulated robot arm. SCARA robots function on 3-axis (x, y, and z), and have a rotary[②] motion as well. SCARA robots excel in lateral movements and are commonly faster moving and have easier integration than Cartesian robots. Typically, SCARA robots are used for assembly and palletizing, as well as bio-med application (see Figure 8-5).

Figure 8-5　SCARA Robots

2.3　Articulated Robots

The mechanical movement and configuration of articulated robots[③] closely resemble a human arm. The arm is mounted to a base with a twisting joint[④]. The arm itself can feature anywhere from two rotary joints up to ten rotary joints which act as axes, with each additional joint or axis allowing for a greater degree of motion. Most articulated robots utilize four or six-axis. Typical applications for articulated robots are assembly, arc welding[⑤], material handling, machine tending, and packaging (see Figure 8-6).

Figure 8-6　Articulated Robots

---

① selective compliance assembly robot arm：平面关节型机器人
② rotary [ˈrəʊtərɪ] *adj.*旋转的
③ articulated robot：多关节型机器人
④ joint [dʒɔɪnt] *n.*关节
⑤ arc welding：电弧焊

2.4　Cylindrical Robots

Cylindrical robots have a rotary joint at the base and a prismatic joint to connect the links. The robots have a cylindrical-shaped work envelop, which is achieved with rotating shaft and an extendable arm that moves in a vertical and sliding motion. Cylindrical robots[①] are often used in tight workspaces for simple assembly, machine tending, or coating applications due to their compact design (see Figure 8-7).

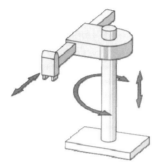

Figure 8-7　Cylindrical Robots

2.5　Delta Robots

Delta robots, or parallel robots[②], possess three arms connected to a single base, which is mounted above the workspace. Delta robots work in a dome-shape[③] and can move both delicately and precisely at high speeds due to each joint of the end effector being directly controlled by all three arms. Delta robots are often used for fast pick and place applications in the food, pharmaceutical[④], and electronic industries (see Figure 8-8).

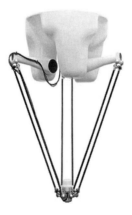

Figure 8-8　Delta Robots

---

① cylindrical robot：圆柱形机器人
② parallel robot：并行机器人
③ dome-shape [dəʊm-ʃeɪp] n.拱顶形
④ pharmaceutical [ˌfɑːməˈsuːtɪkl] adj.制药的

2.6   Polar Robots

Polar robots, or spherical robots[1], have an arm with two rotary joints and one linear joint connected to a base with a twisting joint. The axes of the robot work together to form a polar coordinate[2], which allows the robot to have a spherical work envelope. Polar robots are credited as one of the first types of industrial robots to ever be developed. Polar robots are commonly used for die casting, injection molding[3], welding, and material handling (see Figure 8-9).

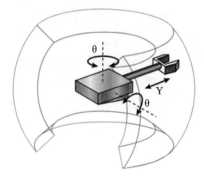

Figure 8-9   Polar Robots

2.7   Collaborative Robots

Collaborative robots[4], or cobots, are robots that can directly and safely interact with humans in a shared workspace. There are numerous types and brands of collaborative robots on the market. Cobots are typically used for pick and place, palletizing[5], quality inspection, and machine tending (see Figure 8-10).

Figure 8-10   Collaborative Robots

---

① spherical robot：球形机器人
② polar coordinate：极坐标
③ injection molding：注塑成型
④ collaborative robot：协作机器人，协同机器人
⑤ palletize ['pælə‚taɪz] v.码垛

3　What Are the Benefits of Industrial Robots ?

Industrial robots create many benefits, including producing consistent quality results. A robot that paints, for example, can paint evenly, without any drips or spills.

Robots make human jobs easier by taking over repetitive tasks. They also reduce mistakes and waste, reduce the risk of human injury[①], and improve productivity and output.

Despite high initial costs, industrial robots do deliver a great return on investment[②] (ROI). When they are consistent and programmed properly, they reduce waste and boost overall product quality.

Because of the many benefits, the use of industrial robots is becoming increasingly popular. Robots can work for hours on end and perform the same tasks for years and years.

4　Industrial Robots Will Only Continue to Improve

Industrial robots will continue to become more popular year after year and into the future. They are making waves in a variety of industries, and in particular, the automotive industry.

Furthermore, they increase productivity, make workplaces safer, and take over monotonous jobs. This way, humans can focus on jobs that require more skills.

Even though the initial costs[③] of industrial robots are high, it is shown that they can save us a lot of money in the long run.

---

① human injury：人身事故
② return on investment：投资回报率
③ initial cost：初始成本，初始花费

Unit 9

扫码听课文

Text A

EDA

1 Definition

Electronic design automation (EDA) is a market segment consisting of software, hardware, and services with the collective goal of assisting in the definition, planning, design, implementation, verification, and subsequent manufacturing of semiconductor devices, or chips. Regarding the manufacturing of these devices, the primary providers of this service are semiconductor foundries, or fabs. These highly complex and costly facilities are either owned and operated by large, vertically integrated semiconductor companies or operated as independent, "pure-play" manufacturing service providers. This latter category has become the dominate business model.

While EDA solutions are not directly involved in the manufacture of chips, they play a critical role in three ways. First, EDA tools are used to design and validate the semiconductor manufacturing process to ensure it delivers the required performance and density. This segment of EDA is called technology computer-aided design, or TCAD.

Second, EDA tools are used to verify that a design will meet all the requirements of the manufacturing process. Deficiencies in this area can cause the resultant chip to either not function or function at reduced capacity. There are also reliability risks. This area of focus is known as design for manufacturability, or DFM.

The third area is relatively new. After the chip is manufactured, there is a growing requirement to monitor the performance of the device from post-manufacturing test to deployment in the field. The goal of this monitoring is to ensure the device continues to perform as expected throughout its lifetime and to ensure the device is not tampered with. This third application is referred to as silicon lifecycle management, or SLM.

Another market segment that is closely associated with EDA is semiconductor intellectual property, or semiconductor IP. This market segment provides pre-designed circuits of varying complexity that may be used as-is or adapted for a particular application. Semiconductor IP allows highly complex chips to be designed in far less time since a lot of existing design work can be reused.

2 Types of EDA Tools

While most EDA products are delivered as software, there are some cases where physical hardware is also used to deliver capabilities. Hardware is typically used when extremely high performance is required. This occurs when a large amount of data must be processed during simulation and verification. In all cases, a dedicated hardware model of the circuit will perform far faster than a software program executing the same model. This dramatic increase in speed is often required to complete various tasks in reasonable amounts of time (hours to days vs. weeks to months).

Very sophisticated and complex software programs mainly use three tools to assist chip design and manufacturing: simulation tools, design tools and verification tools.

2.1 Simulation

Simulation tools take a description of a proposed circuit and predict its behavior before is it implemented. This description is typically presented in a standard hardware description language such as Verilog or VHDL. Simulation tools model the behavior of circuit elements at various degrees of detail and perform various operations to predict the resultant behavior of the circuit. The level of detail required is dictated by the type of circuit being designed and its intended use. If a very large amount of input data must be processed, hardware approaches such as emulation or rapid prototyping are used. These situations occur when a processor's operating system must be run against real-world scenarios, such as video processing. Without a hardware-assisted approach, the runtime for these cases can be untenable.

2.2 Design

Design tools take a description of a proposed circuit function and assemble the collection of circuit elements that implement that function. This assembly process can be a logical one where the correct circuit elements are chosen and interconnected to implement the desired function. Logic synthesis is an example of this process. It can also be a physical process where the geometric shapes that implement the circuit in silicon chips are assembled, placed, and routed together. It can also take the form of an interactive process that is guided by a designer. This is called custom layout.

2.3 Verification

Verification tools examine either the logical or physical representation of the chip to determine if the resultant design is connected correctly and will deliver the required performance. There are many processes that can be used here. Physical verification examines the interconnected geometries to ensure their placement obeys the manufacturing requirements of the fab. These requirements have become very complex and can include far more than 10,000 rules. Verification can also take the form of comparing the implemented circuit with the original description to ensure it faithfully reflects the required function. Layout versus schematic (LVS) is an example of this process. Functional verification of a chip can also use simulation technology to compare actual behavior with expected behavior. These approaches are limited by the completeness of the input stimulus provided. Another approach is to verify the behavior of the circuit algorithmically, without the need for input stimulus. This approach is called equivalence checking and is a part of a discipline known as formal verification.

3　The Importance of EDA

Semiconductor chips are incredibly complex. State-of-the-art devices can contain over one billion circuit elements. All of these elements can interact with each other in subtle ways, and variation in the manufacturing process can introduce more subtle interactions and changes in behavior.

There is simply no way to manage this level of complexity without sophisticated automation, and EDA provides this critical technology. Without it, it would be impossible to design and manufacture today's semiconductor devices.

It is also worth noting that the cost of an error in a manufactured chip can be catastrophic. Chips errors cannot be "patched". The entire chip must be re-designed and re-manufactured. The time and cost of this process is often too long and too expensive, resulting in a failure of the entire project. So, the complexity to design chips is high and the need to do it flawlessly is also required.

Without EDA tools, these challenges cannot be met.

4　Future Trends for EDA

The semiconductor industry is being asked to produce ever more complex integrated circuits (ICs). Semiconductor manufacturers have to supply more complex ICs, such as CPUs and GPUs with hundreds of cores, plus terabytes of memory and multiple high speed communication channels, so they need increasingly sophisticated EDA tools to help them. Advanced driver assistance system (ADAS) is one of the many applications driving the growth of artificial intelligence (AI), and its associated machine learning (ML) and deep learning (DL) technologies.

Additionally, developers often identify a need to optimize their AI performance, without power compromises, by building dedicated logic. Developing the right AI architecture for a given application requires EDA tools that can work with higher levels of abstraction.

This enables AI architects to develop their math code, translate it to C or SystemC, and see upfront which parts of their algorithm should be implemented in hardware and software. They can obtain the ideal architecture sooner than trying to go down to the register transfer (RT) level right away.

While EDA can help with AI solution design, AI can equally be used to improve EDA tools. For the last several years, Mentor's R&D staff has been integrating ML into their own EDA tools. The company currently has five tool offerings commercially available that leverage ML to help deliver better results, and deliver them more quickly.

ML can boost EDA performance because ML requires large volumes of data to be effective, and EDA produces data in large volumes. In fact, EDA data is so readily available that, when leveraging ML for EDA, the question becomes: what data sets can be leveraged effectively for what tool functions?

New Words

collective	[kəˈlektɪv]	adj.共有的；总体的
implementation	[ˌɪmplɪmenˈteɪʃn]	n.实施
verification	[ˌverɪfɪˈkeɪʃn]	n.验证，证明，核实
semiconductor	[ˌsemɪkənˈdʌktə]	n.半导体
foundry	[ˈfaʊndrɪ]	n.代工厂；铸造厂，制造厂
fab	[fæb]	n.晶圆厂
complex	[ˈkɒmpleks]	adj.复杂的；复合的
dominate	[ˈdɒmɪneɪt]	v.在……中占首要地位；控制，支配
ensure	[ɪnˈʃʊə]	v.确保
density	[ˈdensətɪ]	n.密度，密集；浓度
capacity	[kəˈpæsətɪ]	n.容量；生产能力
reliability	[rɪˌlaɪəˈbɪlɪtɪ]	n.可靠性，可信赖
deployment	[dɪˈplɔɪmənt]	n.部署，调集；有效利用
tamper	[ˈtæmpə]	v.干预；篡改
complexity	[kəmˈpleksətɪ]	n.复杂性
dependence	[dɪˈpendəns]	n.依靠；依赖
deliver	[dɪˈlɪvə]	v.交付；发表，宣布；递送
simulation	[ˌsɪmjʊˈleɪʃn]	n.仿真，模仿，模拟
behavior	[bɪˈheɪvjə]	n.行为，表现方式
description	[dɪˈskrɪpʃn]	n.描述，说明
standard	[ˈstændəd]	n.标准
		adj.标准的
element	[ˈelɪmənt]	n.要素，元件
emulation	[ˌemjʊˈleɪʃn]	n.效仿，模仿
situation	[ˌsɪtʃʊˈeɪʃn]	n.情况

runtime	[ˈrʌntaɪm]	n.运行时间，运行期
untenable	[ʌnˈtenəbl]	adj.站不住脚的，不能维持的
assemble	[əˈsembl]	v.组装；聚集，收集
synthesis	[ˈsɪnθəsɪs]	n.合成，综合，综合体
layout	[ˈleɪaʊt]	n.布局，安排，设计；版图
examine	[ɪgˈzæmɪn]	v.仔细检查，审查
representation	[ˌreprɪzenˈteɪʃn]	n.表现；陈述
obey	[əˈbeɪ]	v.服从；遵守
rule	[ruːl]	n.规则，常规
		v.控制
actual	[ˈæktʃʊəl]	adj.真实的，实际的
completeness	[kəmˈpliːtnəs]	n.完全；完全性；完整性
stimulus	[ˈstɪmjələs]	n.刺激；激励
algorithmically	[ælˈgɒrɪθmɪklɪ]	adv.在算法上，算法地
subtle	[ˈsʌtl]	adj.微妙的，巧妙的
catastrophic	[ˌkætəˈstrɒfɪk]	adj.灾难性的；糟糕的
flawlessly	[ˈflɔːləslɪ]	adv.无瑕地，完美地
terabyte	[ˈterəbaɪt]	n.太字节
core	[kɔː]	n.核
developer	[dɪˈveləpə]	n.开发者
optimize	[ˈɒptɪmaɪz]	vt.使最优化
compromise	[ˈkɒmprəmaɪz]	n.折中；妥协方案
		v.妥协
abstraction	[æbˈstrækʃn]	n.抽象
accelerator	[əkˈseləreɪtə]	n.加速器
code	[kəʊd]	n.代码；编码
		v.把……编码，编程序
boost	[buːst]	v.推动；增强，提高

Phrases

business model	商业模式，企业模型
critical role	关键角色，关键作用
be used to do sth.	用于做某事
be known as	被认为是；号称；叫作
post-manufacturing test	制造后测试
pre-designed circuit	预设计电路
adapt for	适应于
rapid prototyping	快速成型，快速原型设计

chip design	芯片设计
video process	视频处理
geometric shape	几何形状
functional verification	功能验证
equivalence checking	等价性检查，等价性验证
formal verification	形式验证
state-of-the-art device	最先进的设备
be leveraged for	被利用

Abbreviations

EDA (electronic design automation)	电子设计自动化
TCAD (technology computer-aided design)	技术计算机辅助设计
DFM (design for manufacturability)	可制造性设计
SLM (silicon lifecycle management)	硅生命周期管理
IP (intellectual property)	知识产权
VHDL (very high speed integrated circuit hardware description language)	超高速集成电路硬件描述语言
SVL (layout versus schematic)	版图和电路比较
GPU (general processor unit)	通用处理器
ADAS (advanced driver assistance system)	高级驾驶员辅助系统
AI (artificial intelligence)	人工智能
ML (machine learning)	机器学习
DL (deep learning)	深度学习
HLS (high level synthesis)	高级综合
SoC (system on chip)	单片系统，片上系统
RT (register transfer)	寄存器传输
R&D (research and development)	研发

参考译文

电子设计自动化

1. 定义

　　电子设计自动化（EDA）是一个由软件、硬件和服务组成的细分市场，其共同目标是协助半导体设备或芯片的定义、规划、设计、实施、验证和后续制造。关于这些设备的制造，这项服务的主要供应商是半导体代工厂或晶圆厂。这些高度复杂且成本高昂的设施要么由大型、垂直整合的半导体公司拥有和运营，要么由独立的"纯粹"制造服务提供商运营。后一类已成为主导的商业模式。

虽然 EDA 解决方案不直接参与芯片制造，但它们在 3 方面发挥着关键作用。首先，EDA 工具用于设计和验证半导体制造工艺，以确保其提供所需的性能和密度。EDA 的这一部分称为技术计算机辅助设计，即 TCAD。

其次，EDA 工具用于验证设计是否满足制造过程的所有要求。这方面的缺陷会导致最终的芯片无法运行或以缩减容量运行，还存在可靠性风险。这个重点领域被称为可制造性设计，即 DFM。

最后一个领域相对较新。芯片制造完成后，从制造后测试到现场部署，对设备性能的监控要求越来越高。此监控的目标是确保设备在其整个生命周期内继续按预期运行，并确保设备不被篡改。这个应用程序称为硅生命周期管理，即 SLM。

另一个与 EDA 密切相关的细分市场是半导体知识产权，即半导体 IP。该细分市场提供了不同复杂性的预先设计的电路，可以按原样使用或针对特定应用进行调整。因为可以重复使用许多现有的设计工作，所以半导体 IP 允许在更短的时间内设计高度复杂的芯片。

2. EDA 工具的种类

虽然大多数 EDA 产品以软件形式交付，但在某些情况下，物理硬件也用于交付功能。当需要极高的性能时，通常会使用硬件。当在仿真和验证期间必须处理大量数据时，就会发生这种情况。在所有情况下，电路的专用硬件模型的执行速度将比执行相同模型的软件程序快得多。在合理的时间内（数小时到数天，而不是数周到数月），完成各种任务通常需要大幅提高速度。

非常精致和复杂的软件程序主要通过三种工具协助芯片的设计和制造：仿真工具、设计工具和验证工具。

2.1 仿真

仿真工具对待选电路进行描述，并在实施之前预测其行为。该描述通常以标准硬件描述语言（如 Verilog 或 VHDL）呈现。仿真工具以不同的详细程度对电路元件的行为进行建模，并执行各种操作预测电路的结果行为。所需的详细程度取决于设计的电路类型及其预期用途。如果必须处理大量的输入数据，则使用硬件方法，如模仿或快速原型设计。当处理器的操作系统必须针对现实世界的场景（如视频处理）运行时，就会出现这些情况。如果没有硬件辅助方法，在这些情况下，运行时间可能无法保证。

2.2 设计

设计工具对待选电路功能进行描述，并组装实现该功能的电路元件集合。这个组装过程可以是一个逻辑过程，选择正确的电路元件并相互连接以实现所需的功能。逻辑综合是这个过程的一个例子。它也可以是一个物理过程，在硅芯片中实现电路的几何形状被组装、放置和布线在一起。它也可以采用由设计师指导的交互过程的形式，这称为自定义布局。

2.3 验证

验证工具检查芯片的逻辑或物理表示，以确定最终设计是否正确连接并提供所需的性能。这里可以使用很多过程。物理验证检查互连的几何形状，以确保它们的放置符合晶圆厂的制造要求。这些要求非常复杂，可能包括超过 10000 条规则。验证还可以采用将实现的电路与原始描述进行比较的形式，以确保它忠实地反映了所需的功能。版图和电路比较（LVS）是此过程的一个示例。芯片的功能验证还可以使用仿真技术将实际行为与预期行为进行比较。这些方法受到提供的输入激励的完整性的限制。另一种方法是通过算法验证电路的行为，无须输入激励。这种方法称为等效性检查，是称为形式验证的学科的一部分。

3. EDA 的重要性

半导体芯片极其复杂。最先进的设备可以包含超过 10 亿个电路元件。所有这些元素都能够以微妙的方式相互作用，而且制造过程中的变化可以引入更微妙的相互作用和行为变化。

如果没有精密的自动化，就没有办法管理这种程度的复杂性，而 EDA 提供了这种关键技术。没有它，就不可能设计和制造当今的半导体器件。

值得注意的是，制造芯片中出现错误的成本可能是灾难性的。芯片错误无法"修补"。整个芯片必须重新设计和重新制造。这个过程的时间往往很长且成本太昂贵，会导致整个项目的失败。所以，设计芯片的复杂度很高，需要做到完美无缺。

如果没有 EDA 工具，就无法应对这些挑战。

4. EDA 的未来趋势

半导体工业被要求生产越来越复杂的集成电路（IC）。半导体制造商必须提供更复杂的集成电路，如具有数百个内核的 CPU 和 GPU，以及 TB 级内存和多个高速通信通道，因此需要越来越复杂的 EDA 工具帮助他们。高级驾驶员辅助系统（ADAS）是推动人工智能（AI）及与其相关的机器学习（ML）和深度学习（DL）技术发展的众多应用之一。

此外，开发人员通常需要通过构建专用逻辑优化他们的人工智能性能，而不损害性能。为给定的应用程序开发正确的人工智能体系结构需要使用更高抽象级别的 EDA 工具。

这使 AI 架构师能够开发他们的数学代码，将其转换为 C 或 SystemC，并预先了解他们的算法的哪些部分应该在硬件和软件中实现。与立即进入寄存器传输（RT）级别相比，他们可以更快地获得理想的体系结构。

虽然 EDA 可以帮助设计 AI 解决方案，但 AI 同样也可以用于改进 EDA 工具。在过去几年中，Mentor 的研发人员一直将 ML 集成到他们自己的 EDA 工具中。该公司目前有 5 种商用工具，它们利用 ML 提供更好的结果，并更快地提供结果。

ML 可以提高 EDA 的性能，因为 ML 需要大量的数据才有效，而 EDA 可以生成大量的数据。事实上，EDA 数据非常容易获得，当利用 ML 进行 EDA 时，问题变为：哪些数据集可以有效地用于哪些工具功能？

Text B

What Is Circuit Simulation?

1　Definition

Circuit simulation is a process in which a model of an electronic circuit is created and analyzed using various software algorithms, which predict and verify the behavior and performance of the circuit. Since fabrication of electronic circuits, especially integrated circuits (ICs), is expensive and time-consuming, it is faster and more cost-effective to verify the behavior and performance of the circuit using a circuit simulator before fabrication.

There are different types of circuit simulators catering to varied needs across the accuracy-performance/capacity spectrum. At one end of the spectrum are analog simulators that solve accurate representations of the electronic circuits. They offer high accuracy and are commonly used to simulate small circuits. At the other end of the spectrum are digital simulators that use functional representations of electronic circuits, typically described using hardware description languages (HDL). These offer the highest performance and capacity, but at relatively lower levels of accuracy. Digital simulators are commonly used to simulate very large circuits.

2　Types of Circuit Simulation

There are three basic types of circuit simulation: analog, digital, and mixed-mode.

Analog circuit simulation involves the use of highly accurate models (i.e., representations) of the electronic circuit to achieve high accuracy. The models include non-linear, linear, and simpler table-based representations of the various electronic devices in the circuit. Analog simulation can run in different modes. These include AC (frequency domain), DC (non-linear quiescent), and transient (time domain). All analog simulators employ algorithms to mathematically analyze the behavior of the electronic circuit in these different modes. They all share the quality of solving matrices to predict the performance of the electronic circuit. Signals are propagated as continuously varying values.

There are two primary types of analog circuit simulators: SPICE and FastSPICE. SPICE simulators use highly accurate non-linear and linear models of electronic devices to analyze the behavior of the circuit. SPICE simulators employ many different integration methods, such as forward Euler, backward Euler, and Newton-Raphson as well as matrix decomposition techniques to compute the response of the entire circuit (i.e., mathematical representation) at every single time point in the simulation period.

By contrast, FastSPICE simulators use simpler table-model representations of electronic devices to analyze circuit behavior. They employ sophisticated algorithms to reduce the complexity of the circuit and partition the circuit based on various criteria, essentially creating a simpler and more modular circuit representation. This representation is then selectively evaluated at a given time point in the simulation period, a process that greatly improves the performance and capacity of the simulation. FastSPICE simulators offer various simulation knobs to help balance the tradeoffs between simulation accuracy and performance.

Digital circuit simulation involves the use of simpler models of the electronic circuit. These models are typically created using HDL. In digital simulation, rather than propagating continuously varying signals, a few discrete voltage levels (primarily logic 0 and logic 1) are propagated.

Analog simulators are used for the analog analyses and digital simulators are used for the digital analyses. Mixed-mode circuit simulation combines the analog and digital simulation approaches. The circuit is partitioned between the two regimes to support the correct level of analysis detail for each part of the circuit. This method of simulation allows for much larger circuits to be simulated in less time with fewer compute resources when compared with analog simulation.

3   Benefits of Circuit Simulation

Circuit simulation provides a critical view into the behavior of electronic circuits. Given the expense and time involved in fabricating electronic circuits, especially ICs, it's much more practical to validate circuit behavior and performance via circuit simulation prior to manufacturing.

Some of the specific areas of validation include:

(1) Memory performance. The read and write access time and latency of memory devices are built from analog circuit simulation of the bit cells and read/write paths inside these memories.

(2) Overall digital simulation accuracy. Digital circuit simulators model the propagation of voltage for logic level 1 and logic level 0. Analog circuit simulation is used to determine the time it takes for a circuit to transition between these voltage levels. This forms the basis for the overall accuracy of the digital circuit simulator.

(3) Noise and crosstalk. Higher level models for noise and crosstalk are developed based on the detailed circuit level analysis of these parasitic effects from analog circuit simulations.

(4) Optimization of high-frequency and high-power circuits. These types of circuits must undergo detailed continuous time analysis to determine their behavior and performance criteria. Analog circuit simulation delivers these important analyses.

(5) Verification. The overall performance and behavior of complex digital circuits (core processors and AI accelerators are examples) are verified with digital circuit simulation.

4　Solutions Synopsys Offers

Synopsys offers a range of analog and digital circuit simulation solutions for a diverse set of use cases and circuit types.

Analog simulation tools include:

(1) PrimeSim Continuum: unified workflow of Synopsys SPICE and FastSPICE simulators.

(2) PrimeSim HSPICE: the gold standard in SPICE simulation.

(3) PrimeSim XA: industry-leading FastSPICE simulator targeting SRAM and custom digital designs.

(4) PrimeSim SPICE: industry's highest performance SPICE simulator targeting analog, RF, and SerDes designs.

(5) PrimeSim Pro: industry-leading FastSPICE simulator targeting DRAM and Flash designs.

(6) PrimeSim Custom Fault: high-performance analog fault simulator targeting full-chip functional safety, test coverage analysis, and chip failure analysis.

(7) PrimeWave Design Environment: newly architected design environment providing comprehensive analysis, improved productivity, and ease of use.

Digital simulation tools include:

(1) VCS: the industry's highest performance digital simulator.

(2) Certitude: functional qualification system.

(3) PowerReplay: early power analysis with RTL simulation data.

(4) Z01X Functional Safety Assurance: high-speed fault simulation solution for IEC 61508 and ISO 26262 compliance.

(5) SaberRD and SaberESD: multi-domain simulation and prototyping and harness design.

New Words

predict	[prɪˈdɪkt]	v.预测，预言
fabrication	[ˌfæbrɪˈkeɪʃn]	n.制造
time-consuming	[ˈtaɪm kənˈsjuːmɪŋ]	adj.费时的；旷日持久的
accuracy	[ˈækjərəsɪ]	n.精确（性），准确（性）
spectrum	[ˈspektrəm]	n.范围；系列
transient	[ˈtrænzrənt]	n.瞬态
		adj.短暂的；转瞬即逝的
matrix	[ˈmeɪtrɪks]	n.矩阵（复数 matrice）
propagate	[ˈprɒpəgeɪt]	v.传播，传送，扩散
employ	[ɪmˈplɔɪ]	v.采用，利用
integration	[ˌɪntɪˈgreɪʃn]	n.结合；整合；一体化
decomposition	[ˌdiːˌkɒmpəˈzɪʃn]	n.分解

compute	[kəmˈpjuːt]	v.计算
response	[rɪˈspɒns]	n.响应，反应
period	[ˈpɪərrəd]	n.阶段；时期
partition	[pɑːˈtɪʃn]	n.划分，分开；分割
		vt.分开，区分；分割
criteria	[kraɪˈtɪərɪə]	n.标准，准则
knob	[nɒb]	n.旋钮，球形把手
balance	[ˈbæləns]	v.平衡，权衡
		n.均衡，平衡（能力）
tradeoff	[ˈtreɪˌɔːf]	n.折衷，权衡
discrete	[dɪˈskriːt]	adj.离散的，非连续
delay	[dɪˈleɪ]	v.延迟，推迟
		n.延期；耽误
validate	[ˈvælɪdeɪt]	vt.验证，证实
access	[ˈækses]	v.访问，存取
latency	[ˈleɪtənsɪ]	n.延迟
cell	[sel]	n.单元
memory	[ˈmemərɪ]	n.内存，存储器
crosstalk	[ˈkrɒstɔːk]	n.串扰
optimization	[ˈɒptəmaɪˈzeɪʃn]	n.最优化
diverse	[daɪˈvɜːs]	adj.不同的，形形色色的
unify	[ˈjuːnɪfaɪ]	vt.统一，使联合，使相同，使一致
workflow	[ˈwɜːkfləʊ]	n.工作流程
coverage	[ˈkʌvərɪdʒ]	n.覆盖范围
failure	[ˈfeɪljə]	n.失败，故障
environment	[ɪnˈvaɪrənmənt]	n.环境
comprehensive	[ˌkɒmprɪˈhensɪv]	adj.全面的；综合性的
assurance	[əˈʃʊərəns]	n.保证

Phrases

circuit simulation	电路仿真
electronic device	电子器件，电子设备
frequency domain	频域
non-linear quiescent	非线性静态
time domain	时域
base on	基于

core processor	核处理器
use case	用例
harness design	线束设计

Abbreviations

DC (direct current)	直流
DRAM (dynamic random access memory)	动态随机存储器
RTL (register transfer level)	寄存器传输级
IEC (International Electrotechnical Commission）	国际电工委员会
ISO (International Organization for Standardization)	国际标准化组织

参考译文

什么是电路仿真?

1 定义

电路仿真是使用各种软件算法创建和分析电子电路模型的过程,这些算法可以预测和验证电路的行为与性能。由于电子电路(尤其是集成电路)的制造既昂贵又耗时,因此在制造之前使用电路仿真器验证电路的行为和性能会更快且更具成本效益。

有不同类型的电路仿真器可以满足精度性能/容量范围内的不同需求。一种是可以精确表示电子电路的模拟仿真器。它们提供高精度,通常用于模拟小型电路。另一种是数字仿真器,它们使用电子电路的功能表示,通常使用硬件描述语言(HDL)进行描述。它们提供最高的性能和容量,但精确度相对较低。数字仿真器通常用于模拟非常大的电路。

2 电路仿真的种类

电路仿真分为三种基本类型:模拟、数字和混合模式。

模拟电路仿真使用电子电路的高精度模型(即表示)实现高精度。这些模型包括电路中各种电子设备的非线性、线性和更简单的基于表的表示。模拟仿真可以在不同模式下运行,包括 AC(频域)、DC(非线性静态)和瞬态(时域)。所有模拟仿真器都采用算法从数学上分析电子电路在这些不同模式下的行为。它们都具有求解矩阵以预测电子电路性能的能力。信号作为连续变化的值传递。

有两种主要类型的模拟电路仿真器:SPICE 和 FastSPICE。SPICE 仿真器使用电子设备的高精度非线性模型和高精度线性模型分析电路的行为。SPICE 仿真器采用许多不同的集成方法，如向前欧拉、向后欧拉、牛顿-拉普森及矩阵分解技术计算整个电路在仿真周期中每个时间点的响应（即数学表示）。

相比之下，FastSPICE 仿真器使用更简单的电子设备的表模型表示来分析电路行为。它们采用精密的算法降低电路的复杂性，并根据各种标准划分电路，从本质上创建更简单、更模块化的电路表示。然后在仿真周期的给定时间点选择性地评估该表示，该过程极大地提高了仿真的性能和容量。FastSPICE 仿真器提供各种仿真旋钮，以帮助权衡仿真精度和性能。

数字电路仿真使用更简单的电子电路模型。这些模型通常使用 HDL 创建。在数字仿真中，不是传递连续变化的信号，而是传递一些离散的电压电平（主要是逻辑 0 和逻辑 1）。

模拟仿真器用于模拟分析，数字仿真器用于数字分析。混合模式电路仿真结合了模拟仿真方法和数字仿真方法。电路在两个机制之间进行划分，以支持电路每个部分的详细分析的正确程度。与模拟仿真相比，这种仿真方法允许在更短的时间内以更少的计算资源对更大的电路进行仿真。

3 电路仿真的好处

电路仿真为研究电子电路的行为提供了一个关键的观点。考虑到制造电子电路（尤其是集成电路）涉及的费用和时间，在制造之前，通过电路仿真验证电路行为和性能是非常实用的。

一些特定的验证领域包括：

（1）内存性能。存储设备的读写访问时间和延迟由这些存储器内的位单元和读/写路径的模拟电路仿真来构建。

（2）整体数字仿真精度。数字电路仿真器模拟逻辑电平 1 和逻辑电平 0 的电压传递。模拟电路仿真用于确定电路在这些电压电平之间转换所需的时间。这构成了数字电路仿真器整体精度的基础。

（3）噪声和串扰。基于对模拟电路仿真中这些寄生效应的详细电路级分析，开发了更高级别的噪声和串扰模型。

（4）高频和大功率电路的优化。这些类型的电路必须经过详细的连续时间分析，以确定它们的行为和性能标准。模拟电路仿真提供了这些重要的分析。

（5）验证。复杂数字电路（以核心处理器和人工智能加速器为例）的整体性能和行为通过数字电路仿真进行验证。

4 Synopsys 提供的解决方案

Synopsys 为各种用例和电路类型提供了一系列模拟和数字电路仿真解决方案。

模拟仿真工具包括：

（1）PrimeSim Continuum：Synopsys SPICE 和 FastSPICE 仿真器的统一工作流程。

（2）PrimeSim HSPICE：SPICE 仿真的黄金标准。

（3）PrimeSim XA：针对 SRAM 和定制数字设计的业界领先的 FastSPICE 仿真器。

（4）PrimeSim SPICE：针对模拟、RF 和 SerDes 设计的业界最高性能的 SPICE 仿真器。

（5）PrimeSim Pro：针对 DRAM 和 Flash 设计的行业领先的 FastSPICE 仿真器。

（6）PrimeSim Custom Fault：针对全芯片功能安全、测试覆盖分析和芯片故障分析的高性能模拟故障仿真器。

（7）PrimeWave Design Environment：全新架构的设计环境提供全面的分析、提高的生产力和易用性。

数字仿真工具包括：

（1）VCS：业界最高性能的数字仿真器。

（2）Certitude：功能鉴定系统。

（3）PowerReplay：使用 RTL 仿真数据进行早期功耗分析。

（4）Z01X 功能安全保证：符合 IEC 61508 和 ISO 26262 标准的高速故障仿真解决方案。

（5）SaberRD 和 SaberESD：多域仿真、原型设计和线束设计。

Exercises

[Ex. 1] Answer the following questions according to Text A.

1. What is electronic design automation (EDA)?

2. What are EDA tools used to do first? What is this segment of EDA called?

3. What are EDA tools used to do second? What is this area of focus known as?

4. What is the goal of monitoring the performance of the device from post-manufacturing test to deployment in the field to do?

5. What are the three tools very sophisticated and complex software programs mainly use to assist chip design and manufacturing artificial intelligence (AI)?

6. What do simulation tools do?

7. What do design tools do?

8. What do verification tools do?

9. What will happen if there is a chip error?

10. Why can ML boost EDA performance?

[Ex. 2] Answer the following questions according to Text B.

1. What is circuit simulation?

2. How many basic types of circuit simulation are there? What are they?

3. What does analog circuit simulation involve?

4. What are the two primary types of analog circuit simulators?

5. What do SPICE simulators and FastSPICE simulators do to analyze the behavior of the circuit?

6. What are the many different integration methods SPICE simulators employ to compute the response of the entire circuit (i.e., mathematical representation) at every single time point in the simulation period?

7. What does digital circuit simulation involve? How are these models typically created?

8. What do some of the specific areas of validation include?

9. What do digital circuit simulators model? What is analog circuit simulation used to determine?

10. What are the digital simulation tools that Synopsys offers?

[Ex. 3] Translate the following terms or phrases from English into Chinese and vice versa.

1. functional verification	1.
2. circuit simulation	2.
3. video process	3.
4. electronic device	4.
5. frequency domain	5.
6. *n.* 标准，准则	6.
7. *v.* 采用，利用	7.
8. *n.* 串扰	8.
9. *n.* 半导体	9.
10. *v.* 干预；篡改	10.

[Ex. 4] Translate the following passage into Chinese.

Simulation of a Circuit Design

Simulation of a circuit design will tell you the electrical behavior of a system for various input signals. The goal is to determine the voltage and current at various locations in the circuit. You could certainly run your simulation by hand, meaning you could calculate the voltage and current throughout the circuit by hand using Kirchhoff's laws and Ohm's law. However, as circuit designs become more complex, writing out calculations by hand can become intractable for even the most skilled engineers. At that point, you can save yourself a considerable amount of time by using a simulation package.

When your design starts to include active or nonlinear devices, such as a diode, the system becomes complicated even further, and a simulation becomes a necessity rather than an option. Although a simulation package does save you a considerable amount of calculation time and expedites analysis, it can be difficult to glean real insights from your simulation without the right analysis strategy.

Some circuits are designed with multiple functional blocks, where each block takes inputs and produces outputs for other portions of the overall circuit. The circuit for a new device can be simulated as an entire system, or the circuit can be simulated in individual blocks. If you design your circuit by dividing it into functional blocks, you can run simulations for each block individually.

Choosing the right type of simulation (analog vs. digital, time domain vs. frequency sweep) really depends on the functionality of the circuit. What type of input signal will the circuit receive? Are you converting between analog inputs and digital data? Is the output intended to be frequency dependent? Is there feedback involved in any portion of the circuit? The answers to these questions and more will help you to make a good choice.

Reading

Top Printed Circuit Design Software

There are many software programs to design printed circuits, whether free of charge or not, from the prototyping phase through to industrialization. How to choose between freeware for DIY[①] fans and complex software suites costing tens of thousands of dollars?

Based on Proto-Electronics client preferences, we have drawn up the top 10 best electronics CAD[②] software programs.

1 EAGLE

EAGLE is a PCB (printed circuit board[③]) design software developed by the German CadSoft Computer GmbH created by Rudolf Hofer and Klaus-Peter Schmidiger in 1988. The company was acquired by Farnell in 2009 and by Autodesk in 2016, a world class software heavyweight with over 2 billion euros of turnover. EAGLE stands for easily applicable graphical layout editor (see Figure 9-1).

---

① DIY: 自己动手做
② CAD: 计算机辅助设计
③ printed circuit board: 印刷电路板，印制电路板

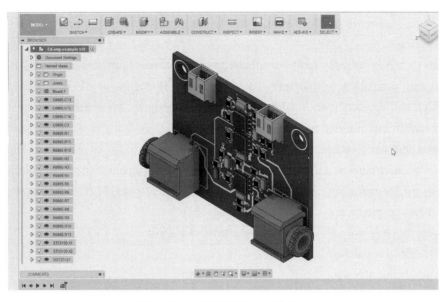

Figure 9-1   EAGLE Work Window

The software is available in 3 versions:

(1) EAGLE Free: the limited trial version for DIY fans.

(2) EAGLE Standard: 99 diagram sheets, 4 signal layers and a 160cm² printed circuit area.

(3) EAGLE Premium: the professional version with 999 diagram sheets, 16 signal layers[1] and an unlimited printed circuit area.

Features and specifications:

(1) Diagram editor (connected to the library[2], electric rules, generation of an interconnection list).

(2) Annotation of changes between the diagram and the PCB.

(3) Diagram hierarchy.

(4) Layout diagram with advanced features.

EAGLE has the advantage of being one of the PCB design software heavyweights. At a reasonable cost of $500/year, it has a significant community[3] that puts tutorials online. It also has an extensive component library and runs in a Mac OS X or Linux environment.

2   Altium Designer

Altium Designer is one of the most popular of the high end PCB design software packages[4] on the market today. It is developed and marketed by Altium Limited. It includes a schematic PCB

---

① layer ['leɪə] *n.*层，层次

② library ['laɪbrərɪ] *n.*库

③ community [kə'mjuːnətɪ] *n.*社区，社团

④ software package: 软件包，程序包

module, and an auto-router and differential pair[①] routing features. It supports track length tuning and 3D modeling.

Altium Designer includes tools for all circuit design tasks: from schematic and HDL design capture, circuit simulation, signal integrity analysis, PCB design to FPGA[②]-based embedded system design and development. In addition, the Altium Designer environment can be customized to meet a wide variety of users' requirements.

Features and specifications:

(1) Design environment with diagrams, layout-routing, documentation and simulation.

(2) Design for manufacturing[③] (DFM) to guarantee that your PCB designs are functional, reliable and easy to produce.

(3) Easy data migration[④] using powerful conversion tools.

(4) 3D[⑤] flex-rigid design.

(5) Printed circuit design.

(6) Diagram design.

(7) Production file output.

3 Proteus

The Proteus electronic CAD solution was developed by Labcenter Electronics Ltd., a company founded by John Jameson in 1988 in the United Kingdom. Widespreaded, Proteus is marketed in over 50 countries (see Figure 9-2).

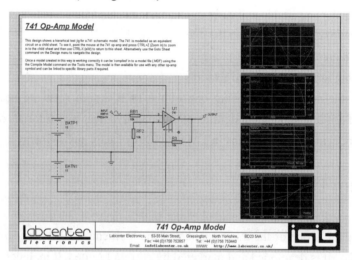

Figure 9-2 Proteus Work Window

---

① differential pair: 差分对

② FPGA: 现场可编程门阵列

③ design for manufacturing: 可制造性设计，面向制造的设计

④ migration [maɪˈɡreɪʃn] n.迁移

⑤ 3D: 三维的

This suite has two main software programs:

(1) Proteus ISI: diagram creation and electric simulation.

(2) Proteus ARES: printed circuit routing solution with automatic component positioning①.

Other available Proteus modules:

1) Proteus VSM

(1) Full built-in workflow.

(2) Diagram design.

(3) Simulation.

(4) Measurement and analysis.

(5) Bug② correction.

(6) Troubleshooting.

2) Proteus PCB design software

(1) PCB design with up to 16 layers of copper.

(2) 14 million components in the library.

(3) Interactive manual routing.

3) Proteus Visual Designer

Combined with Proteus VSM, it provides a complete solution to edit flow diagrams③ and a hardware gallery for a built-in Arduino and Raspberry Pi development environment.

4　KiCad

KiCad is an open source, free printed circuit design software suite. It was developed by Jean-Pierre Charras from the Grenoble IUT in France in 1992. This design software includes diagram management, PCB routing and 3D modelling possibilities for electronics engineers (see Figure 9-3).

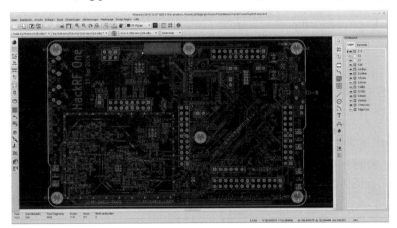

Figure 9-3　KiCad Work Window

---

① positioning [pəˈzɪʃnɪŋ] *n*.配置，布置；定位

② bug [bʌg] *n*.故障

③ flow diagram: 流程图，作业图；框图

Features and specifications:

(1) KiCad: project manager.

(2) Eeschema: electric diagram editor.

(3) Pcbnew: printed circuit editor.

(4) Cvpcb: utility to select the physical imprints[①] of components used on the diagram.

(5) Gerbview: Gerber file viewer.

(6) Pcbcalculator: design aid tool to calculate resistance values, track widths, etc.

5　Cadence OrCAD PCB Designer

Born in 1988 of the merger of SDA Systems and ECAD, Cadence Design Systems is currently a leader on the electronics CAD software market.

Cadence publishes Allegro PCB Designer and OrCAD.

Features and specifications:

1) Diagrams, layout and routing:

(1) Interactive, real time routing with built-in constraints.

(2) Automatic shape creation and update.

(3) Automatic BGA[②] assistance.

2) PSpice simulation and analysis:

(1) Performance and reliability improvement while optimizing costs.

(2) Automatic circuit validation.

(3) Electronic circuit mechanical and electric simulation.

3) OrCAD diagrams:

(1) Symbol editor.

(2) Built-in electronic component search.

(3) Built-in design constraints.

6　DesignSpark

DesignSpark is an electronic CAD software program born of the collaboration between the world leading component distributor RS Components and the Number One Systems software developer (see Figure 9-4).

Features and specifications:

(1) Diagram entry.

(2) Routing and automatic component positioning.

---

① imprint [ɪmˈprɪnt] *n*.印记，痕迹；特征
② BGA: 球栅阵列封装

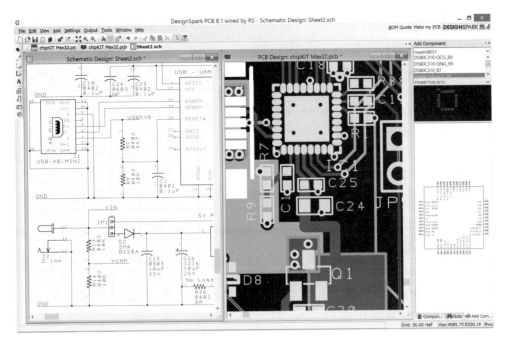

Figure 9-4   DesignSpark Work Window

(3) Project interface to organize design files.

(4) 3D viewer.

(5) Gerber and Excellon drilling file generation.

7 Cadstar

Cadstar is another design tool for the simplest to the most complex multi-layer PCBs.

Cadstar is a full printed circuit board design environment, from initial design to product manufacturing.

Features and specifications:

(1) Printed circuit topology and routing.

(2) Diagram capture.

(3) Analysis, measurement and checks (reliability, signal integrity).

(4) Library management.

(5) Design review for project managers.

8 Sprint-Layout

Sprint-Layout is an electronic prototype design software published by Abacom. Using good ergonomics and capacities worthy of professional software, combined with a very competitive price, Sprint-Layout has become unavoidable for electronics engineers.

Features and specifications:

(1) Automatic PCB routing on two sides.

(2) Extensive traditional and component library.

(3) New component creation.

(4) Gerber and Excellon file generation.

(5) Design-Rule-Check.

9　PADS PCB

PADS is another drawing software program developed by CADLOG, the European leader in industrial electronics software.

Features and specifications:

(1) Diagram entry.

(2) Component libraries (ParQuest integration, Digikey integration).

(3) Project rules.

(4) PCB topology (powerful, interactive routing, DFM and DFT[①] checks, RF[②] module).

(5) Archive management.

---

① DFT: 可测试性设计

② RF: 射频

Unit 10

Text A
Internet of Things (IoT)

扫码听课文

1　What Is Internet of Things (IoT)?

Internet of things, or IoT, is a system of interrelated computing devices, mechanical and digital machines, objects and people that are provided with unique identifiers (UIDs) and the ability to transfer data over a network.

A thing in the internet of things can be a person with a heart monitor implant, a farm animal with a biochip transponder, an automobile that has built-in sensors to alert the driver when tire pressure is low or any other natural or man-made object that can be assigned an internet protocol (IP) address and is able to transfer data over a network.

2　How Does IoT work?

An IoT ecosystem consists of web-enabled smart devices that use embedded systems, such as processors, sensors and communication hardware, to collect, send and act on data they acquire from their environments. IoT devices share the sensor data they collect by connecting to an IoT gateway or other edge devices where data is either sent to the cloud to be analyzed or analyzed locally. Sometimes, these devices communicate with other related devices and act on the information they get from one another. The devices do most of the work without human intervention, although people can interact with the devices — for instance, to set them up, give them instructions or access the data.

3　The Three Layers of IoT Architecture

Even though there's no single IoT architecture that's universally agreed upon, the most basic and widely accepted format is a three-layer architecture It proposes three layers: perception, network and application (see Figure 10-1).

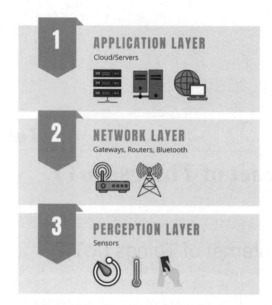

Figure 10-1   Three-Layer IoT Architecture

3.1   Perception

This is the physical layer of the architecture. This is where the sensors and connected devices come into play as they gather various amounts of data as per the need of the project. These can be the edge devices, sensors, and actuators that interact with their environment.

3.2   Network

The data that's collected by all of these devices needs to be transmitted and processed. That's the network layer's job. It connects these devices to other smart objects, servers, and network devices. It also handles the transmission of all of the data.

3.3   Application

The application layer is what the user interacts with. It's responsible for delivering application specific services to the user. This can be a smart home implementation, for example, where users tap a button in the app to turn on a coffee maker.

4   The Four Stages of IoT Architecture

Your infrastructure needs to be able to support the internet of things architecture. The four primary stages listed below are of crucial importance to the overall viability of an IoT implementation (see Figure 10-2).

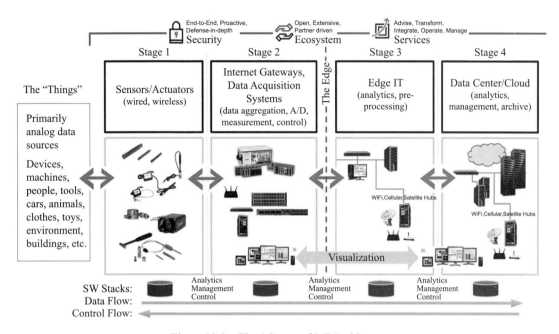

Figure 10-2　The 4 Stages of IoT Architecture

4.1　Connected Objects

An internet of things implementation wouldn't exist without the presence of connected or "smart" objects. These can be wireless sensors or actuators. They react with the environment and make the data they collect available for analysis.

Actuators take this one step further since they are able to interact with the environment in a significant way. For example, they can be used to shut off valves when the water reaches a certain level or simply to switch off a light when the sun rises.

4.2　Internet Gateway

Once the sensors send in the data, it has to be aggregated and converted into digital form so that it can be processed. The second stage of the IoT architecture is to make this happen. It essentially gets the data ready for processing.

The actual task of aggregating and converting the data is up to the data acquisition system. It is connected to the sensors and actuators. It compiles all of their data and then converts it into digital form so that it can be routed over the network by the internet gateway.

4.3　Edge IT Systems

Pre-processing and enhanced analytics of the data are performed in the third stage of an IoT architecture. Edge IT systems are responsible for carrying out these tasks. Since IoT systems collect a significant amount of data and consequently require a lot of bandwidth, these Edge IT systems perform a vital task in reducing the load on the core IT infrastructure.

Edge IT systems use machine learning and visualization technologies to generate results from the collected data. Machine learning algorithms provide insights while the visualization technology presents the data in a way that's easy to understand.

4.4 Data Centers and Cloud Storage

The data needs to be stored for further in-depth analysis. This is why data storage is such an important stage of an IoT architecture. It helps with follow-up revision for feedback as well. Cloud storage is the preferred storage method in IoT implementations.

5 IoT Standards

There are several emerging IoT standards, including the following:

(1) 6LoWPAN (IPv6 over Low-Power Wireless Personal Area Networks) is an open standard defined by the Internet Engineering Task Force (IETF). 6LoWPAN standard enables any low-power radio to communicate with the internet, including 804.15.4, bluetooth low energy (BLE) and Z-Wave (for home automation).

(2) ZigBee is a low-power, low-data rate wireless network used mainly in industrial settings. ZigBee is based on the Institute of Electrical and Electronics Engineers (IEEE) 802.15.4 standard. The ZigBee Alliance created Dotdot, the universal language for IoT that enables smart objects to work securely on any network and understand each other.

(3) LiteOS is a UNIX-like operating system (OS) for wireless sensor networks. LiteOS supports smartphones, wearables, intelligent manufacturing applications, smart homes and the internet of vehicles (IoV). The OS also serves as a smart device development platform.

(4) OneM2M is a machine-to-machine service layer that can be embedded in software and hardware to connect devices. The global standardization body, OneM2M, was created to develop reusable standards to enable IoT applications across different verticals to communicate.

(5) DDS (data distribution service) was developed by the Object Management Group (OMG) and is an IoT standard for real-time, scalable and high-performance M2M communication.

(6) AMQP (advanced message queuing protocol) is an open source published standard for asynchronous messaging by wire. AMQP enables encrypted and interoperable messaging between organizations and applications. The protocol is used in client-server messaging and in IoT device management.

(7) CoAP (constrained application protocol) is a protocol designed by the IETF that specifies how low-power, compute-constrained devices can operate in the internet of things.

(8) LoRaWAN (long range wide area network) is a protocol for WANs designed to support huge networks, such as smart cities, with millions of low-power devices.

6   IoT Devices

6.1   What Are IoT Devices?

IoT devices are the computing devices that are connected to a network and have the ability to transmit data. These devices can communicate and interact over the internet. They can also be remotely monitored and controlled.

6.2   How Do IoT Devices Work?

IoT devices vary in terms of functionality, but IoT devices have some similarities in how they work. First, IoT devices are physical objects designed to interact with the real world in some way. The devices might be sensors on an assembly line or intelligent security cameras.

The devices themselves include an integrated CPU, network adapter and firmware. They are usually built on an open source platform. In most cases, IoT devices are connected to a DHCP (dynamic host configuration protocol) server and they acquire an IP address that the devices can use to function on the network. Some IoT devices are directly accessible over the public internet, but most are designed to operate exclusively on private networks.

Although not an absolute requirement, many IoT devices are configured and managed through a software application.

6.3   What Is IoT device management?

Several challenges can hinder the successful deployment of an IoT system and its connected devices, including security, interoperability, power/processing capabilities, scalability and availability. Many of these can be addressed with IoT device management either by adopting standard protocols or using services offered by a vendor.

Device management helps companies integrate, organize, monitor and remotely manage internet-enabled devices at scale. Such features include:

(1) Device registration and activation.

(2) Device authentication/authorization.

(3) Device configuration.

(4) Device provisioning.

(5) Device monitoring and diagnostics.

(6) Device troubleshooting.

(7) Device firmware updates.

7 IoT Security and Privacy Issues

IoT connects billions of devices to the internet and involves the use of billions of data points, all of which need to be secured. Due to its expanded attack surface, IoT security and IoT privacy are cited as major concerns.

Because IoT devices are closely connected, what a hacker has to do is to exploit one vulnerability to manipulate all the data, and render it unusable. Manufacturers that don't update their devices regularly — or at all — leave them vulnerable to cybercriminals.

Additionally, connected devices often ask users to input their personal information, including names, ages, addresses, phone numbers and even social media accounts — information that's invaluable to hackers.

Hackers aren't the only threat to IoT. Privacy is another major concern for IoT users. For instance, companies that make and distribute consumer IoT devices could use those devices to obtain and sell users' personal data.

Beside leaking personal data, IoT poses a risk to critical infrastructure, including electricity, transportation and financial services.

New Words

interrelate	[ˌɪntərɪˈleɪt]	v.相互关联，相互影响
biochip	[ˈbaɪətʃɪp]	n.生物芯片
built-in	[ˌbɪlt ˈɪn]	adj.嵌入的；内置的
man-made	[ˌmæn ˈmeɪd]	adj.人造的，人工的
collect	[kəˈlekt]	v.收集
gateway	[ˈgeɪtweɪ]	n.网关；入口；途径
intervention	[ˌɪntəˈvenʃn]	n.介入，干涉，干预
perception	[pəˈsepʃn]	n.感知，知觉，觉察
stage	[steɪdʒ]	n.阶段
pre-processing	[priː ˈprəsesɪŋ]	n.预处理，前处理
wearable	[ˈweərəbl]	adj.可穿戴的，可佩带的
platform	[ˈplætfɔːm]	n.平台
standardization	[ˌstændədaɪˈzeɪʃn]	n.标准化
reusable	[ˌriːˈjuːzəbl]	adj.可再用的，可重用的
asynchronous	[eɪˈsɪŋkrənəs]	adj.异步的
accessible	[əkˈsesəbl]	adj.可访问，可进入
interoperability	[ˈɪntərɒpərəˈbɪlɪtɪ]	n.互用性，协同工作的能力
availability	[əˌveɪləˈbɪlətɪ]	n.可用性；有效性

registration	[ˌredʒɪˈstreɪʃn]	n.登记，注册
activation	[ˌæktɪˈveɪʃn]	n.激活
authentication	[ɔːˌθentɪˈkeɪʃn]	n.身份验证；认证
authorization	[ˌɔːθəraɪˈzeɪʃn]	n.批准；授权
diagnostic	[ˌdaɪəɡˈnɒstɪk]	adj.诊断的
		n.诊断，诊断程序
firmware	[ˈfɜːmweə]	n.固件
security	[sɪˈkjʊərəti]	n.安全；保护，防护
privacy	[ˈprɪvəsɪ]	n.隐私，秘密
exploit	[ɪkˈsplɔɪt]	vt.利用
vulnerability	[ˌvʌlnərəˈbɪləti]	n.弱点；脆弱性
render	[ˈrendə]	v.致使，造成
cybercriminal	[ˈsaɪbəˈkrɪmɪnəl]	n.计算机罪犯，网络犯罪
threat	[θret]	n.威胁

Phrases

biochip transponder	生物芯片应答器
smart device	智能设备
edge device	边缘设备；边界设备
physical layer	物理层
application layer	应用层
smart home	智能家居
shut off	停止，关掉
carry out	执行，进行；完成
intelligent manufacturing	智能制造
open source	开放源码，开源
smart city	智慧城市
device management	设备管理

Abbreviations

IoT (internet of things)	物联网
UID (unique identifier)	唯一标识符
IP (internet protocol)	互联网协议
6LoWPAN (IPv6 over low power wireless personal area networks)	低功耗无线个人区域网络上的 IPv6

IETF (Internet Engineering Task Force)	互联网工程任务组
BLE (bluetooth low energy)	蓝牙低能量
IEEE (Institute of Electrical and Electronics Engineers)	电气电子工程师学会
IoV (internet of vehicles)	车联网
DDS (data distribution service)	数据分发服务
OMG (Object Management Group)	对象管理组织
AMQP (advanced message queuing protocol)	高级消息队列协议
CoAP (constrained application protocol)	受限应用协议
LoRaWAN (long range wide area network)	远程广域网
DHCP (dynamic host configuration protocol)	动态主机配置协议

参考译文

物 联 网

1 什么是物联网?

物联网（IoT）是一个由相互关联的计算设备、机械和数字机器、物体和人员组成的系统，这些设备具有唯一标识符（UID），并且能够通过网络传输数据。

物联网中的物体可以是一个植入了心脏监护仪的人、一个带有生物芯片应答器的农场动物、一辆内置了在轮胎压力低时提醒驾驶员的传感器的汽车，或者任何其他可以分配互联网协议（IP）地址并能够通过网络传输数据的自然或人造物体。

2 物联网是如何工作的?

物联网生态系统由支持网络的智能设备组成，这些设备使用嵌入式系统（如处理器、传感器和通信硬件）收集、发送和处理从环境中获取的数据。物联网设备通过连接到物联网网关或其他边缘设备共享它们收集的传感器数据，在这些设备中，数据被发送到云端进行分析或在本地分析。有时，这些设备与其他相关设备通信，并根据彼此获得的信息采取行动。尽管人们可以与这些设备进行交互，如设置它们、给它们指令或访问数据，但这些设备在没有人工干预的情况下完成了大部分工作。

3 物联网的三层结构

尽管没有一种物联网结构得到普遍认可，但最基本、最广泛被接受的格式是三层结构。它提出了三个层次：感知、网络和应用，如图 10-1 所示。

（图略）

3.1 感知

这是三层结构的物理层,是传感器和连接设备发挥作用的地方,因为它们根据项目的需要收集不同数量的数据。它们可以是与环境交互的边缘设备、传感器和执行器。

3.2 网络

所有这些设备收集的数据都需要传输和处理。这是网络层的工作。它将这些设备连接到其他智能物体、服务器和网络设备。它还处理所有数据的传输。

3.3 应用

应用层与用户交互。它负责向用户提供特定应用程序的服务。这可以是一个智能家居实现,如用户单击应用程序中的按钮打开咖啡机。

4 物联网结构的 4 个阶段

基础设施需要能够支持物联网结构。下面列出 4 个主要阶段,这对物联网实施的整体可行性至关重要,如图 10-2 所示。

(图略)

4.1 连接物体

如果没有互联或"智能"物体,就不可能实现物联网。它们可以是无线传感器或执行器。它们会对环境做出反应,并使它们收集的数据可用于分析。

执行器更进一步,因为它们能够以一种重要的方式与环境进行交互。例如,当水位达到一定水平时,它们可以用来关闭阀门,或者在太阳升起时简单地关灯。

4.2 互联网网关

传感器发送数据后,必须将其聚合并转换为数字形式,以便进行处理。物联网结构的第二阶段实现这一点。它本质上是为处理数据做准备。

聚合和转换数据的实际任务由数据采集系统完成。它与传感器和执行器相连。它编译所有数据,然后将其转换为数字形式,以便通过互联网网关在网络上传输。

4.3 边缘 IT 系统

在物联网体系结构的第三阶段执行数据的预处理和增强分析。边缘 IT 系统负责执行这些任务。由于物联网系统收集大量数据,因此需要很大的带宽,这些边缘 IT 系统在降低核心 IT 基础设施的负载方面发挥着至关重要的作用。

边缘 IT 系统使用机器学习和可视化技术从收集的数据生成结果。机器学习算法提供洞察力，而可视化技术以易于理解的方式呈现数据。

4.4 数据中心和云存储

数据需要存储起来，以便进一步深入分析，这就是为什么数据存储是物联网结构中如此重要的一个阶段。这也有助于对反馈进行后续修改。云存储是物联网实施中的首选存储方法。

5 物联网标准

有几种新兴的物联网标准，包括：

（1）6LoWPAN（低功耗无线个人区域网络上的 IPv6）是互联网工程任务组（IETF）定义的开放标准。6LoWPAN 标准允许任何低功率无线电设备与互联网通信，该标准包括 804.15.4、蓝牙低能量（BLE）和 Z-Wave（用于家庭自动化）。

（2）ZigBee 是一种低功耗、低数据速率的无线网络，主要用于工业环境。ZigBee 基于电气电子工程师学会（IEEE）的 802.15.4 标准。ZigBee 联盟创建了物联网通用语言 Dotdot，使智能物体能够在任何网络上安全工作并相互理解。

（3）LiteOS 是用于无线传感器网络的类 UNIX 操作系统（OS）。LiteOS 支持智能手机、可穿戴设备、智能制造应用程序、智能家居和车联网（IoV）。该操作系统还可以作为智能设备开发平台。

（4）OneM2M 是一种机器到机器的服务层，可以嵌入软件和硬件以连接设备。全球标准化机构 OneM2M 的成立是为了开发可重复使用的标准，使不同垂直领域的物联网应用程序能够进行通信。

（5）DDS（数据分发服务）由对象管理组织（OMG）开发，是实时、可扩展和高性能 M2M 通信的物联网标准。

（6）AMQP（高级消息队列协议）是一个开源、针对有线异步消息传递发布的标准。AMQP 支持组织和应用程序之间的加密和互操作消息传递。该协议用于客户-服务器消息传递和物联网设备管理。

（7）CoAP（受限应用协议）是 IETF 设计的一种协议，用于指定低功耗、计算受限的设备如何在物联网中运行。

（8）LoRaWAN（远程广域网）是一种用于广域网的协议，旨在支持具有数百万低功耗设备的大型网络，如智能城市。

6 物联网设备

6.1 什么是物联网设备？

物联网设备是连接到网络并具有传输数据能力的计算设备。这些设备可以通过互联网进行通信和交互。它们也可以被远程监控和控制。

6.2　物联网设备如何工作？

物联网设备在功能上各不相同，但在工作方式上有一些相似之处。首先，物联网设备是以某种方式与现实世界交互的物理物体。这些设备可能是装配线上的传感器或智能安全摄像头。

这些设备本身包括一个集成的 CPU、网络适配器和固件。它们通常建立在开源平台上。在大多数情况下，物联网设备连接到 DHCP（动态主机配置协议）服务器，并获取设备可用于在网络上运行的 IP 地址。一些物联网设备可以通过公共互联网直接访问，但大多数设备设计为仅在专用网络上运行。

虽然不是绝对要求，但许多物联网设备都通过软件应用程序进行配置和管理。

6.3　什么是物联网设备管理？

一些挑战可能会阻碍物联网系统及其连接设备的成功部署，包括安全性、互操作性、电源/处理能力、可扩展性和可用性。通过采用标准协议或使用供应商提供的服务，物联网设备管理可以解决其中许多问题。

设备管理帮助公司大规模集成、组织、监控和远程管理支持互联网的设备。这些功能包括：

（1）设备注册和激活。

（2）设备认证/授权。

（3）设备配置。

（4）设备置备。

（5）设备监控和诊断。

（6）设备故障排除。

（7）设备固件更新。

7　物联网安全和隐私问题

物联网将数十亿台设备连接到互联网，涉及数十亿个数据点的使用，所有这些数据点都需要得到保护。由于其攻击面扩大，物联网安全和物联网隐私被列为主要问题。

由于物联网设备紧密相连，黑客要做的就是利用一个漏洞操纵所有数据，并使其无法使用。不定期或根本不更新设备的制造商容易受到网络罪犯的攻击。

此外，联网设备通常会要求用户输入个人信息，包括姓名、年龄、地址、电话号码、社交媒体账户，这些信息对黑客来说非常宝贵。

黑客不是物联网的唯一威胁。隐私是物联网用户的另一个主要担忧。例如，生产和分销消费物联网设备的公司可以使用这些设备获取和销售用户的个人数据。

除了泄露个人数据，物联网还对电力、交通和金融服务等关键基础设施构成风险。

扫码听课文

Text B

Cloud Computing

1　What Is Cloud Computing?

The internet is changing the way we conduct business and interact. Traditionally, hardware and software are fully contained on a user's computer. This means that you access your data and programs exclusively within your own computer.

Cloud computing allows you to access your data and programs outside of your own computing environment. Rather than storing your data and software on your personal computer or server, it is stored in "the cloud". This could include applications, databases, email and file services.

A common factor to consider when using cloud computing is renting versus buying. Essentially, you rent capacity (server space or access to software) from a cloud service provider, and connect over the internet. Instead of buying your own IT requirements, you are renting from a service provider, paying for only the resources you use.

Cloud computing has 4 models in terms of different access and security options. Before you move your data into the cloud, you will need to consider which model works best for your business and data needs.

1.1　Private Cloud

A private cloud is where the services and infrastructures are maintained and managed by you or a third party. This option reduces the potential security and control risks, and will suit you if your data and applications are a core part of your business and you need a higher degree of security or have sensitive data requirements.

1.2　Community Cloud

A community cloud exists where several organizations share access to a private cloud, with similar security considerations. For example, a series of franchises have their own public clouds, but they are hosted remotely in a private environment.

1.3　Public Cloud

A public cloud is where the services are stored off-site and accessed over the internet. The storage is managed by an external organization such as Google or Microsoft. This service offers the greatest level of flexibility and cost saving; however, it is more vulnerable than private clouds.

1.4 Hybrid Cloud

A hybrid cloud model takes advantages of both public and private cloud services. By spreading your options across different cloud models, you gain the benefits of each model.

For example, you could use a public cloud for your emails to save on large storage costs, while keeping your highly sensitive data safe and secure behind your firewall in a private cloud.

2 How Does Cloud Computing Work?

There are three main types of cloud computing service models available, commonly known as software as a service (SaaS), infrastructure as a service (IaaS) and platform as a service (PaaS).

Depending on your needs, your business could use one of these service models, or a mixture of the three.

2.1 Software as a Service

SaaS is the most common form of cloud computing for small businesses. You can access internet-hosted software applications using a browser, rather than traditional applications stored on your own PC or server. The software application host is responsible for controlling and maintaining the application, including software updates and settings. You, as a user, have limited control over the application and configuration settings. A typical example of a SaaS is a Web-based mail service or customer relationship management system.

2.2 Infrastructure as a Service

IaaS typically means buying or renting your computer power and disk space from an external service provider. This option allows you to access through a private network or over the internet. The service provider maintains the computer hardware including CPU processing, memory, data storage and network connectivity.

2.3 Platform as a Service

PaaS can be described as a crossover of both SaaS and IaaS. Essentially you rent the hardware, operating systems, storage and network capacity that IaaS provides, as well as the software servers and application environments. PaaS offers you more control over the technical aspects of your computing setup and the ability to customize to suit your needs.

3   Benefits of Cloud Computing

Cloud computing offers your business many benefits. It allows you the flexibility of connecting to your business anywhere any time. With the growing number of Web-enabled devices used in today's business environment (e.g. smartphones, tablets), it is even easier access to your data. There are many benefits to moving your business to the cloud.

3.1   Reduced IT Costs

Moving to cloud computing may reduce the cost of managing and maintaining your IT systems. Rather than purchasing expensive systems and equipment for your business, you can reduce your costs by using the resources of your cloud computing service provider. You may be able to reduce your operating costs because:

(1) The cost of system upgrades, new hardware and software may be included in your contract.

(2) You no longer need to pay wages for expert staff.

(3) Your energy consumption costs may be reduced.

(4) There are fewer time delays.

3.2   Scalability

Your business can scale up or scale down your operation and storage needs quickly to suit your situation, allowing flexibility as your needs change. Rather than purchasing and installing expensive upgrades yourself, your cloud computer service provider can handle this for you. Using the cloud frees up your time so you can get on with running your business.

3.3   Business Continuity

Protecting your data and systems is an important part of business continuity planning. Whether you experience a natural disaster, power failure or other crisis, having your data stored in the cloud ensures it is backed up and protected in a secure and safe location. Being able to access your data again quickly allows you to conduct business as usual, minimize any downtime and loss of productivity.

3.4   Collaboration Efficiency

Collaboration in a cloud environment gives your business the ability to communicate and share more easily outside of the traditional methods. If you are working on a project across different locations, you could use cloud computing to give employees, contractors and third parties access to the same files. You could also choose a cloud computing model that makes it easy for you to share your records with your advisers. For example, you could share accounting records with your accountant or financial adviser in a quick and secure way.

3.5   Flexibility of Work Practices

Cloud computing allows employees to be more flexible in their work practices. For example, you have the ability to access data from home, on holiday, or via the commute to and from work. If you need access to your data while you are off-site, you can connect to your virtual office, quickly and easily.

3.6   Access to Automatic Updates

Access to automatic updates for your IT requirements may be included in your service fee. Your system will regularly be updated with the latest technology by your cloud computing service provider. This could include up-to-date versions of software, as well as upgrades to servers and computer processing power.

4   Risks of Cloud Computing

Before considering cloud computing technology, it is important to understand the risks involved when moving your business into the cloud. You should carry out a risk assessment before any control is handed over to a service provider.

4.1   Privacy Agreement and Service Level Agreement

You will need to have suitable agreements in place with your service providers before services commence. This will safeguard you against certain risks and also outline the responsibilities of each party in the form of a service level agreement (SLA). You should read the SLA and ensure that you understand what you are agreeing to before you sign. Make sure that you understand the responsibilities of the service provider, as well as your own obligations.

4.2   Security and Data Protection

You must consider how your data will be stored and secured when outsourcing to a third party. This should be outlined in the agreement with your service provider, and must control security risks. It must cover who has access to the data and the security measures must be in place to protect your data.

4.3   Location of Data

Cloud computing service providers can be located at home or abroad. Before committing, you should investigate where your data is being stored and which privacy and security laws will apply to the data.

New Words

interact	[ˌɪntərˈækt]	v.交互，交流，沟通；相互作用；互相影响
analogy	[əˈnælədʒɪ]	n.类似，相似；类推
option	[ˈɒpʃn]	n.选项；选择权
suit	[suːt]	vt.适合于
		vi.合适，相称
degree	[dɪˈgriː]	n.程度；度数
off-site	[ˈɔːfˈsaɪt]	adv.站外；装置外
flexibility	[ˌfleksəˈbɪlətɪ]	n.柔韧性，机动性，灵活性
spread	[spred]	v.伸开，展开；（使）传播，（使）散布
set	[set]	vt.设置，放置，安置
setup	[ˈsetʌp]	n.设置，安装
continuity	[ˌkɒntrɪˈnjuːətɪ]	n.连续性，继续
disaster	[dɪˈzɑːstə]	n.灾难
crisis	[ˈkraɪsɪs]	n.危机；决定性时刻，紧要关头
collaboration	[kəˌlæbəˈreɪʃn]	n.合作，协作
record	[ˈrekɔːd]	n.记录，记载；档案
accountant	[əˈkaʊntənt]	n.会计人员，会计师
responsibility	[rɪˌspɒnsəˈbɪlɪtɪ]	n.责任，职责
obligation	[ˌɒblɪˈgeɪʃn]	n.义务，责任
outsource	[ˈaʊtsɔːs]	vt.外购，外包
location	[ləʊˈkeɪʃn]	n.位置，场所

Phrases

cloud computing	云计算
personal computer	个人计算机
server space	服务器空间
cloud service provider	云服务提供商，云服务提供者
in terms of	根据；就……而言
private cloud	私有云，专用云
third party	第三方
community cloud	社区云
public cloud	公共云
cost saving	节省成本
hybrid cloud	混合云
customer relationship management	客户关系管理
disk space	磁盘空间

be described as	被描述为
operating cost	运营成本
energy consumption cost	电力消耗成本，能源消耗成本
natural disaster	自然灾难
financial adviser	财务顾问
virtual office	虚拟办公室

Abbreviations

SaaS (software as a service)	软件即服务
IaaS (infrastructure as a service)	基础设施即服务
PaaS (platform as a service)	平台即服务
SLA (service level agreement)	服务水平协议，服务等级协定

参考译文

云 计 算

1 什么是云计算?

互联网正在改变人们开展业务和交互的方式。传统上，硬件和软件完全包含在用户的计算机中，这意味着用户只能访问自己计算机上的数据和程序。

云计算使用户可以访问自己的计算环境之外的数据和程序。它不是将数据和软件存储在个人计算机或服务器上，而是存储在"云"中。这可能包括应用程序、数据库、电子邮件和文件服务。

使用云计算常常需要考虑租赁还是购买。本质上，用户是从云服务提供商租用容量（服务器空间或对软件的访问权），然后通过互联网连接。用户无须购买自己的IT需求，而是从服务提供商处租用，仅需为使用的资源付费。

就不同的访问和安全选项而言，云计算有4种模型。在将数据移到云中之前，用户需要考虑哪种模型最适合业务和数据需求。

1.1 私有云

私有云是用户或第三方维护和管理服务和基础设施的地方。如果用户的数据和应用程序是业务的核心部分，并且需要更高级别的安全性或对数据要求很在意，该选项可降低潜在的安全和控制风险，非常适合。

1.2 社区云

社区云是多个组织出于相似的安全考虑，共享对私有云的访问。例如，一系列专营商都有自己的公共云，但是它们是在私有环境中远程托管的。

1.3 公共云

公共云将服务存储在异地并通过互联网访问。存储由外部组织（如谷歌或微软）管理。该服务提供了最大程度的灵活性且节省成本，但是它比私有云更容易受到攻击。

1.4 混合云

混合云模型利用了公共云服务和私有云服务的优势。通过将选择分散在不同的云模型中，可以获得每种模型的好处。

例如，可以将公共云用于电子邮件，以节省大量存储成本，同时把高度敏感的数据保存在防火墙后面的私有云中，使其安全。

2 云计算如何工作?

共有三种主要类型的云计算服务模型，通常称为软件即服务（SaaS）、基础设施即服务（IaaS）和平台即服务（PaaS）。

根据需求，企业既可以使用其中一种服务模型，也可以混合使用这三种服务模型。

2.1 SaaS

SaaS 是小型企业中最常见的云计算形式。可以使用浏览器访问互联网托管的软件应用程序，而不是使用传统的存储在自己的 PC 或服务器上的应用程序。软件应用程序主机负责控制和维护应用程序，包括软件更新和设置。用户对应用程序和配置设置的控制有限。SaaS 的典型示例是基于 Web 的邮件服务或客户关系管理系统。

2.2 IaaS

IaaS 通常意味着从外部服务提供商那里为计算机购买或租用性能和磁盘空间。该选项使用户可以通过专用网络或互联网访问资源。服务提供商维护计算机硬件（包括 CPU 处理、内存、数据存储）和网络连接。

2.3 PaaS

PaaS 可以描述为 SaaS 和 IaaS 的交叉。本质上租用了 IaaS 提供的硬件、操作系统、存储和网络容量，以及软件服务器和应用程序环境。PaaS 使用户可以更好地管理计算设置。并可以进行定制以适应需求。

3 云计算的好处

云计算为业务带来许多好处。它使用户可以随时随地灵活地连接业务。随着当今商业环境中使用的支持网络的设备（如智能手机、平板电脑）数量的不断增加，访问数据变得更加容易。将业务迁移到云有很多好处。

3.1 降低 IT 成本

迁移到云计算可以减少管理和维护 IT 系统的成本。可以通过使用云计算服务提供商的资源降低成本，而不必为企业购买昂贵的系统和设备。可能能够降低运营成本，因为：

（1）合同中可能包含系统升级、新的硬件和软件的成本。

（2）不再需要为专业人员支付工资。

（3）能源消耗成本可能会减少。

（4）时间延迟更少。

3.2 可扩展性

企业可以根据情况快速扩展或缩减运行和存储需求，并根据需求的变化提供灵活性。云计算机服务提供商可以解决此问题，升级时不必自己购买和安装昂贵的设备。使用云可以节省时间，以继续经营自己的业务。

3.3 业务连续性

保护数据和系统是业务连续性计划的重要组成部分。无论遇到自然灾害、电源故障还是其他危机，将数据存储在云中都可以确保在安全的位置备份和保护数据。可以再次快速访问数据使用户能够照常开展业务，从而最大限度地减少停机时间和生产力损失。

3.4 协作效率

在云环境中的协作使企业能够在传统方法之外更轻松地进行通信和共享。如果用户正从事的项目跨越不同位置，则使用云计算能让员工、承包商和第三方访问相同的文件。还可以选择一种云计算模型，以轻松地与顾问共享记录。例如，可以快速安全地与会计或财务顾问共享会计记录。

3.5 工作方式的灵活性

云计算使员工可以更加灵活地开展工作。例如，可以在家中、度假时或上下班途中访问数据。如果需要不在现场时访问数据，则可以快速轻松地连接到虚拟办公室。

3.6 访问自动更新

服务费中可能包含对 IT 要求的自动更新的访问权限。云服务提供商将定期使用最新技术对系统进行更新。这可能包括软件版本更新及服务器和计算机处理能力的升级。

4 云计算的风险

在考虑云计算技术之前，重要的是要了解将业务迁移到云中时涉及的风险。在将任何控制权移交给服务提供商之前，应该进行风险评估。

4.1 隐私协议和服务水平协议

服务开始之前，需要与服务提供商达成适当的协议。这将保护用户免受某些风险的侵害，并以服务等级协定（SLA）的形式概述各方的责任。应该阅读 SLA，并确保在签署前了解将同意的内容，包括服务提供商的职责及用户自己的义务。

4.2 安全性和数据保护

当外包给第三方时，必须考虑如何存储和保护数据。在与服务提供商的协议中应该对此进行概述，并且必须控制安全风险。它必须涵盖有权访问数据的人员，并且必须采取安全措施保护数据。

4.3 数据位置

云计算服务提供商可以位于国内或国外。在提交之前，应该调查数据的存储位置及哪些隐私和安全法将适用于该数据。

Exercises

[Ex. 1] Answer the following questions according to Text A.

1. What is internet of things (IoT)?

2. What does an IoT ecosystem consist of?

3. What are the three layers of IoT architecture?

4. What is the application layer responsible for?

5. What are the four stages of IoT architecture?

6. What does 6LoWPAN standard enable?

7. What is OneM2M?

8. What are IoT devices?

9. What does device management help companies to do?

10. What do connected devices often ask users to do?

[Ex. 2] Answer the following questions according to Text B.

1. What does cloud computing allow you to do?

2. What is a private cloud? What does this option do?

3. Where does a community cloud exist? Please give an example.

4. What is a public cloud? How is the storage managed? What does this service offer?

5. How many main types of cloud computing service models are available? What are they commonly known as?

6. What is SaaS?

7. What does IaaS mean? What does this option allow you to do?

8. Why may you be able to reduce your operating costs?

9. What doe collaboration in a cloud environment do? If you are working on a project across different locations, what could you use cloud computing to do?

10. What is it important to do before considering cloud computing technology?

[Ex. 3] Translate the following terms or phrases from English into Chinese and vice versa.

1. application layer	1.
2. intelligent manufacturing	2.
3. smart device	3.
4. cloud computing	4.
5. edge device	5.
6. *n.*可用性；有效性	6.
7. *n.*固件	7.
8. *vt.*利用	8.
9. *n.*柔韧性，机动性，灵活性	9.
10. *adj.*可穿戴的，可佩带的	10.

[Ex. 4] Translate the following passage into Chinese.

What Is Cloud Storage?

Cloud storage is a service model in which data is transmitted and stored on remote storage systems, where it is maintained, managed, backed up and made available to users over a network — typically, the internet. Users generally pay for their cloud data storage on a per-consumption, monthly rate.

Cloud storage is based on a virtualized storage infrastructure with accessible interfaces, near-instant elasticity and scalability, multi-tenancy, and metered resources.

Advantages of cloud storage:

(1) Pay as you go. With a cloud storage service, customers only pay for the storage they use, eliminating the need for big capital expenses. While cloud storage costs are recurring, rather than a one-time purchase, they are often so low that, even as an ongoing expense, they may still be less than the cost of maintaining an in-house system.

(2) Utility billing. Because customers only pay for the capacity they use, cloud storage costs can decrease as usage drops. This is in stark contrast to using an in-house storage system, which will likely be over configured to handle anticipated growth. A company will pay for more than it needs initially, and the cost of the storage will never decrease.

(3) Global availability. Cloud storage is typically available from any system, anywhere and at any time; users do not have to worry about operating system (OS) capability or complex allocation processes.

(4) Ease of use. Cloud storage is easy to access and use, so developers, software testers and business users can get up and run quickly without having to wait for an IT (information technology) team to allocate and configure storage resources.

(5) Off-site security. By its very nature, public cloud storage offers a way to move copies of data to a remote site for backup and security purposes. Again, this represents a significant cost savings when compared to a company maintaining its own remote facility.

Reading

The Important Applications of Internet of Things (IoT)

The internet of things (IoT) is a term that refers to the connection of objects to each other and to humans through the Internet.

The applications of IoT technologies are multiple, because it is adjustable[1] to almost any technology that is capable of providing relevant information about its own operation, about the performance of an activity and even about the environmental conditions that we need to monitor and control at a distance.

Nowadays, many companies are adopting this technology to simplify, improve, automate and control different processes. Here, we'll show some of the surprising practical applications of the IoT.

---

① adjustable [ə'dʒʌstəbl] *adj.*可调整的，可调节的

1 Wearables①

Virtual glasses, fitness bands to monitor for example calorie expenditure② and heart beats, or GPS tracking belts are just some examples of wearable devices that we have been using for some time now. Companies such as Google, Apple, Samsung and others have developed and introduced the Internet of Things and the application thereof into our daily lives.

These are small and energy efficient devices③, which are equipped with sensors, with the necessary hardware for measurements and readings, and with software to collect and organize data and information about users.

2 Health

The use of wearables or sensors connected to patients allows doctors to monitor a patient's condition outside the hospital and in real-time. Through continuously monitoring certain metrics and automatic alerts on their vital signs④, the internet of things helps to improve the care for patients and the prevention of lethal events in high-risk patients.

Another use is the integration of IoT technology into hospital beds, giving way to smart beds, equipped with special sensors to observe vital signs, blood pressure and body temperature, among others.

3 Traffic Monitoring

The internet of things can be very useful in the management of vehicular traffic in large cities.

When we use our mobile phones as sensors, which collect and share data from our vehicles through applications such as Waze or Google Maps, we are using the internet of things to inform us and at the same time contribute to traffic monitoring — showing the conditions of the different routes, and feeding and improving the information on the different routes to the same destination, distance, estimated time of arrival.

4 Fleet⑤ Management

The installation of sensors in fleet vehicles helps to establish an effective interconnectivity between the vehicles and their managers as well as between the vehicles and their drivers. Both the driver and the manager/owner can know all kinds of details about the status, operation and needs of the vehicle, just by accessing the software in charge of collecting, processing and organizing the

---

① wearable ['weərəbl] *adj.*可穿戴的；*n.*可穿戴物
② calorie expenditure：热量消耗
③ energy efficient device：节能装置，节能设备
④ vital sign：生命体征
⑤ fleet [fliːt] *n.*车队；船队

data. They can even receive alarms in real time of maintenance incidents without having been detected by the drivers.

The application of the internet of things to fleet management assists with geolocation[①] (monitoring of routes and identification of the most efficient routes), performance analysis, telemetry[②] control and fuel savings, the reduction of polluting emissions to the environment. It can even provide valuable information to improve the driving of vehicles.

5　Agriculture

Smart farms are a fact. The quality of soil is crucial to produce good crops, and the Internet of Things offers farmers the possibility to access detailed knowledge and valuable information of their soil condition.

Through the implementation of IoT sensors, a significant amount of data can be obtained on the state and stages of the soil. Information such as soil moisture[③], level of acidity, the presence of certain nutrients, temperature and many other chemical characteristics helps farmers control irrigation, make water use more efficient, specify the best times to start sowing, and even discover the presence of diseases in plants and soil.

6　Hospitality

The application of the IoT to the hotel industry brings with it interesting improvements in the quality of the service. With the implementation of electronic keys[④], which are sent directly to the mobile devices of each guest, it is possible to automate various interactions.

Thus, the location of the guests, the sending of offers or information on activities of interest, the realization of orders to the room or room service, the automatic charge of accounts to the room or the request of personal hygiene supplies are activities that can be easily managed through integrated applications using the Internet of Things technology.

With the use of electronic keys, the check-out process is automated, disabling the operation of doors, offering information about the rooms immediately available, and even assigning housekeeping tasks to maintenance personnel.

7　Smart Grid[⑤]　and Energy Saving

The progressive use of intelligent energy meters, or meters equipped with sensors, and the

---

① geolocation [dʒɪɒləʊˈkeɪʃn] n.地理定位
② telemetry [təˈlemətrɪ] n.遥感勘测，遥测
③ soil moisture：土壤湿度
④ electronic key：电子钥匙
⑤ smart grid：智能电网

installation of sensors in different strategic points that go from the production plants to the different distribution points allows better monitoring and control of the electrical network.

By establishing a bidirectional communication[①] between the service provider company and the end user, information of enormous value can be obtained for the detection of faults, decision making and repair thereof.

It also offers valuable information to the end user about their consumption patterns and about the best ways to reduce or adjust their energy expenditure.

8 Water Supply

If a sensor is incorporated or adjusted externally to water meters, and it is connected to the Internet and accompanied by the necessary software, It can help to collect, process and analyze data, which allows understanding the behavior of consumers, detecting faults in the supply service and offering courses of action to the company that provides the service.

Likewise, it offers final consumers the possibility of tracking their own consumption information through a web page and in real time, even receiving automatic alerts in case of detecting consumption out of range to their average consumption record.

9 Maintenance Management

One of the areas where the application of IoT technology is most extensive is precisely maintenance management. Through the combination of sensors and software specialized in CMMS[②]/EAM[③] maintenance management, a multifunctional[④] tool is obtained which can be applied to a multiplicity[⑤] of disciplines and practices, with the purpose of extending the useful life of physical assets, while guaranteeing asset reliability and availability.

When the characteristics of the software in charge of processing and arranging the data collected by the sensors are designed to specifically address the maintenance management needs of physical assets, their application is almost unlimited.

The real-time monitoring of physical assets allows determining when a measurement is out of range and it is necessary to perform condition-based maintenance[⑥] (CBM), or even applying AI algorithms such as machine learning or deep learning to predict the failure before it happens.

---

① bidirectional communication：双向通信
② CMMS：计算机维护管理系统
③ EAM：企业资产管理系统
④ multifunctional [ˌmʌltɪˈfʌŋkʃənl] adj.多功能的
⑤ multiplicity [ˌmʌltɪˈplɪsətɪ] n.多种；多样性
⑥ condition-based maintenance：视情维修

Unit 11

Text A

Artificial Intelligence (AI)

Artificial intelligence (AI) is the simulation of human intelligence processes by machines, especially computer systems. These processes include learning (the acquisition of information and rules for using the information), reasoning (using rules to reach approximate or definite conclusions) and self-correction. Particular applications of AI include expert systems, speech recognition and machine vision.

AI can be categorized as either weak or strong. Weak AI, also known as narrow AI, is an AI system that is designed and trained for a particular task. Virtual personal assistants, such as Apple's Siri, are a form of weak AI. Strong AI, also known as general artificial intelligence, is an AI system with generalized human cognitive abilities. When presented with an unfamiliar task, a strong AI system is able to find a solution without human intervention.

Because hardware, software and staffing costs for AI can be expensive, many vendors are including AI components in their standard offerings, as well as access to artificial intelligence as a service (AIaaS) platforms. AI as a service allows individuals and companies to experiment with AI for various business purposes and sample multiple platforms. Popular AI cloud offerings include Amazon AI services, IBM Watson Assistant, Microsoft Cognitive Services and Google AI services.

While AI tools present a range of new functionality for businesses, the use of artificial intelligence raises ethical questions. This is because deep learning algorithms, which underpin many of the most advanced AI tools, are only as smart as the data they are given in training. Because a human selects what data should be used for training an AI program, the potential for human bias is inherent and must be monitored closely.

Some industry experts believe that the term artificial intelligence is too closely linked to popular culture, causing the general public to have unrealistic fears about artificial intelligence and improbable expectations about how it will change the workplace and life in general. Researchers and marketers hope augmented intelligence, which has a more neutral connotation, will help people understand that AI will simply improve products and services and will not replace the humans that use them.

1 Types of AI

Arend Hintze, an assistant professor of integrative biology and computer science and engineering at Michigan State University, categorizes AI into four types, from the kind of AI systems that exist today to sentient systems which do not yet exist. His categories are as follows.

Type 1: reactive machines. An example is Deep Blue, the IBM chess program that beat Garry Kasparov in the 1990s. Deep Blue can identify pieces on the chess board and make predictions, but it has no memory and cannot use past experiences to inform future ones. It analyzes possible moves — its own and its opponent — and chooses the most strategic move. Deep Blue and Google's AlphaGO were designed for narrow purposes and cannot easily be applied to another situation.

Type 2: limited memory. These AI systems can use past experiences to inform future decisions. Some of the decision-making functions in self-driving cars are designed this way. Observations inform actions happening in the not-so-distant future, such as a car changing lanes. These observations are not stored permanently.

Type 3: theory of mind. This psychology term refers to the understanding that others have their own beliefs, desires and intentions that impact the decisions they make. This kind of AI does not yet exist.

Type 4: self-awareness. In this category, AI systems have a sense of self, have consciousness. Machines with self-awareness understand their current state and can use the information to infer what others are feeling. This type of AI does not yet exist.

2 Examples of AI Technology

AI is incorporated into a variety of different types of technology. Here are some examples.

Automation: what makes a system or process function automatically. For example, robotic process automation (RPA) can be programmed to perform high-volume, repeatable tasks that humans normally performed. RPA is different from IT automation in that it can adapt to changing circumstances.

Machine learning: the science of getting a computer to act without programming. Deep learning is a subset of machine learning that, in very simple terms, can be thought of as the automation of predictive analytics. There are three types of machine learning algorithms:

(1) Supervised learning: data sets are labeled so that patterns can be detected and used to label new data sets.

(2) Unsupervised learning: data sets aren't labeled and are sorted according to similarities or differences.

(3) Reinforcement learning: data sets aren't labeled but, after performing an action or several actions, the AI system is given feedback.

Machine vision: the science of allowing computers to see. This technology captures and analyzes visual information using a camera, analog-to-digital conversion and digital signal processing. It is often compared to human eyesight, but machine vision isn't bound by biology and can be programmed to see through walls, for example. It is used in a range of applications from signature identification to medical image analysis. Computer vision, which is focused on machine-based image processing, is often conflated with machine vision.

Natural language processing (NLP): The processing of human — and not computer — language by a computer program. One of the older and best known examples of NLP is spam detection, which looks at the subject line and the text of an email and decides if it's junk. Current approaches to NLP are based on machine learning. NLP tasks include text translation, sentiment analysis and speech recognition.

Robotics: a field of engineering focused on the design and manufacturing of robots. Robots are often used to perform tasks that are difficult for humans to perform or perform consistently. They are used in assembly lines for car production or by NASA to move large objects in space. Researchers are also using machine learning to build robots that can interact in social settings.

Self-driving cars: these use a combination of computer vision, image recognition and deep learning to build automated skill at piloting a vehicle while staying in a given lane and avoiding unexpected obstructions, such as pedestrians.

3 AI Applications

AI has made its way into a number of areas. Here are six examples.

AI in healthcare. The biggest bets are on improving patient outcomes and reducing costs. Companies are applying machine learning to make better and faster diagnoses than humans. One of the best known healthcare technologies is IBM Watson. It understands natural language and is capable of responding to questions asked of it. The system mines patient data and other available data sources to form a hypothesis, which then presents with a confidence scoring schema. Other AI applications include chatbots, a computer program used online to answer questions and assist customers, to help schedule follow-up appointments or aid patients through the billing process, and virtual health assistants that provide basic medical feedback.

AI in business. Robotic process automation is being applied to highly repetitive tasks normally performed by humans. Machine learning algorithms are being integrated into analytics and CRM platforms to uncover information on how to better serve customers. Chatbots have been incorporated into websites to provide immediate service to customers. Automation of job positions has also become a talking point among academics and IT analysts.

AI in education. AI can automate grading, giving educators more time. AI can assess students and adapt to their needs, helping them work at their own pace. AI tutors can provide additional support to students, ensuring they stay on track. AI could change where and how students learn, perhaps even replacing some teachers.

AI in finance. AI in personal finance applications, such as Mint or Turbo Tax, is making a break in financial institutions. Applications such as these collect personal data and provide financial advice. Other programs, such as IBM Watson, have been applied to the process of buying a home. Today, software performs much of the trading on Wall Street.

AI in law. The discovery process, sifting through documents, in law is often overwhelming for humans. Automating this process is a more efficient use of time. Startups are also building question-and-answer computer assistants that can sift programmed-to-answer questions by examining the taxonomy and ontology associated with a database.

AI in manufacturing. This is an area that has been at the forefront of incorporating robots into the workflow. Industrial robots used to perform single tasks and were separated from human workers, but as the technology advanced that changed.

4   Security and Ethical Concerns

The application of AI in the realm of self-driving cars raises security as well as ethical concerns. Cars can be hacked, and when an autonomous vehicle is involved in an accident, liability is unclear. Autonomous vehicles may also be put in a position where an accident is unavoidable, forcing the programming to make an ethical decision about how to minimize damage.

Another major concern is the potential for abuse of AI tools. Hackers are starting to use sophisticated machine learning tools to gain access to sensitive systems, complicating the issue of security beyond its current state.

Deep learning-based video and audio generation tools also present bad actors with the tools necessary to create so-called deepfakes, convincingly fabricated videos of public figures saying or doing things that never took place.

5   Regulation of AI Technology

Despite these potential risks, there are few regulations governing the use of AI tools, and where laws do exist, they typically pertain to AI only indirectly. For example, federal fair lending regulations require financial institutions to explain credit decisions to potential customers, which limit the extent to which lenders can use deep learning algorithms, which by their nature are typically opaque. Europe's GDPR puts strict limits on how enterprises can use consumer data, which impedes the training and functionality of many consumer-orientated AI applications.

New Words

acquisition   [ˌækwɪˈzɪʃn]   n.获得

reasoning	['ri:zənɪŋ]	n.推理，论证
		v.推理，思考；争辩；说服
		adj.推理的
approximate	[ə'prɒksɪmɪt]	adj.极相似的
		vi.接近于，近似于
	[ə'prɒksɪmeɪt]	vt.靠近，使接近
definite	['defɪnɪt]	adj.明确的；一定的；肯定
conclusion	[kən'klu:ʒn]	n.结论；断定，决定；推论
self-correction	[ˌself-kə'rekʃn]	n.自校正；自我纠错；自我改正
particular	[pə'tɪkjələ]	adj.特别的；详细的；独有的
		n.特色，特点
vision	['vɪʒn]	n.视觉
narrow	['nærəʊ]	adj.狭隘的，狭窄的
virtual	['vɜːtʃuəl]	adj.（计算机）虚拟的；实质上的，事实上的
cognitive	['kɒɡnɪtɪv]	adj.认知的，认识的
ability	[ə'bɪlɪti]	n.能力，资格；能耐，才能
unfamiliar	[ˌʌnfə'mɪlɪə]	adj.不熟悉的；不常见的；陌生的；没有经验的
experiment	[ɪk'sperɪmənt]	n.实验，试验；尝试
		vi.做实验
commitment	[kə'mɪtmənt]	n.承诺，许诺；委任，委托
ethical	['eθɪkl]	adj.道德的，伦理的
underpin	[ˌʌndə'pɪn]	vt.加固，支撑
unrealistic	[ˌʌnrɪə'lɪstɪk]	adj.不切实际的；不现实的；空想的
fear	[fɪə]	n.害怕；可能性
		vt.害怕；为……忧虑（或担心、焦虑）
		vi.害怕；忧虑
expectation	[ˌekspek'teɪʃn]	n.期待；预期
neutral	['nju:trəl]	adj.中立的
connotation	[ˌkɒnə'teɪʃn]	n.内涵，含义
integrative	['ɪntɪɡreɪtɪv]	adj.综合的，一体化的
sentient	['sentɪənt]	adj.有感觉能力的，有知觉力的
reactive	[rɪ'æktɪv]	adj.反应的
prediction	[prɪ'dɪkʃn]	n.预测，预报；预言
opponent	[ə'pəʊnənt]	n.对手
observation	[ˌɒbzə'veɪʃn]	n.观察，观察力
psychology	[saɪ'kɒlədʒi]	n.心理学；心理特点；心理状态
intention	[ɪn'tenʃn]	n.意图，目的；意向
self-awareness	[self-ə'weənɪs]	n.自我意识
consciousness	['kɒnʃəsnɪs]	n.意识，观念；知觉

circumstance	[ˈsɜ:kəmstəns]	n.环境，境遇
similarity	[ˌsɪmɪˈlærɪtɪ]	n.相像性，相仿性，类似性
signature	[ˈsɪɡnɪtʃə]	n.签名；署名；识别标志
identification	[aɪˌdentɪfɪˈkeɪʃn]	n.鉴定，识别
detection	[dɪˈtekʃn]	n.检查，检测
junk	[dʒʌŋk]	vt.丢弃，废弃
		n.废品；假货
consistently	[kənˈsɪstəntlɪ]	adv.一贯地，坚持地
pilot	[ˈpaɪlət]	n.引航员；向导
		vt.驾驶
vehicle	[ˈvi:ɪkl]	n.车辆；交通工具
obstruction	[əbˈstrʌkʃn]	n.阻塞，阻碍，受阻
pedestrian	[pəˈdestrɪən]	n.步行者，行人
		adj.徒步的
healthcare	[ˈhelθkeə]	n.卫生保健
diagnose	[ˈdaɪəɡnəʊz]	vt.诊断；判断
		vi.做出诊断
hypothesis	[haɪˈpɒθəsɪs]	n.假设，假说；前提
chatbot	[tʃætbɒt]	n.聊天机器人
appointment	[əˈpɔɪntmənt]	n.预约
repetitive	[rɪˈpetɪtɪv]	adj.重复的，啰嗦的
overwhelming	[ˌəʊvəˈwelmɪŋ]	adj.势不可挡的，压倒一切的
taxonomy	[tækˈsɒnəmɪ]	n.分类学，分类系统
ontology	[ɒnˈtɒlədʒɪ]	n.本体，存在；实体论
forefront	[ˈfɔ:frʌnt]	n.前列；第一线；活动中心
incorporating	[ɪnˈkɔ:pəreɪtɪŋ]	v.融合，包含；使混合
realm	[relm]	n.领域，范围
accident	[ˈæksɪdənt]	n.意外事件；事故
unclear	[ˌʌnˈklɪə]	adj.不清楚的，不明白的，含糊不清
unavoidable	[ˌʌnəˈvɔɪdəbl]	adj.不可避免的，不得已的
minimize	[ˈmɪnɪmaɪz]	vt.把……减至最低数量[程度]，最小化
damage	[ˈdæmɪdʒ]	n.损害，损毁；赔偿金
		v.损害，毁坏
deepfake	[ˈdi:pfeɪk]	n.换脸术
convincingly	[kənˈvɪnsɪŋlɪ]	adv.令人信服地，有说服力地
regulation	[ˌreɡjʊˈleɪʃn]	n.规章，规则
		adj.规定的
credit	[ˈkredɪt]	n.信誉，信用；[金融]贷款
		vt.相信，信任

opaque	[əʊˈpeɪk]	adj.不透明的；含糊的
		n.不透明
strict	[strɪkt]	adj.严格的；精确的；绝对的
impede	[ɪmˈpiːd]	vt.阻碍；妨碍；阻止
lawmaker	[ˈlɔːmeɪkə]	n.立法者

Phrases

human intelligence	人类智能
expert system	专家系统
speech recognition	语音识别
machine vision	机器视觉
weak AI	弱人工智能
virtual personal assistant	虚拟个人助理
strong AI	强人工智能
artificial general intelligence	通用人工智能
for ... purpose	为了……目的
a range of	一系列，一些，一套
deep learning algorithm	深度学习算法
computer science	计算机科学
sentient system	感觉系统
self-driving car	自动驾驶汽车
not-so-distant future	不远的将来
a sense of ...	一种……感觉
predictive analytic	预测分析
supervised learning	有监督学习
unsupervised learning	无监督学习
reinforcement learning	强化学习
analog-to-digital conversion	模（拟）数（字）转换
medical image analysis	医学图像分析
machine-based image processing	基于机器的图像处理
be conflated with ...	与……混为一谈
spam detection	垃圾邮件检测
text translation	文本翻译
sentiment analysis	情感分析，倾向性分析
assembly line	（工厂产品的）装配线，流水线
social setting	社会环境，社会场景，社会情境
image recognition	图像识别
confidence scoring schema	置信评分模式

virtual health assistant	虚拟健康助理
talking point	话题；论题；论据
financial institution	金融机构

Abbreviations

AIaaS (artificial intelligence as a service)	人工智能即服务
RPA (robotic process automation)	机器人流程自动化
NLP (natural language processing)	自然语言处理
NASA (National Aeronautics and Space Administration)	美国国家航空航天局
CRM (customer relationship management)	客户关系管理
GDPR (General Data Protection Regulation)	普通数据保护条例

参考译文

人 工 智 能

　　人工智能（AI）是机器，特别是计算机系统对人类智能处理的模拟。这些过程包括学习（获取信息和使用信息的规则）、推理（使用规则达到近似或明确的结论）和自我校正。人工智能的典型应用包括专家系统、语音识别和机器视觉。

　　人工智能可以分为弱人工智能与强人工智能两类。弱人工智能，也称为窄人工智能，是为特定任务而设计和训练的人工智能系统。虚拟个人助理，如 Apple 的 Siri，是一种弱人工智能。强人工智能，也称为通用人工智能，是一种具有广泛人类认知能力的人工智能系统。当提出一项不熟悉的任务时，强人工智能系统能够在没有人为干预的情况下找到解决方案。

　　由于人工智能的硬件、软件和人员成本可能很昂贵，因此许多供应商在其标准产品中包含人工智能组件及访问人工智能即服务（AIaaS）平台。人工智能即服务允许个人和公司为各种商业目的进行人工智能试验，并对多个平台进行抽样调查。流行的人工智能云产品包括 Amazon AI 服务、IBM Watson Assistant、Microsoft Cognitive 服务和 Google AI 服务。

　　虽然人工智能工具为企业提供了一系列新功能，但人工智能的使用引发了伦理问题。这是因为深度学习算法是许多最先进的人工智能工具的基础，它们的智能仅与训练时提供的数据匹配。因为由人类选择用何种数据训练人工智能程序，而人类本身可能有偏见，所以必须密切监控。

　　一些业内专家认为，人工智能这一术语与流行文化联系太紧密，导致普通大众对人工智能产生不切实际的恐惧，以及对人工智能如何改变工作场所和生活方式抱有不太可能的期望。研究人员和营销人员希望增强智能（具有更中性内涵）会帮助人们明白人工智能只能改进产品和服务，而不是取代使用它们的人。

1 人工智能的类型

密歇根州立大学综合生物学和计算机科学与工程助理教授 Arend Hintze 将人工智能分为 4 类，从现有的人工智能系统到尚未存在的感觉系统。他的分类如下。

类型 1：反应机器。Deep Blue（深蓝）是一个例子，它是一个在 20 世纪 90 年代击败 Garry Kasparov 的 IBM 国际象棋程序。Deep Blue 可以识别棋盘上的棋子并进行预测，但它没有记忆，无法使用过去的经验指导未来的棋子。它分析了可能的行动（它自己的和它的对手的）并选择最具战略性的举措。Deep Blue 和 Google 的 AlphaGO 专为特定目的而设计，不能轻易应用于其他情况。

类型 2：有限的存储。这些人工智能系统可以使用过去的经验指导未来的决策。自动驾驶汽车的一些决策功能就是这样设计的。观察结果可以告知在将来发生的行动，如换车道。这些观察结果不会被永久存储。

类型 3：心智理论。这个心理学术语指的是他人有自己的信念、欲望和意图，这会影响他们的决策。这种人工智能尚不存在。

类型 4：自我意识。在这个类别中，人工智能系统具有自我意识感和知觉。具有自我意识的机器了解其当前状态，并可以使用该信息推断其他人的感受。这种类型的人工智能尚不存在。

2 人工智能技术的例子

人工智能被整合到各种不同类型的技术中。以下是一些例子。

自动化：可以使系统或过程自动运行。例如，机器人过程自动化（RPA）可以通过编程执行通常由人类执行的大量的可重复的任务。RPA 与 IT 自动化的不同之处在于它可以适应不断变化的环境。

机器学习：使计算机无须编程即可行动的科学。深度学习是机器学习的一个子集，简言之，它可以被认为是自动化进行预测分析。有三种类型的机器学习算法：

（1）监督学习：标记数据集，以便可以检测模式并用于标记新数据集。

（2）无监督学习：不标记数据集，并根据相似性或差异性进行排序。

（3）强化学习：不标记数据集，但在执行一个或多个行动后，人工智能系统会得到反馈。

机器视觉：让计算机具有视觉的科学。该技术使用相机、模数转换和数字信号处理捕获和分析视觉信息。它通常被比作人类的视力，但机器视觉不受生物学的约束，如可以通过编程以透视墙壁。它用于从签名识别到医学图像分析的各种应用中。计算机视觉是基于机器的图像处理，它通常与机器视觉混为一谈。

自然语言处理（NLP）：通过计算机程序处理人类（而不是计算机）的语言。其中一个较早且最著名的 NLP 示例是垃圾邮件检测，查看主题行和电子邮件的文本并确定它是否为垃圾邮件。目前的 NLP 方法基于机器学习。NLP 任务包括文本翻译、情感分析和语音识别。

机器人技术：一个专注于机器人设计和制造的工程领域。机器人通常用于执行人类难以执行或一直执行的任务。它们用于汽车生产的装配线或由 NASA 用于在太空中移动大型物体。研究人员还利用机器学习构建可在社交场合进行交互的机器人。

自动驾驶汽车：结合计算机视觉、图像识别和深度学习，使用自动化技能驾驶车辆，遇到意外障碍（如行人）时在给定车道上停车。

3　人工智能应用

人工智能已经进入了许多领域，以下列举 6 个示例。

人工智能应用于医疗保健领域。最大的好处是改善患者的治疗效果和降低成本。公司正在应用机器学习来做出比人类更好更快的诊断。IBM Watson 是最著名的医疗保健技术之一。它理解自然语言，并能够回答所提出的问题。系统挖掘患者数据和其他可用数据源以形成假设，然后它将给出一个置信评分模式。其他人工智能应用程序包括聊天机器人。聊天机器人是一个计算机程序，用于在线回答问题和帮助客户、帮助安排后续预约或自动计费，以及提供基本医疗反馈的虚拟健康助理。

人工智能应用于商业领域。机器人过程自动化正被应用于通常由人类执行的高度重复的任务。机器学习算法正在集成到分析和客户关系管理平台，发现信息以更好地为客户服务。聊天机器人已被纳入网站，为客户提供即时服务。工作岗位的自动化也成为学术界和 IT 分析师的话题。

人工智能应用于教育领域。人工智能可以自动评分，节省教师时间。人工智能还可以评估学生并应对他们的需求，帮助他们按照自己的进度工作。人工智能导师可以为学生提供额外的支持，确保他们处于正确轨道上。人工智能也可以改变学生学习的地点和方式，甚至可以取代一些教师。

人工智能应用于金融领域。个人理财应用程序中的人工智能（如 Mint 或 Turbo Tax）正在进入金融机构。这些应用程序收集个人数据并提供财务建议。其他程序（如 IBM Watson）已经应用于购买房屋的过程。如今，华尔街很大一部分交易都是由软件完成的。

人工智能应用于法律领域。在法律上，对人们来说，发现过程（筛选文件）是非常困难的工作。自动化地完成此项工作可以大大节省时间。创业公司还在构建计算机回答助手，通过编程检查与数据库相关的分类和本体，可以筛选出问题的答案。

人工智能应用于制造业。这个领域一直处于将机器人纳入工作流程的最前沿。工业机器人曾经执行单一任务并与人类工作人员分开，但随着技术的进步这一现象已经发生了变化。

4　安全和伦理问题

人工智能在自动驾驶汽车领域的应用带来了安全和伦理方面的问题。汽车可以被黑客入侵，当自动驾驶汽车涉及事故时，责任不清楚。自动驾驶汽车也可能处于无法避免事故的情况，迫使编程人员就如何最大限度地减少损坏做出伦理决定。

另一个主要问题是滥用人工智能工具的可能性。黑客们开始使用复杂的机器学习工具访问敏感系统，使安全问题越来越复杂化。

基于深度学习的视频和音频生成工具也为不良行为者提供了所谓换脸所需的工具，他们可以制作公众人物的视频，尽管这些公众人物从未说过这些话，也从未做过这些事，但这些视频却让人不得不信。

5 人工智能技术的规范

尽管存在这些潜在的风险，但很少有关于使用人工智能工具的法规，而且即便有法规，它们通常也只是间接地涉及人工智能。例如，联邦公平贷款法规要求金融机构向潜在客户解释信用决策，这些法规限制了贷方可以使用深度学习算法的程度，这些算法本质上通常是不透明的。欧洲的 GDPR 严格限制企业使用消费者数据的方法，这阻碍了许多面向消费者的人工智能应用程序的训练和功能。

扫码听课文

Text B

Big Data

Big data is changing the way people work together within organizations. It is creating a culture in which business and IT leaders must join forces to realize the value from all data. Insights from big data can enable all employees to make better decisions — deepening customer engagement, optimizing operations, preventing threats and fraud, and capitalizing on new sources of revenue.

1 Basic Attributes

1.1 Value

This is indeed the holy grail of big data and what we are all looking for. One has to demonstrate value that can be extracted from big or small data in order to justify the investments, whether on big data or on traditional analytics, data warehouse or business intelligence tools, whatever may be the buzzing nomenclature. There seems to be an increasing interest related to the value of big data, as indicated by the number of Google searches looking for similar terms over the last two years.

1.2 Volume

There is no doubt that the information explosion has redefined the connotation of volumes. It is getting more and more difficult to track data. To measure such data, we need to add various prefixes to "bytes". Since there is a "helluva lot of data", the term "hellabyte" has been coined beyond petabytes, exabytes, zettabytes and yottabytes. However, since these measures will be superseded by the likes of brontobytes and more, lets move on!

1.3 Velocity

Similarly, velocity refers to the speed at which the data is generated. Some of the factors that exacerbate this trend are the proliferation of social media and the explosion of IoT (internet of things). In the context of business operations that have not yet been touched by social media or IoT, the velocity arises from sophisticated enterprise applications that capture each and every minute detail involved in the completion of a particular business process. Enterprise applications have traditionally captured such information but the world has woken up to the power of such information largely in the big data era.

1.4 Variety

The last of the original attributes of big data is variety. Since we are living in an increasingly digital world where technology has invaded into our glasses and watches, the variety of data that is generated is mind-boggling. The computing power available is able to process unstructured text, images, audio, video and data from sensors in the IoT (internet of things) world that capture (almost) everything around us. This attribute of big data is more relevant today than it ever was.

1.5 Veracity or Validity

Veracity or validity of data is extremely important and fundamental to the extraction of value from the underlying data. Veracity implies that the data is verifiable and truthful. If this condition is violated, the results can be catastrophic. More importantly, there are several cases in which the data is accurate but may not be valid in the particular context. For instance, if we are trying to ascertain the volume of searches on Google related to big data, we will also obtain results pertaining to the hit single "dangerous" from "big data".

1.6 Visible

Information silos have always existed within enterprises and have been one of the major roadblocks in the attempt to extract value from data. Relevant information should not only exist, but also be visible to the right person at the right time. Actionable data needs to be visible transcending the boundaries of functions, departments and even organizations for value unlocking. Individuals might have believed that information in their hands is power but in the age of big data, collective information available to the world at large is truly omnipotent!

1.7   Visual

We live in an increasingly visual world and the statistics of increase in the number of images and videos shared on the Internet is staggering. According to official statistics, 300 hours of video are uploaded every minute on YouTube. In a business context, appropriate visualization of data is critical for the management to be able to extract value from their limited time, resources and even more limited attention span!

2   More Contenders

In addition to the 7Vs described above, there are several other Vs that may be considered:

2.1   Volatility

With more applications such as SnapChat and IoT sensors, we may have data in and out in a snap. Volatility of the underlying data sources may become one of the defining attributes in the future.

2.2   Variability

One of the cornerstones of traditional statistics is standard deviation and variability. Whether or not it makes to an extended list of Vs relating to big data, it can never be ignored.

2.3   Viability

Embedded in the concept of value is the need to check the viability of any project. Big data projects can scale up to gigantic proportions and guzzle a lot of resources very quickly. Those who do not learn this fast and get fascinated with fads will funnel funds towards futility resulting in failure. In a nutshell, viability of any project needs to be established and big data projects do not have the liberty of exemption, whether or not it remains a trending buzzword.

2.4   Vitality

Vitality or criticality of the data is another concept that is crucial and is embedded in the concept of Value. Information that is more meaningful or critical to the underlying business objective needs to be prioritized. Analysis paralysis needs to be replaced with a more pragmatic approach. Technology allows marketers to create segments of one, but is such extreme segmentation vital or even aligned to the organizational strategy?

2.5   Vincularity

Derived from Latin, it implies connectivity or linkage. This concept is very relevant in today's connected world. There is significant value arbitrage potential by connecting diverse information sets. For instance, the government has forever been trying to connect the details of major expenditure heads and correlating the same with the income declared in tax returns to identify concealment of income. The same purpose may now be achieved by drawing information from social media posts.

3　An Example of Big Data

An example of big data might be petabytes or exabytes of data consisting of billions to trillions of records of millions of people — all from different sources (e.g. web, sales, customer contact center, social media, mobile data and so on). The data is typically loosely structured data that is often incomplete and inaccessible.

New Words

realize	[ˈriːəlaɪz]	vt.认识到，了解，实现，实行
engagement	[ɪnˈɡeɪdʒmənt]	n.参与度，敬业度
fraud	[frɔːd]	n.欺骗，欺诈行为
indeed	[ɪnˈdiːd]	adv.真正地，确实；当然
nomenclature	[nəˈmenklətʃə]	n.系统命名法；命名；术语；专门名称
analytics	[ˌænəˈlɪtɪks]	n.分析学，解析学，分析论
redefine	[ˌriːdɪˈfaɪn]	v.重新定义
staggering	[ˈstæɡərɪŋ]	adj.令人惊愕的，难以置信的
helluva	[ˈheləvə]	adj.很大的
hellabyte	[ˈheləbaɪt]	n.海字节，缩写为 HB，1HB=2^{90} byte
petabyte	[ˈpɪtəbaɪt]	n.拍字节，缩写为 PB，1PB=2^{50} byte
exabyte	[ˈeksəbaɪt]	n.艾字节，缩写为 EB，1EB=2^{60} byte
zettabyte	[ˈzetəbaɪt]	n.泽字节，缩写为 ZB，1ZB=2^{70} byte
yottabyte	[ˈjɔtəbaɪt]	n.尧字节，缩写为 YB，1YB=2^{80} byte
brontobyte	[ˈbrɒntəbaɪt]	n.布字节，缩写为 BB，1HB=2^{90} byte
velocity	[vəˈlɒsəti]	n.时效性；速度，速率
exacerbate	[ɪɡˈzæsəbeɪt]	vt.增剧，使加剧
trend	[trend]	n.倾向，趋势
proliferation	[prəˌlɪfəˈreɪʃn]	n.增殖，扩散
explosion	[ɪkˈspləʊʒn]	n.爆发，爆炸
era	[ˈɪərə]	n.时代，纪元，时期
variety	[vəˈraɪəti]	n.多样性；品种，种类

attribute	[əˈtrɪbjuːt]	n.属性，品质，特征
mind-boggling	[maɪnd ˈbɒglɪŋ]	adj.令人难以置信的
unstructured	[ʌnˈstrʌktʃəd]	adj.非结构化的，未组织的
veracity	[vəˈræsətɪ]	n.真实性
validity	[vəˈlɪdətɪ]	n.有效性；合法性，正确性
extremely	[ɪkˈstriːmlɪ]	adv.极端地，非常地
fundamental	[ˌfʌndəˈmentl]	adj.基础的，基本的
		n.基本原则，基本原理
verifiable	[ˈverɪfaɪəbl]	adj.能证实的
truthful	[ˈtruːθfl]	adj.诚实的，说实话的
violate	[ˈvaɪəleɪt]	vt.违犯，冒犯，干扰；违反
visible	[ˈvɪzəbl]	adj.看得见的，明显的，显著的
		n.可见物
transcend	[trænˈsend]	vt.超越，胜过
boundary	[ˈbaʊndrɪ]	n.边界，分界线
omnipotent	[ɒmˈnɪpətənt]	adj.全能的，无所不能的
span	[spæn]	n.跨度，跨距，范围
contender	[kənˈtendə]	n.竞争者
volatility	[ˌvɒləˈtɪlɪtɪ]	n.波动率；波动性；波动
variability	[ˌveərɪəˈbɪlətɪ]	n.变异性；可变性
cornerstone	[ˈkɔːnəstəʊn]	n.奠基石，基础，最重要部分
viability	[ˌvaɪəˈbɪlətɪ]	n.可行性，切实可行，能办到；生存能力
gigantic	[dʒaɪˈgæntɪk]	adj.巨人般的，巨大的
proportion	[prəˈpɔːʃn]	n.比例；均衡；部分
		vt.使成比例；使均衡，分摊
guzzle	[ˈgʌzl]	vt.狂饮，暴食；消耗
fascinate	[ˈfæsɪneɪt]	vt.使着迷，使神魂颠倒
		vi.入迷，极度迷人
fad	[fæd]	n.时尚，一时流行的狂热，一时的爱好
funnel	[ˈfʌnl]	vt.&vi.把……灌进漏斗；使成漏斗状；使汇集
		n.漏斗；漏斗状物
futility	[fjuːˈtɪlətɪ]	n.无益，无用
nutshell	[ˈnʌtʃel]	n.简而言之，一言以蔽之
exemption	[ɪgˈzempʃn]	n.解除，免除
vitality	[vaɪˈtælətɪ]	n.时效性；动态性，灵活
criticality	[krɪtɪˈkælɪtɪ]	n.临界点；临界状态；紧急程度，危险程度
prioritize	[praɪˈɒrətaɪz]	vt.把……区分优先次序
pragmatic	[prægˈmætɪk]	adj.实际的，注重实效的
arbitrage	[ˈɑːbɪtrɑːʒ]	n.套汇，套利交易

correlate	[ˈkɒrəlet]	vt.使相互关联
		vi.和……相关
incomplete	[ˌɪnkəmˈpliːt]	adj.不完全的，不完善的

Phrases

big data	大数据
capitalize on	充分利用；资本化
holy grail	无处寻觅的稀世珍宝，努力却无法得到的东西
extracted ... from	从……中抽取，从……中提取
data warehouse	数据仓库
business intelligence tool	商业智能工具
information explosion	信息爆炸，知识爆炸
be superseded by ...	被……取代
wake up	活跃起来；引起注意；（使）认识到
invade into	侵入
unstructured text	非结构化文本
underlying data	源数据；基础数据；基本数据
pertain to	属于，关于，附属
in the attempt to	试图，企图
at large	普遍的；一般的；整体的
according to	依照
in a snap	立刻，马上
standard deviation	标准差，标准偏差
scale up	按比例增加，按比例提高
get fascinated with	迷上，沉溺于
in a nutshell	简而言之，一言以蔽之
analysis paralysis	过度分析
be replaced with	由……代替
be aligned to	与……一致
draw from...	从……抽取
consist of	构成，组成
customer contact center	客户联络中心，客户服务中心

Abbreviations

| IT (information technology) | 信息技术 |

参考译文

大　数　据

　　大数据正在改变组织内部人们协同工作的方式。它正在创造一种文化，使业务和 IT 领导必须联合起来，以便实现所有数据的价值。大数据让所有员工能够更好地做出决策，包括深化客户参与度、优化运营、防止威胁和欺诈行为和开辟新的收入来源。

1　基本属性

1.1　价值

　　这是大数据的梦想，也是人们在寻找的目标。从大大小小的数据中获得价值，以证明投资所值，无论是大数据分析或传统分析、数据仓库或商业智能工具，或许只是不同的名称而已。根据谷歌搜索过去两年寻找类似条目的数量，似乎表明人们对大数据的价值越来越感兴趣。

1.2　数据量

　　毫无疑问，信息爆炸已经重新定义数据量的含义。要跟踪数据越来越难了，要度量这样的数据需要给"字节"前面加上种种前缀。因为有"巨量的数据"，新创造出的术语 hellabyte 已经超越 petabyte、exabyte、zettabyte 和 yottabyte。然而，这些度量单位将被 brontobyte 等替代。

1.3　时效性

　　时效性指产生数据的速度。社交媒体的扩散和 IoT（物联网）的爆炸式增长是加剧这一趋势的因素。在尚未被社交媒体或物联网影响的业务运营中，时效性来自复杂的企业应用，它捕捉了每个特定业务流程的每一个微小的细节。企业应用捕获这些信息，在大数据时代，这些信息就是力量。

1.4　多样性

　　最后一个大数据的原始属性是多样性。我们生活在一个日益数字化的世界里，技术已经侵入眼镜和手表，多样性产生的数据是令人难以置信的。可用的计算能力能够处理非结构化的文本、图像、音频、视频及来自物联网传感器的数据，这几乎可以捕获我们周围的一切。如今，大数据的这个属性与人们生活的联系比以往更紧密。

1.5　真实性或有效性

　　数据的真实性或有效性对提取基础数据的价值非常重要。真实性意味着数据是可验证的和真实的。如果违反这个条件，其结果可能是灾难性的。在某些情况中，数据是准确的，但在特定情况下无效。例如，如果试图确定谷歌中"大数据"的搜索量，我们也会获得有关"大数据"的"危险"的结果。

1.6 可见性

信息孤岛一直在企业中存在，并且一直是从数据中提取价值的主要障碍之一。不仅应该有相关信息，还应该在合适的时间给合适的人看到。可操作的数据需要超越职能部门甚至组织的界限，并能够呈现，才能释放价值。个人可能会认为在他们手中信息就是力量，但在大数据时代，大量的对全球有效的整合信息才是真正无所不能的。

1.7 视觉性

我们生活在一个日益视觉化的世界，统计表明在互联网上共享的图像和视频的数量以惊人的速度增加。据官方统计，每分钟有 300 小时的视频被上传到 YouTube。在商业环境中，适当的可视化数据对管理者是至关重要的，他们能够在有限的时间和资源甚至更有限的注意力中获得价值。

2 更多的属性

除了上述的 7 个属性，可能还有其他几个属性：

2.1 波动率

随着应用越来越多，如 SnapChat 和物联网传感器，可能即时产生一些输入和输出数据。基础数据源的波动率将来可能成为其定义属性之一。

2.2 变异性

传统统计的一个基石是标准差和变异。无论它在不在大数据的扩展列表中，都绝不能被忽略。

2.3 可行性

每个项目的可行性都需要检查，这包含在价值概念之中。大数据项目可占据巨大的比例并非常快地消耗大量资源。不快速学习并沉浸其中，就会耗尽资金而失败。简而言之，任何项目都要进行可行性研究，大数据项目也不例外，无论它是否仍然是一个流行词。

2.4 时效性

数据的时效性或关键性是另一至关重要的概念，它包含在价值概念之中。应该优先考虑对实现基础商业目标更有意义或更重要的信息。需要用更务实的方法取代过度分析。技术允许营销人员创建一个细分市场，但这样极端的细分对组织重要吗？与组织战略一致吗？

2.5 连通性

vincularity 这个词汇源于拉丁语，意思是连通性或链接。这个概念与当今的互联世界密切相关。连接不同信息集合可以得到潜在的套利价值。例如，政府一直尝试把主要支出的细节相连，并将其与收入报税单关联以发现是否隐瞒收入。而这一目的可以通过从社交媒体的帖子上提取信息来实现。

3 一个大数据的示例

大数据的一个例子可能是 PB 或 EB 级数据，它包含了数百万人的数十亿的记录，这些记录来自不同信息源，如网络、销售、客户联络中心、社交媒体及移动数据等。该数据通常结构性不强，而且往往是不完整的和难以访问的。

Exercises

[Ex. 1] Answer the following questions according to Text A.

1. What is artificial intelligence? What do these processes include?

2. What do particular applications of AI include?

3. What can AI be categorized as? What are they respectively?

4. What does AI as a service allow individuals and companies to do?

5. What do researchers and marketers hope the label augmented intelligence will do?

6. How many types does Arend Hintze categorize AI into? What are they?

7. What are some examples that AI is incorporated into a variety of different types of technology?

8. How many types of machine learning algorithms are there? What are they?

9. What are the areas AI has made its way into?

10. What did the National Science and Technology Council (NSTC) do in 2016?

[Ex. 2] Answer the following questions according to Text B.

1. What can insights from big data do?

2. What does velocity refer to? What are some of the factors that exacerbate this trend?

3. Why is the variety of data that is generated is mind-boggling?

4. What does veracity imply?

5. What have always existed within enterprises and have been one of the major roadblocks in the attempt to extract value from data?

6. What should relevant information be?

7. How many hours of video are uploaded every minute on YouTube according to official statistics?

8. What is one of the cornerstones of traditional statistics?

9. What kind of information needs to be prioritized?

10. Where is the word vincularity derived from? What does it imply?

[Ex. 3] Translate the following terms or phrases from English into Chinese and vice versa.

1. expert system	1.
2. image recognition	2.
3. reinforcement learning	3.
4. supervised learning	4.
5. data warehouse	5.
6. *vt.*诊断；判断 *vi.*做出诊断	6.
7. *n.*鉴定，识别	7.
8. *n.*规章，规则 *adj.*规定的	8.
9. *n.*属性，品质，特征	9.
10. *n.*时效性；速度，速率	10.

[Ex. 4] Translate the following passage into Chinese.

Strong Artificial Intelligence (Strong AI)

Strong artificial intelligence is an artificial intelligence construct that has mental capabilities and functions that mimic the human brain. In the philosophy of strong AI, there is no essential difference between the piece of software, which is the AI, exactly emulating the actions of the human brain, and actions of a human being, including its power of understanding and even its consciousness.

Strong artificial intelligence is also known as full AI.

Strong artificial intelligence is more of a philosophy rather than an actual approach to creating AI. It is a different perception of AI wherein it equates AI to humans. It stipulates that a computer can be programmed to actually be a human mind, to be intelligent in every sense of the word, to have perception, beliefs and have other cognitive states that are normally only ascribed to humans.

However, since humans cannot even properly define what intelligence is, it is very difficult to give a clear criterion as to what would count as a success in the development of strong artificial intelligence. Weak AI, on the other hand, is very achievable because of how it stipulates what intelligence is. Rather than try to fully emulate a human mind, weak AI focuses on developing intelligence concerned with a particular task or field of study. That is a set of activities that can be broken down into smaller processes and therefore can be achieved in the scale that is set for it.

Reading

What Is Machine Learning?

Artificial intelligence and machine learning are among the most trending technologies these days. Artificial intelligence teaches computers to behave like a human, to think, and to give a response like a human, and to perform the actions like humans perform.

1   What Is Machine Learning?

As the name suggests, machine learning means the machine is learning.

This is the technique through which we teach the machines about things. It is a branch of artificial intelligence and I would say it is the foundation of artificial intelligence. Here we train our machines using data. If you take a look into it, you'll see that it is something like data mining. Actually, the concept behind it is that machine learning and data mining are both data oriented[①]. We work on data in both of situations. Actually, in data sciences or big data, we analyze the data and make the statistics out of it and we work on how we can maintain our data, how we can conclude[②] the results and make a summary of it instead of maintaining the complete comprehensive bulk[③] of data. But in machine learning, we teach the machines to make the decisions about things. We teach the machine with different data sets and then we check the machine for some situations and see what kind of results we get from this unknown scenario. We also use this trained model for prediction in new scenarios[④].

We teach the machine with our historical data, observations, and experiments. And then, we predict with the machine from these learnings and take the responses.

As I already said, machine learning is closely related to data mining and statistics.

Data mining — concerned with analytics of data.

Statistics — concerned with prediction-making/probability.

---

① data oriented: 数据导向

② conclude [kən'kluːd] vt.得出结论；推断出；决定

③ bulk [bʌlk] n.大块，大量；大多数，大部分

④ scenario [sə'nɑːrɪəʊ] n.设想；可能发生的情况；剧情梗概

2 Why Do We Need Machine Learning?

In this era, we're using wireless communication[①], internet etc. Using social media, or driving cars, or anything we're doing right now, is actually generating the data at the backend[②]. If you're surprised about how our cars are generating the data, remember that every car has a small computer inside which controls your vehicle completely, i.e., when which component needs the current, when the specific component needs to start or switch. In this way, we're generating TBs (terabytes) of data.

But this data is also important to get to the results. Let's take an example and try to understand the concept clearly. Let's suppose a person is living in a town and he goes to a shopping mall and buys something. We have many items of a single product. When he buys something, now we can generate the pattern of the things he has bought. In the same way, we can generate the selling and purchasing patterns of things of different people. Now you might be thinking about a random person who comes and buys something and then he never comes again, but we have the pattern of things there as well. With the help of this pattern we can make a decision about the things people most like and when they come to the mall again. They will see the things they want just at the entrance. This is how we attract the customer with machine learning.

3 How Do Machines Learn?

Actually, machines learn through the patterns of data. Let's start with the data sets of data. The input we give to the machine is called X and the response we get is Y. Here we've three types of learning.

(1) Supervised Learning.

(2) Unsupervised Learning.

(3) Reinforcement Learning.

3.1 Supervised Learning

In supervised learning, we know about the different cases (inputs) and we know the labels (output) of these cases. And here we already know about the basic truths, so here we just focus on the function (operation) because it is the main and most important thing here (see Figure 11-1).

Here we just create the function to get the output of the inputs. And we try to create the function which processes the data and try to give the accurate outputs (Y) in most of the scenarios (see Figure 11-2).

---

① wireless communication: 无线通信

② backend [bӕkend] n.后端

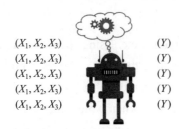

Figure 11-1　Inputs and Output of Supervised Learning　　Figure 11-2　Function of Supervised Learning

Because we've started with known values for our inputs, we can validate the model and make it even better.

And now we teach our machine with different data sets. Now it is the time to check it in unknown cases and generate the value.

Note: Let's suppose you've provided the machine a data set of some kind of data and now you train the model according to this data set. Now the result comes to you from this model on the basis of this knowledge set[①] you've provided. But let's suppose if you delete an existing item in this knowledge set or you update something then you don't expect the results you get according to this new modification you've made in the data set.

3.2　Unsupervised Learning

It is quite different from supervised learning. Here we don't know about the labels (output) of different cases. And here, we train the model with patterns by finding similarities. And then these patterns become the cluster.

Cluster = Collection of similar patterns of data

And then, this cluster is used to analyze and to process the data.

In unsupervised learning, we really don't know if the output is right or wrong. So here in this scenario, the system recognizes the pattern and tries to calculate the results until we get the nearly right value.

3.3　Reinforcement Learning

It is like reward based learning. The example of reward based is, suppose your parents will give you a reward on the completion of a specific task. So here you know you've to complete this task and the time you need to complete it. The developer decides himself what reward he'll give on the completion of this task.

It is also feedback oriented learning. Now you're doing some tasks and on the basis of these tasks, you're getting feedback. And if the feedback is positive then it means you're doing it right

---

① knowledge set: 知识集

and you can improve your work on your own. And if the feedback is negative then you know as well what was wrong and how to do it correctly. And feedback comes from the environment where it is working.

It makes the system more optimal① than the unsupervised scenario, because here we have some clues like rewards or good feedback to make our system more efficient.

4　Steps in Machine Learning

There are some key point steps of machine learning when we start to teach the machine.

4.1　Collect Data

As we already know machine learning is data oriented. We need data to teach our system for future predictions.

4.2　Prepare the Input Data

Now you've downloaded the data, but when you're feeding② the data, you need to make sure of the particular order of the data to make it meaningful for you machine learning tool to process it; i.e. .csv file (comma separated value). This is the best format of the file to process the data because comma separated values help a lot in clustering.

4.3　Analyzing Data

Now, you're looking at the patterns in the data to process it in a better way. You're checking the outliers (scope & boundaries) of the data. And you are also checking the novelty (specification) of the data.

4.4　Train Model

This is the main part of the machine learning when you are developing the algorithm where you are structuring the complete system with coding to process the input and give back the output.

4.5　Test Model

Here you're checking the values you're getting from the system whether it matches your required outcome or not.

---

① optimal [ˈɒptɪməl] *adj.*最佳的，最优的；最理想的
② feed [fiːd] *vt.*馈送；向……提供

4.6　Deploy It in the Application

Let's discuss an example of autonomous cars which don't have human intervention, which run on their own. The first step is to collect the data, and you have to collect many kinds of data. You're driving the car which runs on its owe. The car should know the road signs, it should have the knowledge of traffic signals and when people crossing the road, so that it can make the decision to stop or run in different situations. So we need a collection of images of these different situations, it is our collect data module.

Now we have to make the particular format of data (images) like CSV file where we store the path of the file, the dimensions of the file. It makes our system processing efficient. This is what we called preparing the data.

And then it makes the patterns for different traffic signals (red, green, blue), for different sign boards of traffic and for its environment in which car or people running around. Next it decides the outlier of these objects whether it is static[①] (stopped) or dynamic (running state). Finally it can make the decision to stop or to move in the side of another object.

These decisions are obviously dependent upon training the model, and what code we write to develop our model. This is what we say training the model and then we test it and then we deploy it in our real world applications.

---

① static ['stætɪk] *adj.*静止的；不变的

图书资源支持

感谢您一直以来对清华版图书的支持和爱护。为了配合本书的使用,本书提供配套的资源,有需求的读者请扫描下方的"书圈"微信公众号二维码,在图书专区下载,也可以拨打电话或发送电子邮件咨询。

如果您在使用本书的过程中遇到了什么问题,或者有相关图书出版计划,也请您发邮件告诉我们,以便我们更好地为您服务。

我们的联系方式:

地　　址:北京市海淀区双清路学研大厦 A 座 714

邮　　编:100084

电　　话:010-83470236　010-83470237

客服邮箱:2301891038@qq.com

QQ:2301891038(请写明您的单位和姓名)

资源下载:关注公众号"书圈"下载配套资源。

资源下载、样书申请

书　圈

图书案例

清华计算机学堂

观看课程直播